I0153180

# *Michael, we really have to talk ...*

plus

## A Subversive's Toolkit
### A collection of dissident texts useful for derailing organisational bullies

## Michael O'Neill

Copyright © 2015 Michael O'Neill

All rights reserved. No part of this book may be reproduced, stored in a retrieval system, or transmitted, in any form or by any means without the prior written permission of the publisher, nor be otherwise circulated in any form of binding or cover other than that in which it is published and without a similar condition being imposed on the subsequent purchaser.

First edition published in Australia in 2015 in conjunction with LeftPress by:

Bent Banana Books
24 Lorraine Court
Lawnton, Australia, 4501.

All characters are fictitious and any resemblance to actual persons living or dead is purely coincidental.

A CiP catalogue record for this book is available from the Australian *National Library*

ISBN: 978-0-9925934-4-5

Edited by Bernie Dowling, Bent Banana Books.
Layout and cover design by Ian Curr, LeftPress, Brisbane, Australia.
Cover drawing: Michael O'Neill.

"I had been idling with a pencil and paper, just itemising the essence of each of the previous four and a half days of client contacts, to no purpose that I was aware of. It was a column of crises and resembled an after-the-fact shopping list, one you write when you get home from the supermarket in hell.
For though I penciled words alone, a tortured face looked back."

- Michael O'Neill

For Gibbo

Desire to push the world in a certain direction,
to alter other people's idea of the kind of society
that they should strive after.

George Orwell,
*Why I Write*


We would rather be ruined than changed.
We would rather die in our dread
Than climb the cross of the moment
And let our illusions die.

W H Auden,
*The Age of Anxiety*

# Table of Contents

# Foreword

IN EARLY August 2013, Michael talked with much satisfaction and a touch of pride about the impending publication of this manuscript. It had been a long time in the making.

All his life he had written. Diaries, accounts of personal and political happenings both small and large, poetry, endless records of the small "says" of his children, notes in the margins of books, descriptions of his sketchings, pieces for the student newspaper. He wrote about everything and anything. Despite his yen to write a major work, he had never previously done so. Therefore, his sense of achievement in putting the finishing touches to this manuscript was deep.

Suddenly and unexpectedly on 21 August 2013 he died. He had much unfinished business with the world. Seeing the publication of this book was but one piece of it.

Michael was the most complicated, challenging and interesting man I ever met – a captivating combination. He was introspective and gloomy at times, extroverted and funny at others. He was profoundly intelligent and unafraid.

His sense of justice and fairness and his courage in pursuit of it regardless of all barriers and no matter what the personal cost, were life forces for him. So too were his creativity and his unwavering interest in understanding the true essence of people. At the heart of it, he was an artist who saw, felt and understood the complexity of life – its sadness, its beauty, its ridiculousness – in overwhelming measure.

This manuscript gives but a small glimpse of one aspect of the man and father we knew and loved so deeply. Completing it was a triumph for him. It was a triumph in that he managed to overcome his complex writer's block, of which he gives us a glimpse in the Preface, and a triumph in that he managed to suppress (almost) his penchant for complete forensic examination of all facets of a situation or person in order to tell the story.

His story of organisational life is the story of scores of people. The power of organisations and their impact on both the behaviour of people while operating within them and on the people themselves is compelling material. Michael's unique position as counsellor to those struggling with the brutality of organisational life gave him a ringside view of this each day. It was a story he felt obliged to tell and has done so through his own experience.

Completing the manuscript was not only a great triumph for Michael but it was also therapeutic for him. It refreshed both his emotional state and his creative spirit and allowed the artist to once again emerge and thrive and pursue artistic endeavours. These had been, through necessity, on hold during his working life as a counsellor, when the bulk of his creative energies were directed towards assisting his clients.

We, his family, have put the final finishing touches to the manuscript in Michael's absence, and in so doing have had to make some choices. We have tried to honour what we believe would have been his wishes. One of our challenges has been to settle on a title for the manuscript. When Michael died, the title he was favouring was "Darkness and Denial". His Preface mentions this title. After much soul searching, we have settled on "Michael we really have to talk..." a direct quote from the manuscript.

Michael was a man of many talents. Above all, he was a devoted, proud and creative father and an unwaveringly supportive, interesting and loving partner. This manuscript reflects one small aspect of the man we loved.

We are greatly indebted to Ian and Bernie for their patience and for making the eventual publication of this manuscript possible.


Julie (his partner)

Jess & Gabe (Michael & Maria's children)
Bram & Nell (our children)

# Preface

A LITTLE while after I began to scribble this I thought of it as something you might read one day. I felt pressure to categorise it. First I called it a meditation. That was a compromise, since it was also yarn, lecture, reminiscence, diatribe and howling frustration. I was not only compromising, I was highfaluting as well, unconsciously reacting to my vengeful feelings about the incident that was now boiling over into print. Eventually, I took meditation out of the title. You decide.

The book is also a mystery, though not in the Agatha Christie sense. Just a mystery to me.

Finally, it's also an exercise in Gestalt therapy, with a very big couch on which I put no less than the world and progress from one little excrescence to its soul, which I find in very poor condition.

You have noticed by now, I expect, that I didn't have a plan when I set out. No, I did have a plan, but I was avoiding it. It was a simple plan, the sort you set out for a recalcitrant. Paul Gibney, my clinical supervisor, made it up for me one day when I had finished telling him a story about some casework I did in my counselling job.

That's the way clinical supervision works. I tell him what I have been doing to my clients and then we talk. Mostly, though, we laugh. Not at my clients, not even at me. Rather, because life is, from one point of view, hilarious. Often it's wry laughter, because life is also often false. Phoney, i.e., as Holden Caulfield said so often. Anyway, I did sit down one day and make an attempt to follow Gibbo's plan, but this book happened instead, growing out of a detour I took. I'm good at digression.

I used to think Holden was overdoing it. But working inside an organisation in a job that forces your focus on to the internal workings of the organisation itself makes you appreciate what Salinger was doing with his teenage alter ego. That's because, while phonies are everywhere, they especially accumulate in the upper reaches of organisations. (One is probably a phoney oneself, but other people will have to write a book about that.) Now, I know life is more than what happens in large organisations, and therefore it's not fair to say life as a whole is sometimes false, but when I try to add up all the bits of my history that were not influenced, or downright sat upon, by some large organisation, I come up with ten minutes. So I can say my life is often false. Was often false, at least. I'm retired now and they have less interest in you after you retire.

Anyway, the plan. With a stitch in his side one day, Paul said, "You have to write a book. This is priceless." Then he went serious and said, "It needs to be out there, for the sake of all the people who fall victim to them." His was that I write an introduction and a conclusion, a top and tail, and in between write up ten cases, with a rave attached to each one drawing out some principle of therapy. Paul wasn't the first clinical supervisor to say this to me, but for some reason, maybe because at sixty something I felt like a grown up at last, or maybe at sixty something, having failed to feel grown up for so long, I forsook the quest and decided to just be what I was and let everyone see it. At any rate, I took him seriously. At the beginning, at least.

I soon hit the detour and so wrote the wrong book. Another way to say that is I avoided. I prefer digressed. The way I did it was to side-track on to reminiscence while researching old emails connected with my casework with one of the persons I was going to write up. Instead of collecting emails connected with that particular case, I began to remember the case of a particular email, one that didn't relate to a particular person in trouble, but to the idea of people in trouble. And the extraordinary syndrome of reactions of people in trouble sometimes provokes.

Well, following that side-track wherever it led turned out to be a very effective avoidance technique, and if you persist beyond this preface, you can decide whether it was also fruitful. But I don't want you to skip to the main bit just yet. First I'd like you to read this stuff about working with a client. For a couple of reasons: One, it'll give you some idea of what goes on behind the closed door of the counselling room and might make me seem a bit credible; and, Two, I don't want you blabbing to Paul that I am a complete truant.

What I did with Levina, I had done with countless other clients over the previous twenty-five years. I attempted to help her clarify the situation she was caught up in, and in her particular case, the intersecting binds, one emotional and one organisational, that defined it.

Levina's voicemail came in at 12:41pm. It was a busy day and I didn't listen to it until after 4pm. Having no such luxury as a receptionist, I had adjusted to being unable to return my clients' calls immediately, and had learned both to suppress my uneasiness about delaying help and to merely hope they would be OK in the meantime. Levina's request was simply for an appointment, but there was something in the tone of her recorded voice that undid my complacency. So, late as it was, I dialled her number. She was still at her desk and I could hear relief in her voice when I identified myself. I asked if it was urgent we meet. She asked could it be tomorrow.

At ten the next morning I ushered her into the room and pointed at a chair. She was in her thirties and wore a long dress of the kind her mother might have worn back when we thought the world was about to opt for love and peace. Levina's face seemed creased with anxiety, like the visible expression of what I heard in her voice the day before.

She hadn't been sleeping, she told me. Her doctor had ordered her to take time away from work and she had done so, spending the better part of a week at home. She had not wanted to accept the prescription for "something to help you sleep", but he insisted, telling her she might be glad of it later. After three days doing it tough, she had relented. The sleeping medication, however, had not proven effective. A couple of hours a night was the best she had been able to get, she told me, on the nights she got any sleep at all.

I waited for her to tell me in her own time the events that had reduced her to this state. The story unfolded in a piecemeal fashion, partly because Levina was reluctant. Not reluctant to tell me, just reluctant to believe all this was happening to her. It offended her idea of herself. Information about a past which had built that other idea of herself kept coming out with the story. Eventually, however, the matter around which her present unease had accrued like oedema came clear. She began to describe Melanie, her co-worker.

As the picture of what had gone on in her work area took shape in the space between our two chairs, I began to wonder how the debility I was seeing in her co-existed with what were life skills of an impressive order. Levina had run her own businesses before taking a low level administrative position in a public service department. She had skills far outstripping those required in her job, and, I sensed, a practised ability to get along with other human beings of many kinds.

Neither did she seem anybody's fool. She described her relationship with Leonard, her de facto, a man roughly her own age. He owned his house, as she owned hers. They spent time together and time apart. Leonard was an IT professional and made a comfortable living. They had travelled and planned to travel again. In fact, the travel to come had been Levina's reason for taking the job here.

Hearing all this, I could only speculate about the industrial strength personality disorder which must have existed in Melanie to so scuttle Levina's sangfroid. I never did get a first-hand look at it, as it turned out, for I wasn't to see Levina beyond two sessions and never saw Melanie at all. In any case, Melanie, it also turned out, may as well have been a piece of furniture, a given. How to deal with her was fascinating terrain, but lay beyond the immediate Badlands Levina wandered in right now, and from where she called to me for help.

Levina, hired on by the Department as a general factotum, had recently found herself transferred from a work area which had functioned quite smoothly into the Service Protocols Unit, a group of perhaps a dozen people with a coordinating role, keeping tabs on programs and activities other sections and branches ran to implement the Department's functions.

Whatever success the unit might have had measuring and evaluating the service arrangements it scrutinised in other parts of the organisation, it seemed not to have had much coordinating its own.  Every unit of government, however obscure or high profile its brief, marches on the stomachs of its clerical admin staff.  If letters don't get posted, records archived, phones answered, visitors met, nothing eventuates, no matter how brilliant or energetic the "thinking" echelon of the unit is.  Arriving in the Service Protocols Unit, Levina had quickly perceived that Melanie, although herself a temporary employee, had created a hellish enclave.  She was pushy, loud, demanding, threatening and utterly without insight into her own behaviour.  She had no rank other than a superior decibel capacity, but had assumed the role of deciding who among the three women holding the support positions, i.e., herself, Levina and one other, would do the tasks that fell to their collective responsibility.

For a while Levina's innate skills had got her by.  The senior people in the Unit, with a nod and a wink, made her understand that that was simply the way Melanie was.  One worked around her and kept the peace.  It was unfortunately true that a number of promising staff had left the unit over the twenty months or so Mel had been there, but there had been no formal complaint to act upon and the senior people had consciously taken a do-nothing approach, though that is not the adjective they employed to characterise their response.  Levina wasn't there to run the Unit and had been content to fall in with the prevailing style.  It may have been that as much as her abilities which made her the target for what happened next.

It was at an all-of-unit staff meeting.  Melanie was holding the floor, being critical of an uncooperative and aggressive style displayed by some workers in the sections that the Service Protocols Unit had as "clients" which she found very annoying when she had to deal with them on official Unit business.  It was, as everyone knew, a style she herself displayed.  Furthermore, there was a good chance she found it only where she provoked it in the first place. As Melanie held forth on this there had been the usual embarrassed silence camouflaging the finger-tapping frustration of saying nothing and waiting for her to finish.  Into that silence, however, Levina had ventured on this one and only occasion, gently drawing attention to the fact that "some of us might be equally at fault".

She gave me a full account of what she had said, diplomatic and general, her us enunciated to mean the Unit. Nevertheless, Melanie, perhaps having in some deep recess of her psyche placed herself in the frame, had reacted sharply. Levina had criticised her unfairly, she said, switching her focus adroitly from the clients to her co-worker. She announced that she felt aggrieved and made a speech about it. The discussion trailed away into uncomfortable silence, with only a few face-saving gestures from the senior people.

Later one of those senior people, Donna, came privately to Levina and told her Melanie had insisted on mediation, and a session of that one-size-fits-all panacea was to be organised. Donna was apologetic, but her hands, she told Levina, were tied. She assured Levina that her advent was regarded by herself and the Director, Scott, as the best thing that had happened to the Service Protocols Unit. Her work and interpersonal skills were much admired. In due course, the mediation session took place, conducted by another of the senior managers of the Unit, one now working as a manager but who had once practised as a social worker. Scott was in attendance and, unlikely as it may have seemed, himself became the target of an outburst of righteous ill temper from Melanie.

I must have raised a metaphorical eyebrow, or even a real one, at the decision to have someone from their own management facilitate the mediation, for Levina, as if I had thought out loud, volunteered that she had been a little doubtful herself about how detached this woman could be. In any event, its upshot was an agreement that Melanie and Levina would "talk" together, go for coffee and in general work on their relationship at once whenever anything came up. It was decided, in the spirit of togetherness, that no record need be kept of the mediation, formality, after all, being so unpleasant; and no one outside the unit needed to be aware of the matter. In fact, no one outside the room they mediated in.

The mediation was declared a success, everyone resumed work ... and Levina went down in a heap.

Now, after a week of emotional illness that more than exhausted her sick leave, she was returning to work. She had been back at work one day before coming to see me. Her managers had encouraged her to see me. They felt sure it would help her adjust to "traumatic events", which were unspecified, but their urging was accompanied by vague allusion to other pressures in her life. Unfortunately, they had told her sympathetically, her pay for the fortnight would be affected. She was, as she sat in front of me, a blubbering mess, with no idea why.

I enumerated all the ways in which, on its surface, her situation was good. Her bosses valued her and her work immensely. They had intimated to her in no uncertain terms that they knew what the score really was, and saw through Melanie's distorted representation of what had gone on. They privately sympathised with Levina and admitted that Melanie had been a problem long before Levina's appearance on the scene.

My summary served to further entrench Levina in her bewilderment, as I expected it would. What then, she wondered out loud, was the matter with her? Why was she so upset? I did not discourage her use of that carpetbag epithet, "upset", for it left much room for the more specific space we would need later.

I asked her after a short silence during which we sat with her conundrum to tell me what feelings she was experiencing. Like many people, she avoided admitting that she was harbouring such an unworthy feeling as anger. I let her pile up some of the nicer feelings, the ones that attract pity and don't reflect poorly upon the speaker. It was clear nothing was happening. I waited. Then I asked, is there nothing else there? I had assayed her capable of insight, but, if insight was there, it was an impacted wisdom tooth that would come, or not, in its own time. A half-delivered molar guilty only of indecision might not attract the dentist's attention, but this one was deforming its environment.

I did another little enumeration. "You have a co-worker who abuses people – you now included. Your bosses admit her behaviour is unacceptable, but do not say so to her. You have been recruited into an exercise in futility – the mediation – which has also served as a substitute for supervisory action against Melanie. It is all safely in-house. No record exists. The reputation of the unit is preserved. Scott and Donna have evaded the unpleasantness of taking Melanie to task, and surreptitiously appointed you to rehabilitate Melanie's behaviour via ongoing coffees which they have not even offered to pay for. Confident that I had assessed her feelings a-right, I had made the decision before speaking to throw a tilt into the description: futility, safely, reputation, evaded, surreptitiously, . .

I watched her face as I spoke. There was some movement. The strained confusion that had modelled her features earlier intensified. We were getting close to something, but we weren't going to reach it.

"Are you angry at Melanie?"

Levina's answer was immediate. "No. She is just ignorant. She has no insight. She sincerely believes herself innocent." She thought for a minute. "But, you know," she said, "I am angry." There was another silence, after which she said, "At myself, maybe."

"Well, not at Scott and Donna, certainly," I said. "They are clearly on your side and think you're the ant's pants." This was more tilt, disguised as less.

"Yes," Levina said. Although there was a breath of uncertainty under the word, I saw that her commitment to nice was tenacious. She looked at me. Levina had laid a small sum on the pawnbroker's counter, but full redemption of her heart was going to require something more. I would have to use a scalpel. More sleepless nights were not going to help.

"I think, Levina," I said, "that your feelings have been dammed up by your bosses' approval. They're like a swollen creek that has nowhere to go."

Now she burst into tears afresh, but they weren't like the blubbering earlier. There was focus. Her face seemed to say that she had seen something about herself and it disappointed her. Good, but not enough. I waited, only sliding the box of tissues closer to her along the low table between us.

I took another detour before picking up the blade again. If she could get there under her own steam, I knew there'd be less chance of her relapsing back to stuck.

"You've run two businesses, Levina." She nodded.

"And you've employed people."

She nodded again. "Sales reps. Yes."

"Were they good at what they did?"

"They were feisty, but, yeah, good. It was a hard game. Too mousey, you wouldn't cut it", she said. Her face told me that thinking of those times moderated her anguish.

"How'd you manage them?" I asked. "I mean, did it ever get out of..."

"Well, when you're ultimately responsible for the business, and that includes making enough money to pay them," she said, "you have to draw the line. I just tried to keep the place looking like a business and they soon saw that they had to act professional, too." I could see that reminding her of her successful self was doing a lot of good. But I was after more.

"So, being the boss, you kept the place business-like and professional?" I was purposely re-using her words to inform a bromide from the language of training programs our staff development people ran for new supervisors. It was unlikely someone employed as a temp would have been on it, so she may have heard the phrase somewhere else, or maybe it just clicked for some other reason. At any rate, her face seemed to lighten.

"You're right", she said, responding not to my last question, but to a consequent assertion made by some party in her head. Then, after a pause during which she seemed to be dialoguing with that party, she fulminated. "Those ...!"

The suppressed expletive told me there was one impediment left. "And you are not allowed to mention it because that would be ungrateful. They have been so nice."

Now came the tears again, but these were tears of anger. They didn't last long. After a little while, she seemed to set her jaw. Sometimes you can almost hear the huge boulders grinding and crashing and settling into place again in a person's internal landscape, or maybe it's the sound of teeth locking down on some resolution.

The rest of that session, maybe fifteen minutes, we spent working out some steps she could take back at the office to put the burden back where it belonged. Scott and Donna had been urging her to apply for leave without pay for the time she had been obliged to take off sick. They had not mentioned (as they should have) applying for workers compensation, which would have paid Levina's salary for the days she was unfit, and since the cause was clearly in the workplace, the claim would have had every chance of success. One of the steps she decided upon was to not accept any arrangement to accommodate her absence that disadvantaged her financially.

I saw her once more, a week later. She was sleeping again.

_____ooo_____

CONSIDERED as an abstract feature of our species' praxis, organisation is a human triumph; it can put a footprint on the surface of the moon; but an organisation can, and quite as well, put a boot print on the human heart, as Orwell warned. Organisations provide many nooks and crannies in which our worst traits can flourish, and flourish undisturbed. Their victims often do not understand where the shafts are coming from any more than a watched wren knows someone is inside that hide that looks so much part of the scenery. What one can do as a Staff Counsellor, by definition situated within an organisation, is raise the hide so the bird sees the birdwatcher.

Michael O'Neill

Now, in one sense, that is what good counsel does in any setting, internal or external, hides being as much a feature of our inner schemes of self-ambush as they are of those without. Organisational life, however, is rich in them. It keeps you busy.

It can also keep you off the A list, and render you persona non grata. Years of providing it to members of my organisation did for me (you can read those three words with the emphasis on the first, if you will). What you will soon read will show you how.

1970 Moratorium demonstration in Brisbane - part of national protests against Australia's military involvement in the Vietnam War © Fryer Library, Brisbane.

# 1
## Top of the World, Ma!

SOMETIME in the 1990s I was at a party where there was a man whom many of us remembered marching alongside us in the sixties and seventies, a wry left-wing student radical, irreverent, loud. He was explaining why he had just taken a very well-paid public service position in the upper echelon of the Education Department. He had been living in another state for many years and we didn't know what he had been doing. What we did know was that once he would have roundly reviled the Education Department for its bureaucratic backwardness, so our curiosity about what he had been doing and what he was about to do was tinged with scepticism.

"Comrades," he said, "I have been on the long march through the institutions." There was enough auld-lang-syne in his phrase to resonate with our shared ratbag past, enough residue of our one time reverence for Mao, enough nostalgia for 1968 to dissolve the tension and turn the talk to other things. And though his words could be written off as rationalisation of a cynical surrender to the blandishments of Capital, there was just enough possibility of sincerity in them to earn him the benefit of the doubt. He might still be fair dinkum about change.

So might we. After all, even though our street-fighting days were far in the past and most of us had in at least modest comfort bred a new generation, were housed in government jobs from which we looked comfortably upon the world, the concept of the long march, usually attributed to "Red" Rudi Dutschke, was a powerful anodyne. Many of us had proclaimed the intention to go on that march ourselves all those years ago. So our incipient mandarin's comment recalled our western attempt to be worthy, in spite of the relative comfort of our middle-class revolutionary exertions, of the life and death struggle of our third world comrades. We couldn't march through the wilds of China and we weren't going to realise the socialist paradise next year, so we'd march through the wilds of Whitehall, Washington, Canberra and George Street instead. Nostalgia and shame, in equal measure.

And fatalism: 1968 was a long time ago and we had not hell but kids to raise.

However, the idea, now readmitted to my head, took up residence in a back room. I had never properly examined what long march meant, how Mao translated into now and here in Australia, and I didn't know I was marching until I had half written this book.

It was never clear what we were supposed to do over this long haul, all the while pretending to be fair dinkum, innocent, sincere members of the workforce in whatever institution we were marching through – the public service, the military, the priesthood, the world of private enterprise. Maybe we were meant to independently trigger the overthrow of each of these institutions and begin their replacement with a workers' paradise of love and sisterhood, of brotherhood and plenty at a synchronised moment which we would all be advised of by group email the day before it was to happen.

What did Rudi want from us? What were we supposed to be actually doing as we scuttled and scurried, flimflammers in false moustaches, through life as public servants or soldiers or inmates or sales assistants?

Anyway, walking to work one day, a fifty-minute rumination, I stopped to scribble a note to myself. I had done this a thousand times over the years this book has haunted me, but on this day I got high above it, a long way up, and saw it whole. I had been letting the book and its writer follow their own weird, as Alan Watts advised, and now I realised where that weird was bent, what its route of march was. I wasn't just walking to work, I was marching, and not just to work, but through it. Long marching. I was following orders, Rudi Dutschke's orders, his proposed alternative way of renewing and rehabilitating society.

Max Bruinsma, in his 2001 essay, The Long March, said Dutschke had intended that we should "...go in, behave – and take over". Bruinsma says he called it 'the long march through the institutions' to urge us, we protesting students, to see ourselves as our parents and vice-chancellors kept asking us to, as future leaders, but not to ensure the continuity they hoped cultivating such a self-image would guarantee; rather its opposite. Dutschke wanted us to remember undercover why change was necessary to begin with, so that we blended but did not vanish into the background of our ancien-regime offices leached of passion, but rather kept the faith.[1]

A hard task when one's supply lines stretched over decades, and the temptation to go feral was so strong, the rewards so great. One wonders, like a soldier of Imperial Japan growing old alone in the jungles of Borneo, is anyone still out there. Even Rudi is long since dead. Can one still "take over"? How?

Well, one doesn't; but many might. I began to re-imagine my scribbled pieces of paper as observations of the terrain, a forward scout's tactical intel, that under cover of darkness I must slowly reassemble as a map for those to come.

The task was: Learn. Understand. Put flesh, the flesh of actual experience, upon the theoretical bones of the radical ideas and theory that inspired us in the books and speeches of our youth. See for ourselves the way the reigning paradigm and ideology of the dominant power in the world dictates the style of almost everything we do, everything we think, every local rule and by-law, every manipulative piece of rhetoric that gets developed to govern life in our workplaces, in our homes, on our TV shows. (Now pay attention to what you just read. If you get this, you're less likely to become pissed off at, and more likely to persist with, particular parts of this book where I'll be attempting to hogtie some things that happened so you can see how they link to some big ideas in history, politics, psychology, literature, philosophy and ideology. It's long-bow stuff, but not nut case.)

Rudi wanted us to see how thoroughly the people who are the victims of this oppression remain ignorant of it, resist knowing it, prefer ignorance, quiet and subdued lighting, as once again Orwell

---

[1] http://www.typotheque.com/articles/the_long_march/

made clear[2.] He wanted us to see how well some of us do the bidding of the beast without ever leaving the comfort of our homely understanding of life. To see what happens to any who notice the emperor's wonderful clothes are mere air. To climb out from under.

Maybe I had been too hard on my erstwhile *comrade* at the party.

_____ooo_____

SO the story you've got in front of you looks like lines of prose, but it's the map I am leaving on the track. I've gone on ahead. The pre-map was that short peek inside my consulting room I've already given you, but the map proper starts with a set of coordinates that delimit a tiny bit of territory called Friday Afternoon's Email. We'll start there, with a close analysis of that little contretemps in the office and with luck we'll end with a view from on top of the world, a little like the one that Cody Jarrett could see at the end of White Heat. Cody was Jimmy Cagney's insanely defiant bad guy in that 1949 movie who, pursued by the good guys and with all his companions dead, clambered to the top of an above-ground storage tank at an oil facility, a huge, silver sphere.

---

[2] She knew when to cheer and when to boo, and that was all one needed. If he persisted in talking of such subjects, she had the disconcerting habit of falling asleep . . . Talking to her, he realised how easy it was to present an appearance of orthodoxy while having no grasp whatever of what orthodoxy meant. In a way, the world-view of the party imposed itself most successfully on people incapable of understanding it. They could be made to accept the most flagrant violations of reality, because they never fully grasped the enormity of what was demanded of them, and were not sufficiently interested in public events to notice what was happening. By lack of understanding they remained sane.

They simply swallowed everything, and what they swallowed did them no harm, because it left no residue behind, just as a grain of corn will pass undigested through the body of a bird.

George Orwell, *1984*

From there he looked down at his tormentors, cartoonish little characters like my medieval forebears in the cartographers' guild placed upon their landscapes but now come to life in their suits and peaked caps and ducking for cover behind their shiny automobiles. When I saw him up there some time in the early fifties I was a ten-year-old at the local 'pitchers', but the potential for both him and his pursuers to be blown to Kingdom Come was not lost on me or the cinema full of my fellow worshippers. I am hoping to get you up there by the end of this story, up there with me and Cody, looking down on our tormentors and seeing them for what they are.

The potential in an undeceived view of the world to move us all to the kingdom to come won't be lost on you either, I hope. And, yes, I can smell the scent of risk. In deference to it, and to the ever present hubris, we'll remain silent when Cody, about to die, calls out to his Ma.

# 2
## We Don't Like Talking About That

> Will knew that the man was speaking the truth. But
> it wasn't a welcome truth. It was heavy and painful. The
> man seemed to know that, because he let Will bow his head
> before he spoke again. "There are two great powers," the
> man said, "and they've been fighting since time began.
> Every advance in human life, every scrap of knowledge and
> wisdom and decency we have has been torn by one side
> from the teeth of the other. Every little increase in human
> freedom has been fought over ferociously between those
> who want us to know more and be wiser and stronger, and
> those who want us to obey and be humble and submit.
>
> Philip Pullman, *The Subtle Knife.*

OK, the Friday Afternoon Email story. I'll tell you this story by
letting you listen while I muse to myself about the reaction I got to
what I did. And I'll get to the detail of what I did soon, but first I
need to let you know the minimum you will need to make sense of
it, give you context in which to situate it. It was no big deal, by the
way, so don't slaver. I won't be confessing to the composition and
distribution of salacious pornography. All I did was write a short,
non-obscene email and send it to some people.

Here's the context:

As you've seen already with Levina, I worked as a counsellor
in an organisation, and that's what I was doing when I sent the
thing out. I was called the Staff Counsellor. I counselled the other
workers in the organisation. It was a large organisation with many
functions, and the Levina story may have given the impression my
main work was analysing reported dialogue for clues to damaging
personal quirks, albeit ranged. It was not. There were, as well,
other stimuli which reduced workers to jelly, hurt them, frightened
them and alarmed them. Responding to these was mine as well.

It's Friday, early afternoon, in June some years back, probably
around 2001. I'm metaphorically slumped in my chair after four
and a half days of vicarious exposure to people's traumatic

experiences. I hatch a plan that seems brilliant. Because what I had been exposed to during the week so far – not an atypical week – had made me realise afresh how vulnerable my clients were, what slings and arrows lay routinely in wait for them as they went about their duties, I would send out an email to my colleagues in the human resources network and share this sad realisation with them.

I had been idling with a pencil and paper, just itemising the essence of each of the previous four and half days of client contacts, to no purpose that I was aware of. It was a column of crises and resembled an after-the-fact shopping list, one you write when you get home from the supermarket in hell, for though I pencilled

words alone, a tortured face looked back. Here, I saw, was the communiqué to my colleagues, already written. Those colleagues, my intended audience, were themselves a select segment of the whole body of my vulnerable clients, of course; but since the remaining portion, four thousand people, were their clients as well, towards whom they, like me, had a pastoral duty,

sharing my realisation with this select few seemed like a good idea. As you will see when you read what I sent out, the organisation we were all part of was a large government Department, and its staff was spread out across the state.

"Good idea" was about the extent of my conscious understanding of what I was doing at the moment I set about composing the top and tail for the email. Later, I would be given ample opportunity, and encouragement, to scrutinise that good idea and the motivation it concealed more deeply.

Anyway, this is what I wrote:

Michael O'Neill

Subject: a week in the life

Dear Colleagues

Today I was reflecting on the past week and thinking about some of the things which have happened to [the Department's] staff in five days. I have had contact during the last five days with some members of the HR Network which this email is addressed to. Those among you would know about some part of these happenings but not know about others. Some of you may know of none of them. I wondered if it would be worth letting you all know.

Across the state this week staff involved with the Department's customers have been:-
bashed and hospitalised,
verbally abused to the extent they cannot go on working,
traumatised,
breaking down in tears as a result of being bullied on the street by "customers" of [the Department],
dealing with corpses in the line of duty,
exposed to dead bodies in vehicles aflame,
threatened with bombing,
forced to defend their reputation from slander,
struggling with addiction,
attempting with great trepidation to bring injustice to management attention,
weighed down by personal and family tragedy and attempting to work on,
discredited by "customers" of [the Department] facing potential negative regulatory consequences (fines)...

These people are our clients. You may know of other things they have endured in the last five days which I have not heard about. I would be interested to hear. Perhaps others would too.

    I closed with regards and pushed the fatal send button. Around a hundred recipients were in the email group. Before I tell you what happened next, I'll give you a bit more background. In the meantime, you can be thinking about the email.

    I first began working as a counsellor in employee assistance in 1983, in a different large government department. That's where I learned the trade. Then I moved on, to practise it in another large government department. It's there that the events took place. On the org chart the Employee Assistance Program, or EAP, appeared as a little box labelled "Staff Counsellor", hanging off a slightly bigger box, which in turn hung off an even bigger box. In that biggest box lived the legend "Director, HR Branch". The Branch was the discipline headquarters for human resources matters within the organisation.

Program was rather a grand title for my little bit of the Branch: there was just me.

Most of the rest of the sixty-odd staff of the Branch proper were housed in the same building as I. They were human resources advisers, workplace health and safety advisers, training and staff development people, and so on. More were scattered across the state and in other Divisions of the organisation, satellites floating in deep space, not formally part of the Branch because they were answerable to their local line managers rather than the Director of the human resources branch. Nevertheless, the batteries in their little receivers could still pull in a signal from mission control, if only just, so they formed part of the human resources network. Together we were around one hundred souls.

While the four thousand who made up the department in toto might superficially be seen as constituting "the department", we hundred or so in the HR network knew that wasn't so. The Department was really that deity in the temple's inner sanctum, and we were its priests, its interface with the staff body.

The idea of a public service Department as a deity is not altogether fanciful. The two share some characteristics. Both are notional beings. You can't actually touch either of them. Both command veneration. They may both be merely ideas, but for those who accept their reality and authority, they are ideas with biceps. That is, along with obeisance, they command obedience.

When people speak of an organisation of this kind, especially if their relationship with it is conflicted, they are likely to say something like: "The Department's always been fair (or generous, or cruel) to me, I have to admit." Now, this, of course, always means that someone holding office in the Department has been fair, generous or cruel.  One has to remind oneself that the Department is neither a person nor conscious, qualities pre-requisite in a party being praised for fairness and generosity or accused of cruelty.  If we take a closer look at this linguistic tendency to personify it, a certain similarity is suggested again to the way we personify the power to which we attribute the running of the universe.  Or at least the way those of us given to believing the universe is run by a person and not mere chance do so.  The Department finds itself, in other words, in the company of she/he/it who is known by the names God, Allah, the Great Spirit, etc.  The Department is able to so consort in our minds with the deity because we attribute to it, consciously or not, a like capacity to control our destinies.

This illusion persists for a reason.  The Department had, and has, indeed, the capacity to control our destinies, since we were and are employed by it.  Moreover, we, if I may speak generically and include present and past staff, tend continually to grow abject in its face by enforced participation in the cultural practices of those of its denizens who preceded and inducted us into its all-encompassing milieu.  The style of this relationship is perpetuated by generation after generation of public service recruits, most of whom are quick to learn which side of their bread is buttered.  But some do not. Those were represented, over-represented, in fact, in my clientele.

While I'm on the subject of force and oppression, I had better tell you something else.  I like to watch.  And working in EAP meant that what I got to watch was organisation.  People engaged in organised effort is an engrossing study.  As I hinted above when reflecting upon my work with Levina, organisation has potential not only to lift us to the heavens, but also to save us day to day.  Of course, it already has – one caveperson couldn't rack up as high a score at staying out of the proverbial sabre's teeth as two looking out for each other – but on the whole organised effort gets mixed reviews.

A word about how I came where I could indulge my voyeurism upon organisations, that is, to that large Department. I had the same role in my previous employment, but in that one I had not pursued the role. I happened to be working there as a drudge to keep myself fed while I finished a social work degree, and it happened to be an organisation that employed many social workers, who worked their magic on members of the public. I graduated and did a little stint as a social worker, doing what all the others did. But soon it just kind of happened that I began to act in the Staff Counsellor job after the ex-priest who used to do it resigned.

It was fun of course, seeing the clients; and educational for me, moving slowly, post graduation, towards a journeyman competence. However, what really engaged my heart (and spoke to my ingrained jaundice, perhaps) was having a ringside seat at the ongoing dyadic duelling of detriment and defence, authority and autonomy, boss and subordinate that is organisational life. In their many variations the play of those dyads exposed the still nascent, unconstructed generic nature of organisational life. Sociality – without it there is no humanness. It is our species' thing. Or it should be our thing, at least.

It is sometimes said of parenting that no one is taught how to do it, even though it is the practice that pre-determines all other praxis of human life. Likewise, it could be said, no one ever teaches you how to survive organisational life, and yet it is the mode the species has chosen to midwife almost every other endeavour on the planet. And here I was, as resident shrink, with access to the organisation's refuse, that collection of casualties conveyed endlessly out the back door on a belt, and they magically still are able to talk to me and teach me how it all happened to them.

What if, I used to wonder, some of the people who did it to them, those who commanded (on behalf of the organisation, of course; and what a puzzle that is, finding the dividing line between toxic behaviour in the bully manager and the commission he or she has from the organisation to do its work, dirty or other), what if they could get above their egos and recognise that what these casualties conveyed to me in faint whispers as I smoothed the pillow was, to mangle the bard, caviar for the general? Such intelligence could be parlayed into genuine sustenance, effective remedy. To use it, however, requires recognition that something needs fixing. Generals big enough for that, they who serve their troops rather than have their troops serve them, are few.

But lack of an audience didn't stop me learning my lines. I continued to bone up and though most of it lay unread, I began to pile up reams of good ideas distilled from the pain of others.

_____ooo_____

MY first Department then embraced the foolish fad of downsizing, a reasonless aping of the private sector, practised in the public sector for nought but ideological sucking up reasons. And it was a Department with enormous lung capacity. There was almost no one left to turn off the lights.

Forced, I moved. I resumed hoarding scribbled good advice when I got another job, doing exactly the same role in another large government department. Well, lots of good things lend themselves to hoarding for hoarding's sake, but not good ideas. Those, you want to share. And that's the attitude that got me into trouble. It led to the act I described above, sending out an email to my colleagues. And the trouble it got me into taught me something about the workings of the cultural transmission process within organisations. It gave me a look at the way individuals contribute to, modify, and enshrine a style; how styles are threatened by alternative styles; how individuals' needs, psychological and economic, influence what they pass down to those subordinate to them, and even up to those to whom they are subordinate; though transactions running in that direction, because unable to rely on power's philtre, only work if the influencer is cunningly attuned.

Bit of theory, yes, but don't yawn. Like any good story, this one centres on a conflict and it's coming, it's coming.

With some justice, our nearly four thousand plebeians saw us priests of HR as puissant. We had our collective hand on a spigot at the bottom of a huge reservoir filled with influence under pressure. The jet which that spigot could produce had clout and telescopic reach; it was as trainable as a rifle and equally able to command compliance.

Puissant, yes; but not without internal rupture. Chasms of schism criss-crossed our collective HR self. One particular internal divide rendered me the only person on my side of the line. It concerned the styles of our respective relations with our common clients, the organisation's other 3 900 workers. I felt like I lived in one room and everyone else in the human resources network lived in the next. This was obviously physically true – I did see clients in a private room – and it was, equally obviously, psychologically true, since all staff of an organisation are potentially clients of the Employee Assistance Program; but I began to see my sense of separateness was true in a more immediate and specific way. In my fancy, the imaginary door connecting my room to theirs had a strange property that, though at first I couldn't name it, later revealed itself a trace left over from a bedtime story.

In the room the rest of the network lived in all seemed businesslike, accustomed, ceremonious and steady. They seemed to know what they were doing. Their dealings with our clients followed set procedures. The very weather outside was balmy. But when I stepped back into my room, serenity departed. Here, the squall. One was suddenly not indoors at all, but outside among stinging rain, lightning flashes and gusting wind wrapping scraps of newsprint to your face. Its night and streetlights sputter out, tyres squeal and your feet slip from the wet kerb into gutters running a banker. Detritus everywhere, and moaning, and long, charged periods of staring down the devil for possession of a soul. Yet slip through the door again and, as if by magic, all is calm. One's clothes are dry. The only trace of the disorder left is in the heart, invisible.

My paranormal door might have been one dislodged from the multitude hanging from another conveyor system, the one that snaked like aerial spaghetti through the cavernous factory in which

31

Monsters, Inc. did business in the Disney-Pixar movie of that name. These were the doors the Scarers went through, if the red light on the lintel was illuminated, to exit their own world and find themselves in the normal world, in particular in the bedrooms of its children. Like the Scarers, I could pass from one world to the other and return at will. My clients seemed to exist in both worlds, too. In my room I saw them flesh and blood; in the other room my colleagues spoke their names to me and to each other and had dealings with them, creating them in simulacrum. The names were the same names they had in my room, but hardly any other attributes seemed to match.

I'm not trying to alarm you, Dear Reader. This contrast was not as Jekyll and Hyde as it sounds. It was merely the result of the different planes on which a counsellor and a mainstream HR operative relate to a staff member. I often thought about that difference and about the related fact that much of the anger, hurt and outrage, humiliation and perplexity clients like Levina bring into the consulting room arises out of their dealings with the Department, that deity in the inner sanctum, much of which dealing is via these very colleagues of mine. (I should add that some, of course, of my colleagues in the other room had equal insight into the dolours of our charges, but lacked the remit.)

Anyway, my awareness of these differences led to the "good idea" I acted upon. I think what had unconsciously grown slowly within me was the desire to let my colleagues in the other room have a peek into mine. Eventually, as you've seen, the perfect opportunity arose and I did it; but my act of communication, the Friday afternoon email you read earlier, had consequences I did not predict, and left me licking my wounds for a long time. I didn't mean for it to become famous, or infamous, but soon after I sent it out it developed a life of its own, went about making its own friends and enemies. Shortly it trotted back to me like a pup who's fetched next door's washing and expects a reward, trailing a squabbling retinue which was divided into two warring groups who hectored each other and postured and demanded attention.

# 3
## Email Wars

INSOFAR as I had given any thought at all to the kind of reception this missive might meet, I had expected only to be genially indulged. Ah yes, Michael doing his usual thing, urging gently upon us a more thoughtful attitude towards our clients (i.e., towards the rest of the staff of the Department whose administrative requirements we meet and whose difficulties in relating to the organisation we try to resolve). I knew the email would be read by senior people, just temporarily forgot what its naively truthful message might excite. I had spoken naively to senior people in other places and shouldn't have forgotten, but in those earlier, so other, contexts the surface accidents were different, different enough to make me forget I was speaking truth to power.

And there was in the room on the other side of Disney/Pixar door where all's positive and bright a powerful being who would not brook contagion from my room or any other.

My peers, however, responded to it for a few days with mild interest and even some warmth. There was demur, but it was polite. A well-mannered, network-wide debate started up. Emails referred to my message as "valued feedback" and encouraged others to "take it on board". They drew attention to maxims beloved of organisational boosters, "our people are our most valued resource" and "a happy employee is a productive employee" and thought it good I'd helped them become more aware of the unhappiness that resource was experiencing. They wanted to "respond to the horror" because our "experience as a society patently demonstrates that we can't just expect people who go through trauma to 'just get over it'". They pointed out to each other that the "effects of trauma can run deep and over long time frames". They saw that employers had an "obligation to provide a work environment that is healthy and safe on both a physical and psychological" level. They canvassed ideas for responding to the disorder out there supportively. They allowed that it was quite clear that it's not all wine and roses at the coal face and even suggested I had touched on only a few situations, tip of the iceberg.

Such disapproval as surfaced included friendly comment describing my email as unpleasant because of its "negativity". Polite or friendly their emails might have been, but the underlying existential timidity and fastidiousness which motivated these disapprovers angered one correspondent whom I shall call Spiro. He entered the fray with the following email, addressed to me, but ccd to the whole network, early the next Tuesday morning:

Subject: Re: a week in the life (A Reality Check)

Michael,

Thankyou sincerely for that reality check. It has taken a little while for me to respond as I try not to get involved in the E-Mail debates for obvious reasons. Be they small in numbers the replies to date are pretty surprising. Maybe people would like to hear some nice bedroom stories from your work environment where everyone lives happily ever after and then they can feel warm and comfortable under their cosy HR blanket.
People pull your head out of your ----------- sand pit and realise that as much as [the Department] is trying to improve the situation for our most valued resource, professions like Michael's are going to see the damaged people. Hey all you productivity buffs out there did you know that a happy employee is a productive employee.
If in HR we have to put a positive spin on any bad news we had better have words with our colleagues in [here he mentions a division of the Department which honestly reports on the state's efforts to improve road safety] and see what they can do about putting a positive spin on their road toll statistics when they are up. I prefer what they do at present, give us the tragic facts and then revisit strategies to improve the situation.
Once again Michael thankyou sincerely for that reality check. A final thought, let us take on board this valued feedback and try and make a difference during our planning for the future.

KR,
Spiro

Spiro added a caustic PS:

In case some think preparing this text is a waste of [the Department's] time, I did it at home.

The scathing nature of this Parthian shot reveals not only Spiro's frustration with the look-the-other-way delicacy he is here castigating his colleagues for, but also his long-standing exasperation over the same endemic ostrich behaviour he had seen throughout the whole Department and the public sector generally, which he had experienced in many of its jurisdictions.

When Spiro alludes ominously to "obvious reasons" why he is loath to engage in public debate, he is betraying a premonition which was to prove valid before nightfall.

Another correspondent was also a touch wary of engaging in discussion publicly, yet showed a mature grasp of the debate nevertheless. Rhyll picked up Spiro's notion of the reality check:

Michael,

In the interests of not continuing the whole email debate, I just cc'd to all of us working in the HR area.

The positive outcomes that are achieved throughout [the Department] should be applauded, however a 'reality check' with information such as this is just as important, as many of us in our everyday roles may not be aware of the negative issues that do occur within business areas, due to their sensitive and confidential nature. Being aware of these real-life incidents can only help us in improving our client service when dealing with staff from business areas by increasing our understanding of the difficulties faced by staff.

When HR/Payroll and [other staff] have interaction with clients, the reality is that it may be as a direct or indirect consequence of incidents similar to those [you] described. The best thing for us to do is bear this information in mind, as the person on the end of the next phone call might just have experienced situations like these.
Once again, thank you for the info sharing.

Rhyll

What Rhyll wrote perfectly articulated the value to her and her colleagues of awareness of their clients' vicissitudes. If we had been inhabiting a rational world the plain sense of her comment would have pre-empted the brouhaha that was to come and we could have all got on with it. Her email was reassuring, but the fact that it ccd only a select few of those who had already spoken and not the whole network, saddened me. The prevalence in otherwise confident and well-educated HR practitioners of such wariness about joining the debate in full public view, i.e., cc-ing one's comments and responses to the entire network, is the by-product of one of the very phenomena this book seeks to delineate. But more of that anon.

I also had a response from my immediate boss (whom I shall call Hans). It was not a written response, but a question put to me in a conversation on another matter, which occurred on the Monday, my little email's first full day out in the big world. Our exchange seemed friendly. He asked only for clarification of my purpose. Lesser mortals seemed to have no difficulty figuring that out and his needing to ask should have given me the tip, but, naïve as ever, I didn't realise that under his neutral curiosity he was merely marking time while he sniffed the wind. The reviews had been mostly good in the lively email traffic and the show may yet be a hit, so one needed to keep one's powder dry (and perhaps one's metaphors under control).

Later that day I was able to email Hans a postscript to our discussion because in the meantime I had responded to an email sent not to the whole network, but to me individually at 1:00pm and I used a segment of my reply to it in my email to Hans. In the 1:00pm email a correspondent whom I shall call Marley had put this to me:

> I think, Michael, and correct me if I'm wrong, but the motivation behind your original email was to bring to the HR network's attention the emerging (or emerged!) state of reality at the coal face in customer service roles... 'Pollyanna' statements notwithstanding!

In my response to Marley I articulated, for the first time, what had been tacit to then:

My conscious motivation was to darken the picture the HR operatives have of our clientele. It happens to me and I suspect to others in the HR game. One tends to become glazed over, blasé, seen it too many times before. It's a natural protection we adopt having to be exposed to too much human dissatisfaction or discomfort or pain or tragedy when our resources or ability to right the wrongs and fix the foul-ups is not adequate to the task. Or our courage fails and we need to protect ourselves from shame by shutting down our sensors to the distress and/or insistence of the face across the counter or the voice in the earpiece.

I felt reminded of who and what our vulnerable clients are by my week. I wanted to pass it on. (Unload it?) I wanted to break – once only and knowing it will need to be done again in a week, a day, an hour – through to the heart and let it bleed a little.

Wise? God knows.

My unconscious motivation? By definition, so far at least, unknown.

Anyway, you identified it correctly.

Regards

Michael[3]

It was the first two paragraphs of this response to Marley that I sent to Hans, a little before 4:30pm. After he got it he kept his

---

[3] This went only to Marley. In hindsight, it might have served me well to cc it to the whole network. On the surface my failure to explain myself when the disapprovers first vocalised looks like haughty reserve – if the swine can't tell a pearl, stuff 'em – but I suspect I had begun to feel a dread curiosity about my colleagues' reactions and a fascination (rabbit in the headlights, perhaps, but certainly plain incredulous) about what was coming rather than shyness.

own counsel still for, I thought at the time, the reasons I touched on above. The more likely reason was to emerge later.

And the reference to Pollyanna in Marley's final exclamation must have slipped into my unconscious to wait.

Let me leave this strand of the story for a minute and take you back to Friday to follow another that took a different route, but was soon to intertwine with the main one. Almost as soon as my original email had hit the airwaves, a colleague I shall call Di wrote back to me with this innocent sounding suggestion:

> Michael
>
> I think you should send this to [the Director-General] with the ending:
>
> "And how has your week been [DG]?"
>
> I think he would be astonished to say the least.
>
> Di

I wasn't kidding about naivety. By 4:30 pm on Friday I had done as Di said. I sent my original email to the DG with this brief introduction above it:

> To: The Director-General
> cc:
>
> Subject:      a week in the life
>
> Dear [D-G]
>
> I circulated the email below to members of the HR Network today. One replied to me suggesting I copy it to you.
>
> kind regards
>
> Michael

Note the empty cc field. I had at least enough nous not to publicise to the whole HR network that the D-G had been presented with this nitro, which would have set up a panting public, lying in wait for his response.

When his reply came after the weekend – on Tuesday morning around 10 o'clock – I confess I was relieved at the sensible nature of it. And I need not have been so cautious about face. He himself chose to share his participation in the debate widely. His email began:

Subject: Re: a week in the life

Michael

I refer to your email to the HR network.

As one of the network suggested you copy it to me, I thought I'd cc these thoughts to the network as well.

It is always concerning when our staff are suffering difficulty or trauma. It can be especially so for you and others in the HR network because, as you say, they are your clients. (Of course, they must be of concern to all of us in [the Department] as well!)...

Now, while it is true the DG then went on and, "without in any way detracting from the importance and human impact of the cases you refer to," provided me and the eavesdropping network with some upbeat information about the "huge number of positives" to be recognised as well, he showed no puzzlement about my purpose and even validated my having adverted to these dark phenomena.

He closed by saying,

In linking this back to the HR network, I think it is important that as well as being aware of the tough cases, everyone in the network is able to keep a balanced view of how all staff in the Department are faring, since this must then help in ensuring the best possible services are available to meet all needs.

With Best wishes

Michael O'Neill

In the face of such graciousness it may be churlish to observe that very few people in authority display concern about promoting a "balanced view" when it's the upbeat side of the organisation's behaviour in the centre ring. I have never heard a suit remind the staff when things are going well or "we" are humbly accepting an excellence award to keep steadfastly in mind all the times we've crushed someone's spirit, met a cry for help with silence, as an organisation subjected a worker to long periods of abuse or condoned any other of the thousand unnatural shocks that bosses turn a blind eye to. A mere quibble this, though. Compared with what was to come, the DG's response was civility itself. It didn't come near to disturbing the calm before the storm. And while it's hard to tell through his good manners, my Friday afternoon email doesn't seem to have made the DG uncomfortable.

Nor should it have. For in truth, when one reads the text of my email over and tries to assess its potential to do some kind of damage to the body politic, to fry the corporate *sangfroid*, to undermine decency, to set off a chain reaction of suicides among its readers or let loose the dogs of war – that is, its explosiveness – then absent any knowledge of the creative capacity most of us have for mistaking one's own unresolved hobby-horse shit for the central point of whatever communiqué is being presented to one – one draws, I think, a blank.

But as always, others may opine otherwise. Across the water from the City of Light, the stately barque *Pollyanna* was hove to. Siobhan leant out from her starboard side seeking wrongs to right. Ten hours would see her dock. I was unaware of its pending arrival when conversing with Hans on Monday afternoon about my Friday email. I was still in the dark when I explained my email's purpose to Hans as I had done for Marley. I couldn't guess how Hans felt. Once Siobhan reappeared and acquainted herself with the controversy, however, she would adopt an attitude and it would suck Hans's email into its slipstream at once.

Hans was wise to wait. The Director's attitude was not going to be easy to predict. For though normally she virtually channels Pollyanna (as Marley well knew), Siobhan, was nevertheless human and this situation was going to test her. The facts as I had laid them out like an electronic Cassandra were indisputable, legal tender, exchangeable at any bank for gold ducats of reality; but, if sweetness and light were to prevail, such coin needed to be withdrawn from circulation, declared counterfeit, and those uttering it utterly routed. That kind of annihilation (knowledge management, we sometimes call it) was going to be hard to achieve while remaining *persona grata* inside the borders of Sunshine City. To massacre Truth is villainy, and though the bard himself may set it down in his tables that a man may smile and be a villain, it was not going to prove easy to slash and burn perniciously and be of pretty mien.

Some level of ambivalence, a touch of role strain for her perhaps, was on the cards.

The Director logged on to her email well after close of business Tuesday and found herself amidst the blizzard. At 7:29pm, Siobhan made her contribution to the debate. You can read this straight through without taking notes. We'll be coming back to it. You'll encounter material in brackets as you read. If they're rounded and soft, they enclose Siobhan's words, as befits. The material in square brackets will be mine. (If you forget, just sniff it. Now each in deference to both our Irishness may have an air of Londonderry, so if it has a perfumed air and reprise the *seamróg*, 'tis hers, if mean, sardonic, or redolent of *Diabhal,* why then, 'tis mine.)

Subject:     Re: a week in the life

Dear Folks

I have been out of the office for two days and am just catching up with the latest area of debate.

On first reading your email, Michael, I was trying to work out what was your purpose – a "wave" for assistance perhaps? I subsequently understand from Hans that you considered that you had sufficient mechanisms in place – a professional mentor – to help you with the impact of your casework – so it was not a cry for help.

Michael O'Neill

Therefore, in your role of staff counsellor, I am still unclear what it is you are trying to achieve by sending out this email. We have the function of staff counselling as one way to assist people to move back to normal living when "bad" things happen. We know that, as part of everyday life, members of the community will act in a way towards the people of [the Department] that is unpleasant, and even damaging in some instances. Both the community and [the Department] have responsibilities here – the community to prevent this behaviour through a range of means, and [the Department] to look after our people who are affected.

An important part of your role is to advise, from the "intelligence" you gather in your work, how we can do something concrete to minimize trauma that occurs through circumstances outside our control. There are strategies we could teach people, for example, to assist them not to "take on board" a lot of the rubbish that angry customers can unload. We can assist people to learn positive self-talk to avoid becoming bitter or adopting a long term victim role. I am sure there are heaps of other positive things we could suggest managers do to help people when they experience such a situation. What do you suggest?

No matter how wonderful any organisation is, "bad" things will happen to people – either from outside or from within the workplace. Just as some people are courageous and struggling to survive though personal tragedy, others might damage through intimidation or neglect, while most work hard and do a great job, want to spend time with friends and family, play sport, and lead a balanced life.

The vast majority of people in [the Department] are working to make our workplaces the best we can, and deal with the mixture of human behaviour and the difficulties that stand in the way. Along with that, goes being clear about what is unacceptable behaviour and stopping it. In your role, Michael, you can contribute to the success of shaping positive environments by encouraging and acknowledging the good news that people are generating, and not sending out a message that makes me feel that we are experiencing some unusually large barrage of misery targeted at the people of [the Department]. (Try telling a Family Trauma Services Officer at present that we are doing it tough!).

I am not advocating a denial of the bad things – I am talking about inspiring people, creating energy to copy some of the good things happening, so that we can achieve together, and use some of that energy to help those having a rough time. I do not believe any other way works.

Please make a time to see me to talk this through further (Misha, please arrange.)

Regards

Siobhan

I felt overwhelmed by this cloud of arrows, as if the intended of some modern Boadicea, whose ranks of archers had loosed a thousand feathered bolts at once, obscuring the sky above me, the shafts sliding this way and that, but all homing on my heart. At the same time, nevertheless, I meant to blunt and break the point of each in turn, if I could before their sheer numbers did for me. But mean as I might, I did nothing. A paralysis, which I told myself was detachment, overtook me. For four years, it held me, until I sat down to this long cathartic task. But let me return to then.

At 7:39pm, ten minutes after the first, Siobhan fired off volley number two, a response to Spiro's email.

Spiro – you have met him already – was a particularly resistant spore, having long since passed beyond that career point where he was fazed by the prospect of her ill will, or anyone else's. Clearly, he required special attention. Applying the hot iron to him also provided a chance to make sure no one missed the connection to the source of the contagion, an opportunity she exploited by cc-ing her email doubly, once to the entire network and once to me individually, and obviously. This ensured I got it twice, once as a network member and once as me. That couldn't hurt.

Subject:     Re: a week in the life (A Reality Check)

Dear Spiro

I cannot understand your point here. All I can hear is a lot of anger expressed in a way that I find insulting to HR people and

> what they are trying to achieve in [the Department]. Please make
> a time to see me to discuss what you were trying to achieve with
> this contribution. Debate is acceptable – belittling and sarcasm
> is not!
> Regards
> Siobhan

Having been licked by the same snake ten minutes before, I was alive to the Director's use here of public humiliation. So I wrote to Spiro late Wednesday morning, commiserating, cc-ing no one. I told him that belittling and sarcasm may or may not be a correct description of what he had written, but regardless of that, public castigation and carpeting of him was not acceptable. She had, I said, done it to me too. Shooting from the hip.

The Director's lapse into bad modelling (i.e., disregard of the elementary supervisory etiquette, praise in public, criticise in private) was not only in full view of her troops, among whom such etiquette was second nature, but ensured they see it and be a party to it. It, the lapse, was an indicator of her panic, a panic understandable, if not forgivable, in one now so riven. The demands from Pollyanna, her internal parasite, for sweetness and light contended with the urge to punish the insubordinate doomsayers, and their squabbling was probably deafening. It's hard to think in such a din. Worse still, add the distraction of the faint voice quibbling around the edges of her interior debate, a murmuring, attenuated wraith, now of no fixed address, asking to be remembered, a self of hers that once upon a time itself inhabited the dark, her gollum.

While the Director's emails targeted me and my adherents, it was the liberty of the HR network to engage with vital, if difficult, professional matters such as the purposeful nourishment of the empathy required to practise that was actually in the cross-hairs. On the face of it, counterproductive. One might, rather, have expected engagement in such an endeavour to attract approval from her. And, indeed, Siobhan pretended to such a liberality. At the beginning of her first salvo, the email to me, she speaks of catching up with the latest area of debate. One might take that to imply that debate was a norm around here. Yet both of her contributions so far had included public summonses to private carpetings. In each the covert message is clearer than the apparent argument: I can back up my silver tongue with my silver gun.

Interpersonal communications got seriously weird sometime in the late twentieth century when pen and ink, and laborious, old-fashioned typewriters fell back before the onslaught of electronically fast thought transfer: email. It's got worse since, but skip that for now. E-fast living means we can say before we think. Virtually. In other words, one consequence of this dizzying way of living is the frequent excision of the reflection and editing phase from the process of percolating our felt reactions to another's act or provocation. This is, or used to be, the phase wherein we set down words where they can't abruptly fly away without being shorn of their shrillness by being processed through our rational minds first. Now, one's first draft reply is there pulsating on the screen – have a look at the way a live computer screen comes up in movie scenes to get a sense of the throbbing impatience of it – and its despatch with despatch is often too hard to resist. The cultural notion of the first draft is dying. I mention this because to read this whole yarn through that fascinator may help us read more generously. And even at this remove of years I can use a little generosity.

Now, I want to say something about the values at work here. How could it have come about, this immersion in the geist so complete that fostering ignorance and dissuading empathy among the HR practitioners of the organisation could be perpetrated so publicly, so deliberately and so determinedly and not be seen for what it was?

I imagined Senior Management might answer my question as follows: Oh, that is not the position of the "organisation". The organisation really values wisdom and honesty and empathy. It is merely this particular Director who is aberrant in her ideology. And that, too, might convince, except that Siobhan had in fact great cachet in the organisation. Her opinion and advice was sought at the high table. Still, Senior Management might yet weave and prevaricate and say in the organisation's defence, Aah, but that's merely the result of an excess of delicacy on our part about confronting her silliness, which you may rest assured is seen for what it is. Her advice is sought, sure, but then quietly ignored. And this, too, might mollify for a moment, did it not uncover the even more dispiriting failure of the organisation's upper echelon to confront poor performance among the mighty, to its own cost and that of us below stairs. This was an insight of some poignancy for me, since I had identified this defect in its management practice to the Department in my address to the Board of Management four years earlier when they asked me to tell them what my first few years in the Departmental shrive box had taught me.

[Because there is a danger you will lose fascination with this matter over the next few paragraphs, let me urge you to stay with me for five minutes. It will be worth it. Further down the track there is unfamiliar terrain, and here immediately ahead you will come into possession of one or two $E=MC^2$s to keep in your pocket like matches for when the lights go out.]

So. I realised this nuanced cultivation of Siobhan by those Senior Managers who populated the Board displayed an actual organisational value (as opposed to those *espoused* in Our Mission and Our Vision mottos up on the wall, the recitation of which requires such facial discipline), a value in operation in the executive suite and its environs:

Avoidance of unpleasantness at almost any price

Lower-level staff may eye my identification of that value sceptically. Bitter experience may have taught them senior level bosses' distaste for confronting poor performance among their own is not a failing found among their immediate bosses, the ones down at the level close above them, where, they perceive, there's more relish for the task. Their scepticism is justified. The distinction between mores at the two different organisational altitudes derives from adherence among senior people to another value, one that is, predictably, equally unofficial. Think of this second value as mirroring a tendency found outside, in the upper social classes generally: the inclination to honour an aesthetic that rates the face of higher ranked persons more pulchritudinous and thus more deserving of preservation (that is to say, of saving).

For it is true that things more beautiful are universally seen, *ipso facto,* as more worthy of preservation. That is never contested in relation to, say, architecture. This may be because to object to the preservation of such cultural treasure marks the complainant as ill-bred; but whatever the explanation, the cultural complaisance such silence represents is also pervasive amongst the afore-mentioned senior organisational cohort. Thus, as the superior pulchritude attributed to senior face is never gainsaid, at least in public, none object to its high heritage listing. If there is face to be saved, in other words, this is the face.

And so, tacitly permissioned by our lower-level silence, those at *very* senior levels choose to confront peer bad behaviour with an enthusiasm in indirect proportion to the altitude at which they and the perpetrator live. Time has so burnished this practice that its place in the unofficial pantheon of organisational values is assured. It may, therefore, be academically stated:

Accountability obtains in inverse proportion to altitude.

All right, let me give you some more of the story.

Neither Siobhan's refrigerant nor her cauterizing iron was a total success. Some time passed and there came swimming into the swamp, reckless of the smiling crocodile, two more emailers, both women.

Here's the first of their texts, published the day after the Director's. It illustrates how Siobhan's diatribe email attempting to kill the debate, a purpose she owned up to later, as I describe below, was perceived for what it was by someone bold enough to speak plainly the very next day. I shall call this correspondent Eleanor. For reasons clear in her text, Eleanor's email was not copied to the entire HR network, but it did include among its small number of ccs Siobhan and the Director-General:

Michael O'Neill

Date: 06/06/2001 11:29:23

Subject: Thank You

Hi Michael

I don't usually get involved in email debates and I don't particularly want my comments here to be broadcast to "half the organisation". I am cc-ing only those people who have responded to your original email. [4]

First Michael – thank you. It's important we continually look for positive stories about people and celebrate our many successes, BUT it's equally important we don't lose sight of those members of our [Departmental] "family" who are not faring so well (either because of circumstances in their personal lives and/or work-related issues which impact negatively upon them).

I did not in any way read negativity in your original email. What I did read was some brief detail about what some of my colleagues in the "real" world have to deal with on a regular basis. I really was not aware of many of their issues (although as you know there were one or two my family has been forced to cope with over the last few years – e.g. injustices meted out by several now ex-employees who avoided culpability by conveniently resigning when things got too hot).

I appreciate you sharing your observations with us. Having worked for a long time in "head office" environments and policy-making units in several Government Departments, I find that it's easy to lose touch with reality and see everything with rose-tinted glasses.

It's why I've advocated so hard for "permission" (remember our discussion with [the DG] at Virginia Palms) to approach people management issues on a local basis in a way which best fits each individual work environment. From experience, generalised "people" policy directives are not always meaningful to all people in all situations.

---

[4] Eleanor didn't know that many people sent email responses to me without cc-ing anyone. She probably assumed anyone who responded was unafraid to be open about it.

Back to you . . . what on earth have you done to deserve what I perceived as bordering on personal and public attacks from a number of respondents?

I think you do an exceptionally good job under very difficult, and at times I'm sure – traumatic circumstances. I think you deserve a chocolate Freddo every day!! Seriously, I (and many, many others in [the Department]) appreciate your honest, ethical and doggedly optimistic approach to your job. We need people like you who are not afraid to say what they think and mean what they say.

If you ever have the time, I'd love to catch up with you over a coffee.

Cheers

Eleanor

Then, a full week after Siobhan's chilly chide, came this, from Delilah. Her defiant phalanx of upper case letters would have created an echoing ring in the canyon of scared silence had it been ccd to the whole network, but it was only ccd to me. The addressee was the smiling croc herself:

Date:        12/06/2001 09:35:26

Subject:     A Week in the life . . .

Siobhan,

TO ADD MY 2 CENTS WORTH to the debate, having personal experience of workplace difficulty and being proactive trying to resolve the problem I would like to say that . . . . .[*sic*]

PUBLICATION IS A FORM OF RECOGNITION AND/OR ACKNOWLEDGEMENT – IT IS TOO EASY TO MINIMISE THE PERSONAL TOLL EXPERIENCED BY THE AGGRIEVED BY DEMANDING A BALANCED REPORT WHEN THE PUBLICATION COULD BE VIEWED AS 'FACTS OF WORKLIFE'.

Regards

Delilah

Michael O'Neill

Only two cents worth, maybe, but this widow's mite may have nevertheless lodged like an irritant in the opaque, unclosing eye patrolling the bank. Her point was probably missed by many, however. Her shouting capitals and the fact she admits to distilling her "personal experience" – easy for the eye of party to read in a devaluing 'only' in front of that – to bring us this intelligence tends to depreciate her wisdom in a lackadaisical reader's eyes. Yet her insight is spot on: insisting on *balance* that matches every detriment with an upbeat success story, much as it may suit the suits, serves to minimise improperly the importance and impact of those detriments, to trivialise them, ultimately. And, of course, her insight was a slight to the croc's vision of things.

Like Eleanor's, Delilah's prod drew no immediate or public response from Siobhan on a network level such as Spiro's had provoked, and it was unlikely there was any privately communicated response confidential between Siobhan and Delilah – Siobhan's armamentarium in such matters didn't stretch to the hush-hush deal, the discreet reprimand behind closed doors; sulky silence or muezzin from the minaret was it, nothing in between.

It had been my email address that appeared in the primary address field of Siobhan's first email, but her clear intention ("Dear Folks") had been to address the entire HR network, whom she ccd. The same group who received my Friday afternoon email.[5] Applying the cryogen to me in public was an effective way to pre-empt copycat insurgency. Get the spores before they can germinate. Eleanor and Delilah somehow slipped through.

The day long delay before the Director sat down at her keyboard would have allowed her to spy out the attitudes expressed so far, including that of the DG, whose contribution had then been on the cyber noticeboard some seven hours. Thus one

---

[5] Aside from the group cc to the whole network, Siobhan ccd her email *individually* to only one other person, Misha, her executive assistant and gibbet attendant, to publicly assign her the task of facilitating my carpeting.

might be tempted to explain her unabashed scorn of my email as the consequence of her having slid as smoothly into the slipstream of what she divined to be the real (but diplomatically masked) attitude of the DG as Hans had into hers; but I suspect she, more Catholic than the Pope, needed no specific encouragement to spy out his unspoken desire and prosecute it zealously. In his 1994 judgement in the matter of Phillips vs. Disciplinary Appeal Committee Federal Court Judge Wilcox draws attention to this "commonplace of human experience":

> Alert and ambitious subordinates often take their cue from a superior's known attitude; it is not necessary for the superior to give instructions about a course of action. ... Especially in these days of public service efficiency bonuses, payable at the discretion of a superior officer... (paragraph 70)

Hans, one rung down from Siobhan, represented the common or garden variety specimen of Wilcox, J's "ambitious subordinate". In terms of the level to which his actual administrative abilities would have elevated him, Hans should have peaked three ratlines down, yet his career had carried forward on cunning and tacking skill to his present rank. But his rise looked likely soon to slow. Siobhan, by contrast, was headed for the peerage. Wilcox, J, again, from the same matter:

> The realisation that a leader's unspoken wish can influence a subordinate's actions is at least as old as the murder of St Thomas Becket in 1170. Readers will recall the legend that, on news being brought to him in France of Becket's latest provocative act, King Henry II muttered an irritated, but rhetorical: "Who will rid me of this turbulent priest?" Without more, four knights crossed the Channel and murdered the Archbishop in Canterbury cathedral. (paragraph 69)

Hans was ashore and running.

# 4
## Siobhan's World

SIOBHAN'S capacity with the keyboard was not the extent of her fine motor skills. The play of her rapier across my skin all those years ago was sure as Zorro and the discourse it etched indelible. That long intimacy between us, like getting to know the top-dog con you shared a cell with, means I can present you with this gloss[6]. An impudent one, of course, since impertinence, as either irreverence or digression, is my métier.

### *'Dear Folks'*

The folksiness of *Dear Folks* is sweet and democratic, but contrasted against what follows it is simply sheep's clothing and underlines the tension between Siobhan's incompatible purposes, her (later retrospectively avowed) intention to squash any talk of things being unpleasant in the organisation, and her (equally avowed) ideological determination to adhere to nice. At first glance, of course, these purposes seem compatible enough. They become increasingly incompatible, however, the more unbiddable are the little boys watching the naked emperor process.

---

[6] That long intimacy is a common feature of boss/subordinate dyads, which tend to marriage-like features, good and ill. And, as in real marriages, the less dominant nurtures in silence insights with the potential to strip the public image from the other party. In both institutions it is the natural obstructions to marshalling those insights into cogent, public revelation which almost always save the perp from exposure. For every victim who limps away from episode after episode vowing to expose that bastard or snitch on that bitch big time, then does so successfully, 99 others just get drunk. Hence the long gestation of this book.

*'I have been out of the office for two days and am just catching up with the latest area of debate.'*

She will catch up with it, and then, like the old vaudevillian Napalm-in-the-Morning, she will have to kill it to save it.

With the exception of two women, Eleanor and Delilah, whose emails I presented above, no one from the network risked the Director's wrath after her "contribution to the debate". That it was her intention, rather, to kill debate stone dead was, at risk of understatement, arguably discernible in her email at first reading.

Within a month speculation about alternative readings was redundant. During an acrimonious meeting between Hans, Siobhan and me early in July, she naively and self-righteously conceded, psychological jaw out-thrust, that it had been her conscious intention to kill the debate.

Reflecting upon these events even at this remove, Frustration, as much as Indignation, cries out within me, "What do you guardians think will happen to us if we are allowed to stay for a minute longer than you can tolerate with an unpleasant insight or observation about our world? What are you so afraid of?" I hear John Keats intone, *negative capability, that is when a man is capable of being in uncertainties, mysteries, doubts, without any irritable reaching after fact and reason.*

*'On first reading your email, Michael, I was trying to work out what was your purpose – a "wave" for assistance perhaps?'*

Siobhan here attributes more subtlety and subterfuge to my email than even generosity can find in it. The purpose she initially descried in it was the result of her own wishful thinking, her desire to categorise an uncomfortable phenomenon, plainspoken reportage of the vicissitudes of industrial life for the Department's frontline staff, as something which sweetness might brush away like a child's tears. *Oh, it's not that things are bad out there.*

Michael O'Neill

*Michael's just feeling over-whelmed.* By what, one would want to ask, of course.

**'I subsequently understand from Hans that you considered that you had sufficient mechanisms in place – a professional mentor – to help you with the impact of your casework'**

She would have cleared up her confusion on this matter in the same conversation with Hans in which he cleared up his own confusion about what attitude he had to my email.

**'so it was not a cry for help.'**

Cry for help? My email had not seemed to me a sympathy-seeking suicide threat; though, if I was smarter, its latent capacity to end my industrial life might have been clearer to me. Her employment of the phrase may suggest an unconscious wish or prediction about my fate, perhaps her desire to visit retribution upon me. At any rate, this half-visible vengeance wish has had to be put down following Hans's information. Siobhan handles her disappointment with aplomb.

**'Therefore, in your role of staff counsellor, I am still unclear what it is you are trying to achieve by sending out this Email'**

Try as I might, re-reading my Friday email standing on my head or peering at it through a glass darkly, I cannot find the opacity that so bedevilled Siobhan's and Hans's attempts to fathom it. What part of "Absorb These Ugly Facts" is hard to understand?

**'We have the function of staff counselling as one way to assist people to move back to normal living when "bad" things happen.'**

The quote marks around the word *bad* are a delicate way of saying a naughty word on paper or screen. The three-letter word itself is a concession to the upset state her generic idea of a client might be in when reporting his or her ills to you. It is sweep-it-under-the-carpet level mendacity, describing someone in a rage as "upset".

Siobhan's seems to be of the "there, there" school of counselling. People do tend to go on about their troubles, don't they? We must be kind, however. Really, they just need time to get perspective and see they were never in any real danger.

*'We know that, as part of everyday life, members of the community will act in a way towards the people of [the Department] that is unpleasant,'*

Heavens! This is not exactly an outbreak of authenticity, but it's promising. Being threatened with bombing *is* quite *unpleasant.* We're not quite mobled queen here, but there's hope.

*'and even damaging in some instances.'*

That would be the bashing and hospitalisation. Good, quite good. (But don't get your hopes up.)

*'Both the community and [the Department] have responsibilities here – the community to prevent this behaviour through a range of means, and [the Department] to look after our people who are affected'*

But hang on! Won't that mean *telling* the looker-afterers in the Department (that would be the HR practitioners, wouldn't it) that our people are affected and *how* they are affected, and engaging their creative sympathies in the process, maybe? How would you do that? I know! What about getting someone with first-hand knowledge of our people's distress to tell the looker-afterers?

Michael O'Neill

*'An important part of your role is to advise, from the "intelligence" you gather in your work, how we can do something concrete to minimize trauma'*

Perhaps she *has* noticed my constant stream of intelligence, sans identifying information, to the upper echelon – though, if she has, this is the first sign. There's at least a touch of realism evident in her words here at last. Bad's been morphed into *trauma*, given a passport and allowed to venture out of the house without his quote marks; but she is at least toying with the idea that what I learn from the pattern of wounds on my body of clients enables me to tell her and senior management how well we are doing as an organisation.

*'that occurs through circumstances outside our control.'*

*'Outside our control.'* Hmmm. Maybe not. What our staff suffer is *not* outside our power to prevent.

*'We can assist people to learn positive self-talk to avoid becoming bitter or adopting a long-term victim role.'*

For example, a discussion might go like this: Counsellor: "You know you are a good person. It doesn't really affect you that that 'customer' called you a viciously nasty name and impugned your parentage and was the fourth such offender today. Yes, I'll grant he did lean across and punch you, and you are here at emergency, but the doctor says it's only the cartilage, the bone's OK. So this playing the victim..."

Staff Member: "Oh, I see. It's only a role. I can just drop it, right? Listen, Sweetheart. Boss. This is no chimera. It really is a hospital. I'd like to get some rest. Will you go, or must I use the buzzer?"

*'I am sure there are heaps of other positive things we could suggest managers do to help people when they experience such a situation.'*

Positive is a relief. One has been waiting to get it out of the way. It presages the exhortation to adopt an upbeat tone when managers consult us in response to their people's traumatisation: we shall smile regardless of what the line manager is trying to help.

*'What do you suggest?'*

"Come on, Michael. *I* have just declared there are heaps of things we can do. That's my credibility established. Now it's *your* turn. Put your money where your whining mouth is." This match-me challenge implied that I, as Staff Counsellor, had overlooked my duty to educate line managers in proactive, creative and sympathetic HR tactics they could have used with their staff. It was a master stroke from Siobhan of acid condescension, a pirouette of subtlety, a Michael expungement.

It was, as well, a nuanced nick. That teaching role was one I surely had – albeit a mere gnat to her elephant as Director and "faculty leader" of HR input to the organisation – so this was deft fence, this diversion on to me of blame for the state of ignorance among our line managers, with its implied disappointment over my (presumed) failure to educate. Subtle character assassination delivered with an air of innocence, it left an unhandsome duelling scar on my credibility, and constituted significant real estate captured in the campaign against anyone and everyone who notices and remarks something, anything, untoward.

Don't bring me problems, bring me solutions. On the face of it, a reasonable response to someone who reports a problem? No. Rather, it is clichéd and reactionary, refuge taken in what amounts to just another business mantra, one that sounds assertive and in-your-face. "Don't bring me problems, bring me solutions" is forward defence adopted by managers to whom it's clear that some change is required in the organisation, but who are frightened to act. The higher one has climbed in the organisation, the more one has to lose if one's boat-rocking wrong-foots those above. This fact of organisational life perpetuates one of the distinguishing features of those at higher altitudes: the assumption that onus to repair a defect in the organisation lies with any who point one out. A moment's thought reveals there's no justification for this downward buck passing, but the prospect that one's bad news about the organisation will suddenly land one in the role of fixer, regardless of who has the actual power to effect the change required, is a discourager of such reporting.

*'No matter how wonderful any organisation is, "bad" things will happen to people – either from outside or from within the workplace.'*

Uh-oh! Bad got his shades on again. That "wonderful" is a bit worrying, too. Not a word I often associate with organisations, you would have noticed, but it's been slid in here to suggest many of them are.

Aren't folks wonderful! Round up the sulky discontent of the few and submerge it in the buoyant bubbling ruck of prosperous humanity's determined cooperation with the advertised life.

*'The vast majority of people in [the Department] are working to make our workplaces the best we can, and deal with the mixture of human behaviour and the difficulties that stand in the way.'*

Well, that's a relief.

*'Along with that, goes being clear about what is unacceptable behaviour and stopping it.'*

A clear-sighted recognition, this, that all's not always well in public contact land, but it may not exist beyond the full stop, so I'd better not be banging on about it.

*'In your role, Michael, you can contribute to the success of shaping positive environments by encouraging and acknowledging the good news that people are generating, ...'*

Though it's nice for one so dour as me to be invited, my contribution hardly seems necessary; the market is so saturated already. Platoons of her underlings already crank out positives incessantly. She has so indulged her penchant for pleasantry by cloning herself into the ranks of her subordinate managers that even those running units that one would expect to focus on bad stuff, e.g., staff grievances, complaints, workplace health and safety lapses, industrial disputation, repackage what they do like products from Pleasantville. Until the only bad news agent left is the EAP, and its halloos are less popular than a road agent's. So it has to go.

*'... and not sending out a message that makes me feel that we are experiencing some unusually large barrage of misery'*

However Siobhan's "makes me feel that" is interpreted, things don't look good for her:

*'Makes me feel'*

She's got what is either an evil or deluded official loose in a dangerously influential position. Which means she has, as Sheriff Bulford T. Justice would have phrased it, *a genuine sityuh ation heeyuh,* if not a *total lack of respect for the law.* Perhaps that should be lore. Anyway, everything might unravel at any moment.

When one rides glee club shotgun for the organisation the job description calls for nice and you can't retain authority or a sharp look out on the buckboard, if you're all the time carrying out exorcisms or reduced to jelly. So, if this interpretation of "makes me feel" is correct, then Siobhan is signalling that she stands upon the brink of action, and that action is required urgently.

*'... targeted at the people of [the Department]. (Try telling a Family Trauma Services Officer at present that we are doing it tough!)'*

That's not a knife. THAT'S a knife! The FTSOs for whom Siobhan has such admiration are in a different Department and were at the time being depicted sympathetically in the press as under strain from their work. So Siobhan's enthusiasm for their canonisation, though against her grain, was facilitated by the acceptableness in PR terms of their victimhood.

*'I am not advocating a denial of the bad things –'*

Could have fooled me. Sounds like you want me to stop talking about what I'm doing, what I'm seeing. Anyway, if I close up my baleful bazaar who will service the minacious longings of my special clientele? Where will my "customers" shop for those dark, fertilizing truths so ugly to the taste and so enlivening to the soul?

*'I am talking about inspiring people, creating energy to copy some of the good things happening, so that we can achieve together, ...'*

An invitation to get in harness together, the two of us. Do some really great things. She's inviting me to join her in some high level leadership, tone-setting and emblematic, lovely work for a senior person with vision, compassion, a high public profile and an obligation to raise spirits and productivity. Sorry, Siobhan. I'm a counsellor and I deal with blood, sweat and tears. If you want to get in harness with me and not with some saccharine simulacrum birthed in your brain and safely berthed in your domain, then it's going to need a wide elastic harness, because we're working different sides of the street. We'll arrive at the same corner, maybe at the same time, if we're lucky and if we stay in respectful contact with each other. I'm happy for you to use my intelligence so you know which doors to knock on. But I ain't yuh depity, Ma'am. So, please, take this badge off of me. I cain't use it anymore. Never could.

*'... and use some of that energy to help those having a rough time.'*

Here it is breaking the surface again, that ugly truth: a rough time.

*'I do not believe any other way works.'*

And it sounds like a waste of time to implore her, as Cromwell did his adversaries, to bethink herself in the bowels of Christ she may be wrong. The possibility is not countenanced.

And yet, what long and weary experience of "other ways" is here hinted at. Is it possible she has so traversed this terrible terrain that, if we but fall smiling in behind, we will be spared much horror we are too young to bear? Is there a wisdom here that knows afore what shape our ends will take and would take care of us pre-emptively, were we but able to lose our obstinate self-will? Ah, there's cud to chew. But is it momma, would take care of us, or that Sicilian *Godfather* from Corleone?

Well. Let us step a little north-east and a long way back to the court of another tyrant where we may learn something from another supervisory counselling session, though it is not always clear there who is supervising whom.

Michael O'Neill

This is how Teiresias, in Sophocles' *Oedipus Rex*, reveals his reason for stalling when Oedipus is insisting on hearing the dangerous truth about his own earlier misdeeds, expressing his (Teiresias's) fear that the truth will only make things worse:

> Alas, alas, what misery to be wise
> When wisdom profits nothing! This old lore
> I had forgotten; else I were not here.

In Sophocles' rendition of this age-old myth, Teiresias the seer carries the burden of struggling with the obligation to tell things the way they are and the multi-layered set of rationalisations for engaging in spin and bullshit and self-preservation by cutting one's cloth to suit one's audience. In other versions it is other characters, but the central theme is always the examination of the consequences of truth-telling or avoidance of truth-telling. Sophocles' Teiresias, under pressure to come clean, is troubled by his fear that Oedipus will not profit from the truth, and confesses that he himself is having an equally profitless time being put in such a bind by his professional duty as seer. He is also admitting the distress he feels at being the bearer of bad tidings, expecting to be done for it.

But his stance of lament is a pit stop merely; Sophocles allows him to rest there to give his courage time to overtake his self-interest and his fear. Another eight exchanges with king Oedipus and the discourse will be complete and his truth out. His seemingly definitive stance at the pit stop represents one way: the way of patronising condescension (that would treat Oedipus as a child) and, ironically, fearfulness (that expects the passion his news generates to rebound upon him). A myopic assessment of Teiresias might rest there, taking pit stop for chequered flag. Teiresias's stance viewed whole, however, with his eventual truth-telling included, represents a way other than condescension and fear. It represents the way of faith in the ultimate power of truth to eventually, on the cosmic scale, produce the best, indeed, the Greek would probably insist, the inevitable outcome.

Later we will have need of Sophocles again. For now, let me have some sympathy for the devil.

Let us assume Siobhan is acting in full consciousness. A sympathetic rendering might say she has seen so much loss and grief that she not only agrees with Teiresias that it will profit nothing to acknowledge ugly truths, but also believes in Teiresias's "old lore" of self-preservation; that is, both she and I, if I knew what was good for me, are less liable to payback if we keep mum. Also like Teiresias, she is under pressure. In her case, and in contradistinction to Teiresias's, it is pressure not only to preserve me and herself from harm (i.e., from payback for having revealed too much), but also to preserve *an illusion*. So, she adopts his pit stop way: the way of patronising condescension that would treat all of us as children, and of fearfulness that the increase of sympathy for suffering staff my email generates will rebound upon her precious, pollyannic illusion. But it should be said that Siobhan has adopted this mode of behaviour not in full awareness, but in unconscious compliance with a culture that is both difficult to detect and generically pervasive in organisational life. Would that she had followed him to his final act.

In contrast to Teiresias, however, and perhaps because she is not in the presence of her king – my power to punish was limited – Siobhan feels *authorised* to deprive her lessers of their chance to come to the same, or a different, conclusion for themselves. Hence her umbrage at my insubordinate sabotage of her mother knows best approach. Teiresias says, Don't make me tell you about this, it's too dreadful. But he does it. Siobhan, on the other hand, says, No one else may choose, since *I do not believe any other way works* and it is for me alone – Oh, lonely weight of office! – to decide what you can bear and choose the way.

One last shot of sympathy. (Better not pass it up. As my erstwhile fellow worker in the lord's vineyard and recovering alcoholic, Sister Kate used to say, never pass a tap without having a drink; there's always a drought coming.) Siobhan was unwittingly the beneficiary of a force from the very ether, a particularly virulent bug in present day management atmosphere, riddling the corporate world.

Like many diseases, it is known by its initials: UMO. That stands for unwarranted management optimism. Siobhan, who almost by definition, you might say, especially if it is I who am authorised lexicographer, would have no desire for vaccination or treatment, could hardly have resisted contracting this bug. In the world she aspired to it is *de rigueur*. Just as acerbics have long held that when we fall "in love" we are temporarily psychotic, so with UM *Optimistas*. Dan Lovallo and Daniel Kahneman, two keen epidemiologists upon whom I will call later, have charted the incidence of this infection in an insightful Harvard Business Review article.

> *'Please make a time to see me to talk this through further (Misha, please arrange.)*
> *Regards*
> *Siobhan'*

Hand me that megaphone, Misha. Thanks. Now, come in here that boy, and stand on the carpet in front of my desk.

The ugliness that from time to time flashes from Siobhan's email suggested many of nature's paragons of the genre to which it is analogous; but it is here, in its Parthian paragraph and last parenthetical aside, the public reprimand and instruction to her secretary to organise a "meeting" for me, that its true corollary is revealed: the Scorpion.

Although the Friday afternoon email I published to the HR Network was, in my judgement, innocuous to any reasonable eye, Siobhan's reaction to it, published to the whole HR network, was, in sum, intemperate, I thought, and internally inconsistent. Its intellectual freight and the needlessly public carpeting it announced were, I also thought, ill-considered, but deliberate, acts – the true determinants of which escaped her.

Her rebuke was, however, a reaction not only to the (inevitably) dispiriting information I published, but also to what my publicising action revealed: that her control of the organisation's agenda was imperfect. As a result, she saw she had an EAP problem.

But for the moment this stopgap public reprimand would suffice. She was confident she had silenced me. And it is true I was still, watching the play unfold – on my screen only, as I thought then. If Siobhan was conscious of having in several ways here modelled something less than self-discipline for her troops, her subsequent comportment didn't reveal it. The competitive thrust she couldn't resist and this harked back to her previous job – *Try telling a former Trauma Services Officer that we are doing it tough at present!* – established the pecking order in the call-this-bad?-you-don't-know-you're-alive chook yard and was merely the most egregious among a raft of such beside-the-point displays. Perhaps she didn't regard these small debits to her account as germane, or didn't care, perhaps thinking desperate times called for desperate measures.

At any rate, her main objective had been achieved. I fell Cistercian silent and so, equally frozen by her action, did the HR network. Their Director had expressed open displeasure at having been made, by the publication of facts, to experience uncomfortable feelings. They took it as the reproving finger wag it was. Her email's freight of insult included the implicit comparison of her erstwhile Trauma Services colleagues with the wimps we had working on our frontline. Well aware that their only survival option was to ignore this testosteronic, defiant and rhetorical provocation, the HR network paled into silence, almost to a woman. Two women alone defied her displeasure.

It might have been her indignation at the work of those two recalcitrants, in fact, which eventually galvanised Siobhan to seek more perfect control, for she seems subsequently to have realised that she had not, as Robert Ruark might have advised her, used enough gun. She was about to dry her feet, come at it from a wholly different angle, and correct that mistake. She was about to set things in motion. Her underlings' thirst for the seamy (which I had pimped to) clearly had not been completely expunged and might lead to more Friday emails like mine in the future. Delilah's and Eleanor's irritation may have wound into her secret depths and, cherished more lovingly there than any speck in an oyster, would emerge adamantine and pearl and shaped like a plan.

Because the publicly required appearance on the carpet was never arranged by her secretary, and no word of it had passed between Siobhan and me, I thought I had ceased to exist. All through a nondescript offsite workshop we both politely attended during this interregnum she kept her own counsel. However, my illusion of safety was shattered at last when she invited me to a meeting with the cypher-like Hans a few days after that workshop, on July 3. By now we were roughly a month into the post-furry little famulus period; which is to say, my email had been loose about four weeks.

The meeting was held in Hans's room and I walked through his doorway without noticing it had become circular and dark with a metallic echo and a rifled groove Bart Simpson could have spiralled down on his skateboard. Ruark was there with a satisfied smile, although I couldn't see him.

Siobhan had been working hard during the layoff, and now presented me with her magnum opus draft plan, pearl handle first. Puppy-eager, three bags full Hans, proud as a parent at a speech night panto, but a little apprehensive about the rest of the audience's reaction, telegraphed his role in the plan's birth. Neither of them actually licked their lips, but both seemed to hope I'd put it to my head as soon as my hand closed around its pearly grip.

Siobhan explained that she was about to place the plan before Jody Laden, her own boss, a high level, second tier Senior Executive in the organisation, entitled to a capital S and a capital E. The key proposal in it was to subordinate my role and function (internal provision of counselling to the staff of the Department) to the external EAP provider firm. This was a firm of consulting psychologists I had contracted with some years back to act as my backup when there were too many clients seeking help, and as my locum when I was on leave. Siobhan declared that this restructured EAP would eliminate the need for my clients to log their requests for my help by leaving a message on my answering machine. (Aah, was this the slyly referred to "EAP problem"?) The external firm had a receptionist who actually spoke into the phone. It would be much more personal, nicer. We simply teach Departmental staff a new number to call when they need help, and Voila! Bob's your uncle.

Oh, and by the way, henceforth I would be professionally and clinically supervised by the head of that firm.

It was brilliant, no trace of personal malice, unassailable, out of the blue and as clever as a cat. It was like listening to someone relay my co-ordinates.

The plan had these selling points. A recalcitrant, a doomsayer who had tenure in the organisation and was hard to kill, who created upset for Siobhan at unpredictable moments, whose apprehension of the higher profile functions of the EAP was inhibited by his poor grasp of PR, who just wasn't with the program, unredeemable, would now come under the control of a hired consultant who was completely dependent upon her say-so for the continuation of a quite valuable contract with the Department, renewed (or not) at regular intervals, if delivered upon. No more answering machine. No more back answering machine. I could see her swishing through the gleaming glass and steel foyer of the new university building set in acres of lawn by the sweep of the river on her way to give a guest lecture to ranks of shiny HR101 faces, eager to teach them that all you have to do is, "Get the surface looking right and it'll all happen".

Up to now I had thought of Siobhan's late evening email as a splenetic outburst composed at the end of a long day in a spasm of pique at our unruliness. ***You see what I have to put up with? The cat goes away for a short break and how badly the mice have played!*** But when I reflected later on the events of July 3 with her and Hans in his office, I began to wonder whether she was Machiavelli-gifted at this. Had her email been the first jab of a two-punch knockout play, the second being the plan? I did see her email's perfect fitness to its function, as if it were the crucial bit of stage business some phantom playwright laboured hours to perfect, knowing where it fitted, a tactic in his character's overarching trajectory. It established my second rate-ness in the mind of the audience.

Further, like great artists will, our ghostly playwright (was it she, I now pondered) had provided her lines to speak and acts to act which were, paradoxically, both spontaneous and deliberately crafted. Even Siobhan's email (without which, of course, no book; and I *am* grateful), by now as famous within a confined circle as the one which provoked it ... could it, too, have been devised, its long end foreseen? It had, after all, spelled the end of debate, despite her writing Spiro ten minutes after she despatched it to declare debate was acceptable. Or were these objectives achieved with skill honed beyond the need for thought in the service of her god? While it was attractive, in a way, even to be the target, like being the rat man written up to lasting fame by Freud – I could have lived with it – in the end I had to live rather with the much less glam truth that the whole run of the game had been opportunistic. If Siobhan had shown flair and had recognised opportunities, it was more likely to be the result of her having adopted Pollyanna so long ago.

Be that as it may, its job done, punch number one made way for punch number two: this proposed restructure, the comprehensive *coup de grâce*. All she had to do now was get her boss's endorsement and we had arrived at the final solution.

As things panned out Siobhan did not prevail for another two years, and then by good luck rather than her pearl-handled plan (which in the meantime I had managed to scuttle). And by *deus ex machina*.

But, in the end, prevail she did, even if she could take no credit for it when it eventually happened, and could even plausibly feign sympathy. For all that, however, her ability to grasp the smooth end of things that flew up off the road at her made it clear that Strategic Siobhan was no mere plodding knight. Darkness *would* be banished, and by a prince of light.

The fullness of her commitment to prince of lightism I learned a little while after July 3 in the following way. Provoked to attempt an act of reconciliation by the sharp deterioration of relations at that meeting into embarrassing dysfunctionality, I suggested she and I meet to resolve the hostility between us.

Duly, we met, just Siobhan and me, a cards-on-the-table session. A little hesitantly, I ventured the criticism that she behaved too often like Pollyanna. She floored me by reacting to this with pleasure and with a practised philosophical defence of her Pollyannaism. Floored me twice, in fact: first that she chose to blind her*self* with brightness; second, her assumption that she, by virtue of her principate might impose this delusional Weltanschauung on her staff. It was clearly her belief that occupation of the position of HR Director automatically conferred the moral authority – for clearly no civil authority assigned this remit – to decide what intellectual and philosophical rubric might reign in the minds of those under her, those who guided the operation of the branch and wider HR network. She seemed not to notice that this was a position inimical to her avowed acceptance of the right of her troops to debate matters, an espoused virtue concerning which her PR was as liberal as her practice disingenuous.

But valid moral authority, I wanted (but later, of course) to say to her, is not exercised with blunt instruments (public flogging, open reprimand) in one hand and words, weasel or not, in the other. It is not bundled with the positional authority one acquires when appointed to a management position. Moral authority over persons comes into being when it is voluntarily bestowed upon a person by those intending to be subject to it. That happens when, and only when, undeniable virtue, wisdom, courage and compassion in that person attract it. A leader may demand respect or command respect. This is so for Presidents, Popes, Prime Ministers ... and Directors HR. To behave as if one has moral authority by right or *by appointment* is to succumb to the intrinsic seduction of power merely, to pass on the opportunity, and, indeed, the *moral* obligation to combine moral (or expert) authority with positional authority, an achievement which alone confers true leadership status upon one. To assume it comes with the appointment letter, in other words, is simply to misread the world and the way allegiance and professional integrity function, interact and give birth to each other.

Siobhan's assumption in killing off this debate, misusing her authority and exploiting the cravenness dormant in her staff to do so, rested upon that misreading, but was *sanctioned* by her devotion to her god. It was a theocratic act in no less a way than is the issuing of fatwa or the curtailment of women's right to decide their own medical treatment by governments held hostage to the electoral power of a religious parliamentary rump. Providentially, however, Siobhan's god is a shallow god. If it were not, our oppression might have been tragic rather than merely banal, and our silence in the face of it guilty rather than just deeply shameful, embarrassing and supine.

# 5
## Michael's World

THEN there was Michael Chertoff, the friend the
president had made his secretary of homeland security.
Chertoff said the problem was that the hurricane came in
the middle of a 'second stage review' of disaster planning.
As a consequence, he said, FEMA lacked the 'skill set' for
'preparedness'. It sounded like the hurricane made
landfall before they finished designing the PowerPoint
presentation. Of course, that's how twenty-first-century
public servants talk – like private-sector people.

Don Watson, *American Journeys*

I QUIT the field in strategic retreat. My wound-licking went on, of
course, in the aftermath of these contentions, but gradually
diminished as I got on with seeing clients. Their stories continued
to replicate the ones I had summarised in that fateful Friday
afternoon email, confirming the plain truth of what I had
broadcast, and that added to the background sense of disjunctive
realities. I got used to it. Time passed. The whole experience was
shelved somewhere inside my head.

I continued employed by the department for two years,
ducking and weaving to survive; then a machinery of government
change, or MOG, (a reshuffle of public service departments
presented to the citizens as a measure to increase efficiency),
meant that I had to move – i.e., I was conscripted – to a newly
created organisation called a Shared Service Provider. This shift
meant no change in the clientele I served, nor a move to new digs.
It did, however, mean I answered to different bosses. More of that
soon.

It was about two years into this new arrangement that I
happened to read something fateful, a text that spoke to me
because, as *I* had done, its author observed the simultaneous
existence of two worlds, one of which, like the sunny room I had
always been so surprised by when I stepped from my office through
the magic doorway, was not a naturally-occurring phenomenon,

Michael O'Neill

but one maintained in place by forces that only make their presence felt when the false world they maintain in existence is threatened.

That text had first appeared a generation before my email adventures, in *The New Yorker* of April 18 1970. I first found it quoted in William Shutz's *Here Comes Everybody*. It was commentary about the national debate in the United States about that country's involvement in the war in Vietnam:

> The disparity between the official policy and the reality is now so great that it appears as though policy is developing in accordance with a set of rules that will be responsive to the political situation in America but that the actual conduct of the war is developing according to a completely different set of rules, determined by the conditions of unspeakable brutality and confusion in Vietnam itself.[7]

*The New Yorker*'s analysis, its author unidentified, along with many others like it, had percolated into popular consciousness at a time when the world was ripe for a fresh cycle of scepticism. It confirmed a suspicion held inarticulately by many, and emboldened thousands toward a political agnosticism that meant that persons whose social or political importance formerly protected them from our scepticism could no longer depend on that immunity.

What that subversive text, and its like, had done back then, so it did now, for me; though I didn't see it at once. The morass of paralysed resentment and hurt that was the Friday afternoon email and its sequelae was slowly replaced by a determination to unlock its meaning that fell upon me invisibly, but formed itself around me like a cuirass of hammered bronze.

*The New Yorker* commentary sent me into a brown study and eventually helped me to see that the little, local world I had so naively threatened was the spawn and replicant of a larger version of itself. For Vietnam (the political experience, not the country) taught us this painful lesson: as a society (perhaps as a species) we

---

[7] *The New Yorker*, 18 April 1970, p. 34.

are wont to and want to delude ourselves at the official, public level while continuing to know the truth at the level of unofficial, individual experience. The architects and maintainers of that uberworld were persons of social and political importance, the same whose immunity was now unravelling, and had been unravelling since the Seventies.

Some of these newly vulnerable were real flesh and blood eminences who had bought or been born into that elite; but one was an abstraction whose face first flowered into existence not above a bib but above a nib. Pollyanna, triumph of self-possession, found her way on to the printed page in 1913, then began, having fallen in with folk hungry for her advent, to practice the possession of others. The perfect complement to Horatio Alger's brigade of boys doing well against the odds, Pollyanna commenced colonising the fertile American mind. Everything was going to be all right. Not just in America, but here in Australia as well. Her possessees got here well before the cyclists from Salt Lake City. As time went by, many found work, some of them in the public service. Under deep cover for years, Pollyanna's automatons eventually began to holograph her here in our sandstone civil service structures. Some stepped inside the glowing image. When enough of these worshippers had been absorbed, out she stepped, singular and whole. By the late twentieth century she had once more fallen in, as earlier back home in the US, with folk hungry for her coming. Her group dalliance with them, its flowering, the consequences of it and, ultimately, the threat to its continuation, are the preoccupation of this book.

What you read in the previous chapter is an account of her at work inside Siobhan, one of her possessees. What I want to do now, rather than present you with a detailed thesis on her cultural impact (which I couldn't do even if I cared to), is throw a series of shafts of light upon the phenomenon from many angles until her modus operandi begins to come into focus. This will replicate on paper the process my rattletrap mind – if my mind was a car it would be the used jalopy Jed Clampett bought from Pa Kettle – went through to bring me to an understanding of that cultural impact.

# 6
## Two Worlds Collide

ALONGSIDE those hungering for Pollyanna's help in boosterism, a slowly growing band of malcontents has begun to bugger things up for her. Born out of the disillusion of Vietnam (the political experience), these undesirables have begun to undermine the compact. Pollyanna's spell is beginning to be broken. Now, when she reassures, a very few are more likely to want to know what she is up to behind those innocent, eager and appealing eyes. They burr up when she speaks to them in that way of hers that presumes they are not experiencing life directly, but rather are only capable of engaging the world through the fantasies she constructs. There's plenty of opportunity for blurring when you work in government at any level, where daily life soon confirms for you, unless your rose-tinted glasses are welded on, that the official ideologues of the public service, under Pollyanna's tutelage, intentionally conjure a world with at least as much passion, if not quite as much skill, as Hollywood.

To live it without strain, life in that world requires the same willing suspension of disbelief as living in Hollywood's; and the people who run this cinema frown upon any but a temporary, overnight return to reality after your seven and a quarter hours in that magic light whose function is not to reveal but to obscure. So next day you have to return. And Polly's there, flashlight in hand, to usher you back to your station and cue you, or cure you, if your night release has disoriented you.

But let us look more closely at some distinguishing features of Pollyanna's dalliance with our senior public servants. Where once it was these senior public servants who gave frank and fearless advice to politicians, regardless of how unpalatable it was, now these senior public servants have become amnesic about the British tradition of civil service. Now too often they reverse that advising flow and are at pains to *take* their cue from politicians whom once they cued. This results in their radiating an upbeat picture of the world at all times. No longer circumspect, they are, rather, centrifugal. They reflect their own upbeat picture back upstairs to the politicians from whom they got it in the first place. (A department head and the Minister are sometimes like two kids each with a torch and mirror.) They broadcast it downwards to the public service workers below them (who, knowing what's good for them, less and less dare to unfasten their dutifully pasted-on expressions), and sideways to their own peers, incredibly, for these know as well as they the reality gap being papered over; and they fine-mist it out to the public whom they serve (whose demur, when it comes, is inaudible to them, TV cameras being one-way).

It is a culture of smiles, but one never acknowledged, except in rare circumstances, and only when there is nowhere else to go.

For middle ranked public servants keeping one's warden's license current in this secure facility requires visible vigilance in rooting out any less than enthusiastic account of the world that might be espoused by those below. The visibility is important. It's a gate-keeping service designed for consumption by their betters in senior management who would preserve the shared, essential falsehood, the collusion between themselves and the politicians. By definition not yet at senior levels, middle rankers try hard to adopt the correct coloration, to learn this warden role fast, for it needs to become rote and instinctive before they join the senior rank.

At the bottom of the public service heap were the lower ranks whose helper I was employed to be, and among whom my own public service career began.

So bear with me while we examine the nature and history of this modern collusion between politicians and senior public servants a little more closely, for it partly founds the theoretical understanding I propose below to explain how our social, political and cultural life, what you might call the life of the polis, has come to this.

The collusion is for the most part an unconscious complicity, but nevertheless it is a *tour de force* of that marketing approach to life that eschews the dour in favour of promulgating those moods which reassure and comfort people about their lot in life. This urging, as economic and political commentators are forever telling us, achieves two important things: circulation of the consumer dollar and the reprise of last election's voting patterns. At an impersonal level these achievements, i.e., a smoother, more voluminous torrent of money circulating in the same groove and the perpetuation of present voting patterns are the two steady arms of Atlas that keep the world and its riches exactly where they are.

# 7
## An Era before Sweetness & Light

TO scratch the surface of the historical provenance of the way things are in the public service let us climb back into my rattletrap and revisit some of my personal work history, see if we can't toss off a few more random shafts of light. OK, you strapped in?

I spent most of my working life in the public service of one or other of three jurisdictions, Queensland, where I started, and New South Wales, both at state levels, and in Commonwealth public service. Public service life in Australia wasn't always committed to the delusion of sweetness and light as the way of the world. When I commenced work straight out of school in 1958 no one felt obliged to pretend our little body politic was democratic, that it had no internal skeleton of hierarchy. We weren't all equals within it. The ideology of those times didn't require it. I started in the Clerical division, the *crème de la crème*, of the Queensland Public Service – the capitalization came unbidden: achieving this employment was hot stuff in my demographic. I got into that division by virtue of my two whole years of high school, and it meant I had narrowly escaped becoming one of Huxley's Epsilons: the CAs (clerical assistants) whose lower educational achievement earmarked them for dirty work. They wore the coarse blue cotton apron[8], bibbed. And by day's end it was dirty all right.

The officers to whom I reported and who dealt directly with the citizens manifested no demeanour of servility. They saw themselves more as masters of, than servants to, the public. I do not remember any of them, or anyone at more stratospheric levels of government going out of their way to convince the public, our "customers" (as we would never have called them), their lot was wonderful and our service was exceptional and that they were entitled to expect from us superior care and attention. PR, as we know it today, was a long time in the future. The commonest

---

[8] I wore it, too, in the first years, at least part of the day, working beside real epsilons, who by far provided the best company in the place. But they and I knew that soon enough I would have to hang it up.

sensation a citizen on the receiving end might have experienced was likely to be one of having been browbeaten or at best tolerated.

My bosses in 1958 showed even less interest in the well-being of their subordinates.

For, in the parlance of the time, ours was not to reason why; ours was but to do & die. My mid-century bosses subscribed to this dictum for themselves as well, so discomforts among the lower ranks aroused no sympathy. Anything they had to bear that wasn't actually lethal seemed OK, too OK for the thought of protest to ever arise. Perhaps the still fresh memory of straitened wartime conditions made it so, or the genetic memory – gallantly supported and preserved by our smugly archaic education system – of those other wartime conditions Tennyson reported so proudly from the Valley of Death.

# 8
## Enter the Light

OVER the half-century since public-service life in the Valley of Death, some remarkable changes have come. It is now as conventional within the public service for management to feel or affect an obligation to provide for the emotional well-being of staff, as it was then, not to give a fig. Now, statutory and subordinate legislation prescribe standards of workplace health and safety, while accepted industrial relations practices aim at producing at least a minimum decency in the workplace. The growth in the practice of providing staff with employer-funded welfare officers, as they were still called in early 1980s Australia, later to be known employee assistance programs like mine, or EAPs, (also known as EASs, employee assistance *services*) has been in part a result of this new broom. Unfortunately, the rapid spread of the new way of naming and conceiving this provided resource to employees, i.e., calling them Employee Assistance Programs or Services, coincided with another American import.

Somewhere in that half-century, maybe around the time the *New Yorker* was crystallising its editorial stance, our eminent grey hologram, Pollyanna, smiled her way into a role as consultant without portfolio, got loose in the public service, became soon ubiquitous. When I began just a dozen years later to practice as a counsellor in the employee assistance field in the public service in Queensland I found her well ensconced, though not yet at the peak of her influence.

That peak came after another ten years of IT improvements and simultaneous growth in the general awareness of how useful she could be. Soon her grey pallor vanished and real colour suffused her cheeks. The state was then nearly five years into a newly conscientious era, following upon the revelations of the Fitzgerald inquiry into, among other things, the entrenched deficiencies of its apparatus of administration. Things needed fixing bad, Fitzgerald discovered, and it was going to take time. So, the usual bureaucratic bland stare couldn't cut it, at least for a while, had lost its power to silence the newly awakened demand of people for a responsive public sector. But this interim represented an opportunity for anyone skilled at putting a brave face on things long before they were genuinely fixed. As a result the cachet of Pollyanna and that of her channelers has, over the score of years since Fitzgerald, increased considerably. If you can't fix it, *say* you've fixed it. No part of the public service is now immune from her factitious sweetness and light. My own little consulting room, with its terrible weather and constant stream of savaged people limping through, was not, I guessed, prime real estate and might have seemed too unpalatable or too unimportant a conquest; but, if I thought that, I was merely innocent. In fact, she snuffed the battle with delight since with my darkness I durst affront her light.

My confrontations with her, usually via her embodiment in Siobhan, Director of my Branch, increasingly brought into sharp relief for me the contrast between the two sets of rules the *New Yorker* defined. Living by one set are those who still believe human beings are up to handling the truth. Living by the other set are the boosters who understand the marketplace. Among the boosters, dissent from the all's well is a contaminant to be smiled away, if possible; but sterner measures may be resorted to, if, like the child's sock inadvertently attached to the back of the Scarer George when he returned to the Monsters, Inc. factory from a mission, such dissent's potential to destroy our way of life is understood. In such emergencies, these boosters will drop like shock troops of the dreaded Child Detection Agency (CDA) from the ceiling and decontaminate the dissenter, if necessary shaving his entire furry body. The boosters are Pollyanna's people.

But I continued complacent about my own safety, organisationally speaking. Pollyanna had always been gracious, condescending and warm towards me when she saw me among the unfortunates still under pessimism's power. Life at work seemed to settle down again.

I ducked and wove for two years after the fateful July 3 meeting with Siobhan and my immediate boss. Let me return to that tense meeting. You will recall that the instrument which promised a denouement was at hand in the form of a proposal to contain me, and Siobhan, pitchfork poised and me a netted parcel on the sand, waited only upon the thumbs down from the imperial loge. The owner of that thumb, Jody, was the same Executive Director who would in two years' time deliver the thumbs-down-lite upon Siobhan herself at the HR network retreat. For now, though, she was happy to entertain Siobhan's final solution. For my part, of course, I didn't sit still. Net or no, I presented a paper of my own to Jody which directly, point for point, challenged Siobhan's. The Executive Director, perhaps paralysed by the choice between upholding the patent nonsense of Siobhan's proposal and being the instrument of her loss of face – they were thick – threw up her hands and asked the deputy CEO to call the shot. He had us all to tea and, as luck would have it, supported me.

The disappointment must have been severe for Siobhan. So close and yet no cigar. But her spirits were not wholly crushed and soon rose again. For she had another iron in the fire a full month already and it was shaping up well. This iron had started out more like a golden apple that fell fortuitously into her lap about a month before our tea with the Deputy CEO.

For on the second last day of July a staff member with what was much later determined to be Borderline Personality Disorder had been frantically referred to me by her supervisor. He was desperate to get some help for her, and himself, after a long period during which she had displayed emotional instability in the workplace. She and I spoke once and established what I naively took to be rapport. The next day she became emotional in the workplace again – I had not effected a miracle cure – and explained to her boss, who, as well as being desperate, was, as is not uncommon within dyads where what psychoanalysis terms projective identification flows abundant, over-involved with her, that I had made her worse. In fact, she informed him, I had recommended she commit suicide. Her boss didn't contact me to ask if this had in fact been my counsel to her. Instead he made a recommendation of his own: that she put her allegation in writing and have *me* investigated. When the written complaint arrived in Siobhan's office she commissioned an external consultant, a woman known to her, to investigate it. This would definitely be the final solution.

I was never able to learn, despite many attempts, what terms of reference were given the investigator. Judging by her eventual report, her brief was to examine, on the pretext of looking at my alleged unconventional counselling, the possible termination of the whole operation of the EAP. She couldn't make a finding of fact upon whether I had or had not told this woman to kill herself, since I denied it and no third party had been present in the consulting room, nor would she off her own bat hazard, on the balance of probabilities, that I had or had not. But her report to Siobhan made up for that minor failing by a raft of recommendations about the urgent and necessary restructure of the EAP. The investigator's report was submitted well after the Deputy CEO had come down on my side at the meeting about Siobhan's restructure of the EAP. The proposals in the report bore uncanny resemblance to those in Siobhan's failed final solution drafted two months before and still a current proposal when the investigator began investigating me, but by now a mere stain in the bottom of the Deputy CEO's teacup. But Siobhan's capacity for hope had been, as would have made Pollyanna proud, athletic enough to spring from a dying mount to this fresh one.

Alas, it also was headed for the knacker's yard. The investigator's report was so transparent and written to support an already decided outcome that it fell victim to its own clumsiness and, when I challenged it, was set aside at the same level and by the same person who quashed the final solution. But this quashing came in March of the following year, eight months after the Personality Disordered client came into my consulting room. During those eight months of tension, in the course of which it became clearer to Siobhan with every passing month that the golden back-up apple was corroding rapidly, she saw that her hired gun investigator was going to fail her. So she commissioned one last sortie in her campaign to rid herself of me and my penchant for darkness. For this one she called on the assistance of Hans, loyal and true. This would expunge the EAP problem once and for all.

This final sortie, the final, final, final solution, began on September 27, at a time when the first final solution is a month dead in its teacup, but the second final solution (repackaging all the original final solution recommendations about the EAP problem as recommendations by the investigator looking at my alleged malpractice) is still a goer, though corroding quick. Again, this triple-f solution seems to start out as a fortuitous golden apple delivered into Siobhan's lap by gravity.

On the twenty-seventh of September Hans chaired the fortnightly meeting of all the officers in HR Branch who reported to him. I was one of those officers, as was my colleague, Margaret Mooney. At the meeting a fortnight before, Margaret and I had commented that staff of the Branch had complained that Siobhan continually brought into the Branch people she knew from her past employment in other organisations and appointed them, *sans* any merit selection process, to highly paid positions. We described it as nepotism. Hans could hardly deny it was happening. It was common knowledge and a matter of concern to most people in the Branch, whom it clearly disadvantaged unfairly. Hans resolved, against our demur, to invite Siobhan to our next meeting and this was it. His expectation was that she would explain for herself her recruitment philosophy.

The meeting began and Margaret and I in turn confronted Siobhan with our observations of her peculiar recruitment practices and the loyalty they demonstrated to her once-upon-a-time co-workers compared with the justice they failed to show to her present day subordinates.[9] Siobhan was neither charmed by

---

[9] The justice here juxtaposed with loyalty is deceptively named. That is, justice to Siobhan's present staff might also appear as loyalty. It's hard to settle upon a moral posture here because we feel affection for the idea and affect we call loyalty. It is deeply rooted in us. In fact, it is not until one thinks of loyalty as a specifically tribal virtue that one begins to see where the tension arises. The

our irony, nor struck by our logic, but utterly discountenanced. The gear shifts in the meeting were sudden.

Siobhan wept and raged by turns, favouring me especially with her attention. Chagrin and awkwardness overtook the room utterly. Feeling ran high. Those present not accustomed to taking other than an obsequious posture in the presence of authority were extremely uncomfortable. Voices were raised in angry exchange of emotionally charged commentary camouflaging, and fuelled by, outrage at the impropriety of our confronting Siobhan in a relatively public place with what she could never hope to justify and so must needs be embarrassed by. Someone from the general office area without stepped quietly to the door of Hans's office and closed it soundlessly, eyes averted. Hans, his usually brown nose flushed red, was aghast not only at our temerity, Margaret's and mine, but at his own stupidity in providing us, against our express warnings that it was a dumb move, with the venue and opportunity to so undo his boss.

Eventually Siobhan worked herself into such a state that no one else in the room, contaminated all by her extremity, was capable of resolving the situation. Then, as if by magic, she was saved by the opening of the door and the appearance of her personal assistant with the news that her boss wanted to speak to her on the phone in her office. She left, amid silence, saying nothing. The meeting disintegrated after that, our capacity for further discourse disappearing like water into broken earth.

---

controversial realisation comes that justice and loyalty are not competitors. They belong in different evolutionary periods of our growth towards species maturity. The rule of Law is the death knell of loyalty. I have referred to the "corrosive phenomenon of loyalty" in communications of various kinds in the context of the public service to very little audience acclaim. We don't want to know. Nevertheless, we must.

Professor John Kleinig, Department of Law, Police Science, and Criminal Justice Administration at John Jay College of Criminal Justice, addressed this problem when he visited Brisbane in 1994. His ideas inform Rubric 11 of the *Manual* at Item 6 of *The Subversive's Toolkit*.

# 9
## Michael Has To Go

AT first, I suspect, Hans felt completely at a loss and as close as he could come to being ashamed of his lack of foresight. But the next morning Hans and Siobhan conferred in her office. Soon he was his over-confident self again. He knew what was needed now and he was determined on a course. If, before the meeting, Michael needed to go, and Siobhan's public email response carpeting him for limning out the awful work risks our frontline and counter staff face, left him in no doubt, then he needed now more than ever to go. For now, escalating his sedition beyond toleration, he had made the first rough sketch in public of the pre-equity, pre-merit, pre-everything *ancient regime* that existed under Siobhan's sceptre in the Branch. But Hans faced one difficulty, a single, insurmountable stay to his sword. It was Siobhan who had misbehaved at his meeting.[10] As its chair he knew that. She had done wrong both before it in the practices we had complained of and during it in her response to our discomfiting comments.

No matter. Easily fixed. Just reframe it all. Wordsmith extraordinaire, tongue honed in the service of one Circe (whom I had met before), cunning as a wheelhouse cat ensconced on the binnacle, Hans could rewrite history and reset our course with ease. The crime here – and no one could deny there'd been one committed, just look at all those distressed people, left distraught by the great exit, rudderless and confused like chaotic confetti in the wake of a bride in flight – was clearly Michael's disrespectfulness. Bingo. Do him for that. Take a day or two. Scuttle around and talk to everyone but him about what happened yesterday at the meeting. Imply his guilt. Provide all bar him with a scapegoat to assuage any sense of guilt. Lay a trap. Carefully prepare a charge sheet itemising his misdeeds. Conceal that

---

[10] Let me just detain you once more, Dear Reader, for it would be a waste to tell you my story without exposing you to one of the abiding dilemmas in public service life: the question of loyalty, which looms large not only at this point of the story, but also when I come to the *ménage à trios*.

Siobhan and I, Hans, have conferred, colluded, conspired to realign and rewrite yesterday's goings-on into a more suitable lead up. Lure him to a disciplinary interview dressed up as an invitation to debrief the debacle. Catch him off guard. Read him the riot act. Secure an admission. Demand an apology. Begin the dreaded diminished work performance proceedings.

He did it well, too, by his lights. Fortunately, they were low wattage. I shucked his trap, though not easily and not at once. It took months and consumed thousands of dollars of taxes in special investigator's salary, in the paid time and lost productivity of a dozen members of the Branch whose witness statements about the alleged disrespect and the *mêlée* in general of the staff meeting were recorded, cross-checked, double-checked, verified and pored over. And in the end Hans had to back down profitless. And to add insult, I, in defence of my job, submitted a grievance against his falsely charging me. And won from him, at the end of all those months, a retraction.

Hans's scheme to play white knight to my venomous dragon for the deliverance of Siobhan, distressed maiden, not only to himself but also to her boss, Executive Director, Jody Laden, had drawn her, Jody, into its machination. As things fell out, those three formed a triumvirate discountenanced and frustrated at my once more wriggling loose from their conspiring. Locked together in their triple-berth chariot like Brutus, Cassius and Cassius's dog, seeming never to have heard their whispering slave's *sic transit gloria mundi*, possibly due to the steam of frustration coming out of their ears, they had forged ahead until at last the axle broke. Their planned triumph succumbed to hubris.

But hubris is nothing, if not even-handed. Offstage, Treasury was putting the finishing touches to a wobbly *deus ex machina* and the triumvirate's luck was about to turn. One year on from Hans's defeat, my own would be complete.

It came about as a consequence of the move to something called Shared Services.

Like a slowly massing cloud on the horizon, the government's commitment to a revolutionary approach that would revise the sector's system for supplying itself with corporate services – payroll and information technology administration, maintenance of its fleets of automobiles and people, etc., – had been seeping like doom into the consciousness of public servants, the pre-awareness of something wonderful and terrible, something that dripped with the promise of globalisation and the same dread, something just as universalising. This seeping, in retrospect, is quite obvious, its string and cardboard growing more visible as time passes. The process is fundamental to opinion management, whether softening up public servants to embrace a new mode of work or preparing the electorate to cop the invasion of Iraq. All media are recruited in the lead-up to "inform" and educate their readership about the circumstances of life and wonderful prospect of a solution. The truth was that each Department and agency was going to have to relinquish dozens, maybe hundreds, of staff to the new Shared Service Providers, brand new agencies, called SSPs, reputedly destined to eventually merge into one monster agency, which would "sell" services back to the denuded Departments, who would become its "customers". The plan as publicised, however, was upbeat. The selling started long before the new SSPs were up and running.

The folklore that was growing around this bifurcation adventure in which half of us became "customers" of the other half proclaimed that the inhabitants of the sector, long contemned in the popular imagination (that of the bond slave of Capital, the Media) for their presumed second-rate "public service mentality," would move boldly and at one stroke on to the very catwalk of business style, dressed in bottom lines, draped in business development, comely with competition, *décolletage* with contracts and commerce. The shared service provider push was a progressive force lifting us higher, making us better. We were already calling our agencies businesses, soon we'd be business class for real. Our efficiency and productivity would rocket upwards under the famously energising influence of that way of life. No more poor cousin working in Capital's home as a domestic keeping the house running. We public servants would be participants in the private sector.

Everyone, nearly, agreed quietly to ignore the perfectly predictable failure that would attend this posturing charade and the nakedness that the promenading emperor's arse would shortly exhibit utterly escaped derision and foretelling, due to this very lip-smacking eagerness to be like the private sector.[11]

Getting to that acme of private sectorism, however, necessitated that some eggs be broken. There might be pain. Public service mini-empires might crumble, new ones emerge. The ambitious were positioning themselves for glory or foreshadowing lamentation. Sometimes both at once. Attitudes were fluid; it was hard to know if pessimism or optimism was in. The shadow of this massive cloud (above which the god's contrivance with my name on it creaked) gradually fell over our sandpit like the huge ship's shadow in *Independence Day*. Since Hans, Siobhan and I each performed a corporate services function, the darkness was tinged with a personal threat for us all. The question now became: Which of us might suddenly be yanked from our perennial internecines and absorbing, sand-in-your face infighting and sucked into the comfortless void of the dread new SSP? Although we all qualified for the plank, some of us ate at the captain's table and last minute reprieves might be possible.

---

[11] In late 2004 a Performance Audit by the New South Wales Auditor-General exposed the actual savings for the first real year of that state's shared services exercise, the earlier predictions of whose success were a vital influence upon Queensland's adoption of the idea, as a mere $13.6m, or 5% of the projected accumulated savings by 2006 of $297m, and at the same time revealed the implementation cost to be $79.4m. Queensland's response was to issue an analysis of the NSW audit and to show how we were avoiding that state's errors of implementation. By then we were near a year and half into implementation, and no one suggested stopping. Not in public anyway. Saving, after all, is self-evidently important, face especially.

Well, it's an ill wind. Through this fog of apprehensive ambiguity one clear and unexpected silver lining gleamed to the delight of the triumvirate of Hans, Siobhan and Jody. The answer to the question was me.

Some ideologue in Treasury, apocryphally an American consultant with minor god status in SSP implementation lore, was asked what should be done with departments' EAPs. Whereupon, as I later learned to my chagrin, this deity, in a gesture not quite on a historical par with Lenin's legendary absent-minded tick beside a list of names presented to him, leading to their premature termination, consigned EAPs, generically, to exile from their home departments and into the wasteland of SSP, a fate not quite worse than death. In America, after all, and increasingly here, EAP is just another service which management outsources. That it might have a function as a corrective the organisation applies to itself was outside consideration. This level of unawareness of consequences is to be expected in reform agendas driven by financial agencies and not counter-balanced by advice from a personnel agency. To accept organisation restructure advice of this kind and not predict the profound emotional effect it will have on workers, a government would have to be already in thrall to the mercantile mentality[12]. Ours was. Is.

Melancholy as Romeo leaving Verona, I was marked for export. How sad for you, Michael, my betters in the Department commiserated. Ah, well. Too bad. They hid their glee at their deliverance, from both turbulent priest and their own exile, and carefully smiled not upon the stroke of luck, good theirs, mine ill, that killed their jeopardy. There was admirable discipline in this. These circumstances, as no other, called for inhibition of that exhibition of glee most gorgeous that was usually the major part of Siobhan's unofficial job description. Here only condolence was required. But her po-face belied what must have excited her,

---

[12] I submitted a paper to my superiors arguing that this mercantile mentality would produce a morally deleterious effect upon the public service. The paper is included in the appended *A Subversive's Toolkit*.

nevertheless, as the ideal solution. Delivered at last; and not by
sword or rapier of hers, but by a golden axe wielded by the
Machine's god. Rid of him, but not losing what we want from him.
He is removed from his pillbox that was placed at that crucial
intersection of internal traffic so perfect for taking swipes at the
Department's dysfunction; and because Treasury did it, we won't
antagonise the troops, those whose groundswell affection for him
is so reminiscent of the truck between priest and parishioner that
they can publicly write to him in defiance of our equally public
censure, in terms like Eleanor used:

> I think you deserve a chocolate Freddo every day!! Seriously, I
> (and many, many others in [the Department]) appreciate your
> honest, ethical and doggedly optimistic approach to your job.
>
> We need people like you who are not afraid to say what they think
> and mean what they say.
>
> If you ever have the time, I'd love to catch up with you over a
> coffee.[13]

Notwithstanding the illogicality, the insanity of it, the fiction
was upheld that I could continue as Staff Counsellor – the *sine qua
non* of which position is belonging to the organisation – while
separated from the organisation. To challenge that direction from

---

[13] The triumvirate wouldn't have had access to emails like the one I will quote in
this footnote, but they were well aware of the gratitude felt toward me by the
many staff who'd used the EAP over more than a dozen years. This client had
brought to me his bewilderment at the behaviour of his psychotic partner and
we had worked on it. Later, he sent me this:

> I want to help her so much but am realising that I can only hand her the
> keys. She still does not want to cooperate with the psychologist and still
> maintains that she does not understand why people think that she is not
> normal. I am sitting here with tears streaming down my cheeks...I might pack
> up and go home for a cry...Thank you so much for your time and trust. You have
> helped me so much to better understand her and myself. Take care.

Treasury was beyond the courage of the people who ran the show. Their timidity suited Siobhan down to the ground. And so I went, vanquished.

Let me say something about the mechanism of denial, a deeper look at how it is possible for Siobhan and other denial merchants to be, or appear to be, blind to broken, unfixed things and comfortable in that ignorance. Her email response to me, *in toto,* showed what mobilisation of her forces can do by way of forward defence. Yet what we saw in her email is only the poor, reasonably well-mannered cousin of her more dramatic outbursts in meetings and in the general run of office life, those highly public, but unscripted, events in which her behaviour is even more instructive. Here the earthquake-like way in which her demosthenic fury on occasions removes psychological overburden, composure giving way to white-knuckle angst, as she demolishes any who obstruct, makes plain with how much concentrated, inward- and outward-focussed vigilance she stands ready to fend off of any threatening awareness of the dark and those who might trigger it.

Pollyanna seems to infest her so completely at such moments that one might fancy Siobhan merely a thin overlay, a diaphanous mask worn by her internal and imperious guest now thoroughly in control. And now in control, Pollyanna settles down to home so totally that – and here let's go a step lower into the psyche – an even deeper layer of her emerges, her shadow side. This termagant variant, now briefly discernible, is as haggard as Siobhan/ Pollyanna is normally genial, chubby-cheeked and cheerful. It is as if the skull of Grant Wood's mid-western American Gothic farmer is straining through Pollyanna's skin, and more rabidly with every outing.

In fact, there is something suggestive of paternity in the similarity of this deep *in extremis* layer of Pollyanna to Mr American Gothic.

For this ghastly vision is far truer to the underlying reality of pollyannaism, if we know it by its fruit rather than by its propaganda. The ideology of the Pollyanna we know, though originally, of course, taken over from Eleanor Porter's sunny 1913 literary creation, has long since dispensed with whatever pretty innocence Potter invested it with. That takeover was an inevitable step in the construction of what Marx termed cultural superstructure. Consumer confidence requires an ever upbeat note and a stalking horse was needed beneath which the insatiable voraciousness of the greed that powers the market economy could raven about freely without any of those whom it savaged being any the wiser about the real identity of their attacker. The credo of the little girl with the braids was perfect for the job, making her the obvious target for a hostile takeover; and because the eleven-year-old didn't do hostility, it was candy from a baby.

Yet Siobhan, all literary and metaphysical fancy aside, is not from outer space (or from my fantasy life) and what her actions illustrate lies ghost within us all. Arthur Miller, who might have, had he a little less integrity, stood in for the phantom playwright above to compose Siobhan's email, knew a little of the effects of this phenomenon, being one of those doggedly pursued by the denial-driven House Committee on Un-American Activities as a result of his passion for telling ugly truths to his fellow citizens. If my Friday email, with its modest freight of ugly truths caused me to learn what retribution follows the telling, my discomfiture was a mere grain of sand beside what for Miller was a whole beach. Towards the end of a long life of suffering condemnation for his clear view of things he wrote usefully about the denial which he constantly disturbed in *Timebends A Life* (he poetically omits the conventional colon).

Sifting those drifts of sand, Miller comes to a precious stone. Part of its uncovering occurred during his reflection while on a post-war tour of Europe. He speculated on page 523 about how the farmers and villagers of an area "still famous for its anti-Semitism" must nevertheless have learned not to look up as "trucks packed with people whined up [the] road" to Mauthausen concentration camp, near Hitler's birthplace.

For another score and more pages he riffles through historical and cultural examples of denial ranging through history and across the globe, coming to rest for our edification upon a little classic. He looks at the conviction and ultimate acquittal of a suspect named Reilly, accused of slaying his mother, and the revelation that prosecutors simply denied the existence of evidence which would eventually explode their obsession with Reilly's "guilt" and their convictions about his motivation, which they had explained

Michael O'Neill

as oedipal rage. It was a case Miller had been personally involved with.

On page 556 he writes,

> The Oedipus complex may or may not operate universally, but the sheer animal reflex of bureaucracy in stonewalling against embarrassing truths surely does, and no less so [here in America] than in Russia or China or anywhere else. The vital difference is our right of appeal from its decisions, but appeals are expensive and depend too often on sheer good luck. There is a lawyer in almost all of my plays, perhaps because man is what man is, *nature's denial machine*. In the course of the Reilly case I grew to treasure the law as our last defense against ourselves. (*My emphasis*)

We may be instructed also by someone else who saw one of those same death camps a score of years earlier, when they were still warm, and the confection of sadism and insouciance which made them possible was fresh out of the oven. The Russian author Vasily Grossman came in 1944 to Treblinka with the liberating Red Army. Unfit for military service, he had been assigned a special correspondent for the Red Army newspaper, *Red Star*. What he found and described at Treblinka could, he wrote, render even the strongest person insane. Indeed, he reports that of the 800 prisoners spared the gas chambers and employed burning the corpses of the less fortunate many sought to provoke for themselves the luxury of a German bullet, and fifteen to twenty committed suicide daily because of the terrible moral torment. There were enough replacements.

Grossman reflected upon the same dilemma as us. Directly addressing the predictable squeamishness in his reader, he wrote, of his own report,

> It is infinitely hard even to read this. The reader must believe me, it is as hard to write it. Someone might ask: 'Why write about this, why remember all that?' It is the writer's duty to tell this terrible truth, and it is the civilian duty of the reader to learn it. Everyone who would turn away, who would shut his eyes and

walk past would insult the memory of the dead. Everyone who does not know the truth about this would never be able to understand..."[14]

Even before they exist, Grossman is talking to Holocaust deniers, those among his potential readers who would quibble about the poor taste of directing attention to dark things. *My* potential readers may quibble, too. They may say it is unfair and poor taste to use Grossman's observations anticipating deniers to prosecute my case, since his central subject is the Nazi disregard of human life and values so incomprehensibly evil, so unique, so outside any possible pale, as to be therefore, paradoxically, unavailable for rhetorical deployment to reinforce argument about misdeeds within human scale. But it is the very fact that denial may govern in a thing so large that makes Grossman's insight so pertinent. It testifies to denial's power.

And there is another, more proximate reason Grossman's rhetoric is pertinent here. For Siobhan and her delicates got off lightly. I could equally well have chosen to write that Friday email at the end of any of a dozen other weeks in the life of the Department. On those Fridays my account might have included not only the oblique references which it did to the dead bodies of citizens of the state who are, or were, our clients, but a direct reference to a member of our own staff killed that week: Sometimes in the line of duty, smashed by a truck ignoring the witches' hats, or crushed accidentally in a pug mill that grinds rock into the gravel we used to surface roads; sometimes dead by their own hand, such as in a one-person donga in an isolated road building camp comprising a dozen such huts, and found by co-workers breaking down the door on a mortal threesome – his body in the single bunk entwined in a crowded embrace with a rifle and that god that loves not bribes. Or Siobhan and her delicates may have had to integrate unthinkable events from my work like

[14] Vasily Grossman, *A writer at war: Vasily Grossman with the Red Army 1941-1945,* edited and translated by Antony Beevor and Luba Vinogradova, Harvil, London, 2005, page 301.

visiting and talking to a construction camp foreman who forty-eight hours earlier had to deal with the death by crushing of his own son, a child who had until that morning lived with him and his wife and their other children in one of the camp's family dongas; a child who, with a group of other curious camp children, had dislodged an improperly stored, huge spare wheel from a mammoth piece of road building plant; a child who happened to be where the great wheel of death fell when the group couldn't control it; a child whose father was first brought to the scene by the stunned, bemused, horrified playmates come running to find an adult; a child who died not at once but some short time later, choking in his father's arms; a child whose blood and other tissue filled his father's mouth as his father attempted mouth-to-mouth; a child whose father was not only camp foreman but responsible for the safe disposition of plant and equipment on the site; a child whose father, my client, had now to live with the needless death of his son and his own roles in it; a child whose father's marriage would soon dissolve; a child whose father, though young and fit, would live from that day only about the same number of years as his son had lived.

This inbuilt incline in us (more like a cliff face, perhaps) precipitating us into denial fairly clamours to us to both resist *and* understand it, even as we surrender to it. Denial is almost our default mode, a normal condition nearly, so one baulks at calling it pathological. To help delineate it, let me take advantage of some of the particularly pertinent fare daily spread out for the readers of Queensland's newspapers in the early months of 2006.

At that time commissions of inquiry and the coroner's court were looking at a range of controversial matters in a number of state government departments. One issue being examined was public servants' possible official misconduct – in Queensland "official misconduct" is an act sufficiently heinous to warrant dismissal – of various stripes, including alleged culpable killing at the government hospital in Bundaberg, a regional centre. Naturally, the witnesses were keen to avoid being found to have misbehaved or turned a blind eye to the misbehaviour now under the investigator's microscope. To fall into either category would mean graduating from witness to accused.

Over a period of months, story after story emerged of the occurrence in government departments of self-serving misrepresentation of the facts, suppression of unpleasant or politically damaging information, lower echelon public servants being silenced or "requested" by superiors to "keep this in-house for a while," and staff having it made clear to them that disciplinary action might follow, if they revealed certain information about the internal workings of the Department to outsiders. "Outsiders" in such conversations might refer to the police or specialised investigating agencies and standing commissions of inquiry established some years earlier to eradicate public sector corruption and malpractice. Sadly, almost no-one over a certain age now finds such suppression any longer worthy of remark. And no-one under a certain age knows any different. It is the norm. Why get upset over it. If one gasped in amazement at every revelation that deserved it, one might never breathe properly again. It is tempting, even, to resign from the struggle and say, it's human nature, what can you do. Who taught us so? No one and everyone. As Marx saw, the mode of production, in our case Capital, produces the superstructure, i.e., the culture, it requires. Ours, including our ideas of what's OK, is thoroughly Capitalised. Public image, even for the public service, is everything, justifies everything.

Some of those in Bundaberg accused of failing to react to and prevent medical incompetence which was at once killing and maiming people *and* creating revenue for the hospital were revealed to have justified their refusal to rein the incompetent in by asserting that, "This is not a hospital, it's a business." A business doesn't de-advertise itself. Further, it became clear these officials' arse-up values derived logically from Departmental policy on how to supplement budget allocations and husband resources, policy they sincerely felt virtuous about adhering to. I think we're past *Pollyannaism 101* now. This madness is postgrad.

Indignant amusement at seeing this denial illness writ so large and public and safely located in others is comforting respite. However, it is also defensive. If we are to penetrate the mystery of denial and its acolyte Pollyanna, we will have to go beyond the disbelief, rage and weary despair these revelations generate in us and see our very selves as part of that rather large non-graduating group of flunkers, and denial as more than merely ghost in us. We have to go further than the conventional there-but-for-the-grace-of-God admission of a tendency and acknowledge that we ourselves, at moments of potential embarrassment, try to put the best possible face on things, if not actually lie or deny reality, while scrabbling around for a rationalisation.

As long as I'm in the frame then, let me get some help from Alexander Chase, who added an idea to Gautama Siddhartha's wisdom, when he wrote,

to understand is to forgive, *even oneself.*

So our cycle of rage, resignation, insight and *mea culpa*, might bring these three huge questions to the page:

1. When a challenging truth whose publication has potential to unsettle is put to us *before* it has become so publicly known that it can no longer be hidden, i.e., while it is still known only by those whose silence (we think) can be coerced or cajoled, what fosters in us this readiness to deny?

2. For those truths we ourselves first see and should utter, what stills our tongues? Is it the fear our ribbon to Power's maypole might be cut? Is it Power's pure aphrodisiac subversion of our self-respect? Or is it Power's plain, old-fashioned threat, which we suss and succumb to in an unnoticed instant, thereby sparing Power the embarrassment of those locutions which would unface us both and which it would rather employ only when the chips are down? ("If any of you mention this [report, submission, statistic] outside this room, you may be in breach of your obligations under the Code of Conduct to not bring the Department into disrepute. OK?")

3. If we perceive who or what has offended the Gods and, like blind Teiresias, are asked to speak the unvarnished truth, may we be forgiven for taking refuge with him, in fearful silence, and crying out, "Alas, alas, what misery to be wise/ When wisdom profits nothing!"; forgiven, that is, for our despairing avoidance of those dimly perceived and terrifying insights about ourselves that, like death, have undone so many?

Tradition tells us St Peter, when the cock's crow ended his long dogged night of three declared denials, was dismayed to see he'd lived out this humiliating confirmation of his master's predictive insight. That agonised sense of being subverted by one's own cowardice is utterly aversive. None choose to experience it. So when we have fallen prey to our own denial, we all, I think, work hard and darkly to avoid knowing it. For we know that should we ourselves or anyone else, naïve, confront us with our sin, we will be thrown into crisis.

Such crises *can* be resolved, but it means at least painful self-examination and embarrassed admission, decision to change, upheaval, *then* peace: little George Washington lays his tomahawk down and fesses up. However, if we are inclined to engage in this self-renewal, it may help to wonder first about the mechanism that might be producing and maintaining the tendency to deny.

For example, Siobhan and her delicates, like the Holocaust deniers, prefer a posture of psychotic refusal, eyes resolutely averted, rigid neck twisted up and away to keep the offending darkness out of their field of vision (and out of ours, too, if they can). Perhaps that posture reduces the likelihood of seeing the horror, and that is important. For they fear that seeing the horror will engender a moral exhaustion which will bankrupt them and dissolve their stiff-necked resolve to deny, plunging them into the unbearable. Do they have some ancient, attenuated memory of some piece of darkness once encountered, perhaps when they were too young and frail to withstand it, when sources of support were absent or found it funny or were complicit? Is it the threatened revisiting of this tiny, interred remnant that must be prevented, if life is to continue?

Michael O'Neill

Few, of course, engage in this self-renewal, choosing not to resolve the crisis of knowing the truth, but refusing to see it; and crisis delayed or resisted long enough can end with one flying to one's fate like Oedipus. Remember the lines of Auden.

We would rather die in our dread
Than climb the cross of the moment
And let our illusions die

Therefore, best avoid the crisis altogether. Call in an air strike: attack is the best defence, and easy to do, if all this is set inside an organisation, and if the naïf urging the truth upon us is subordinate to us. Dead messenger, dead easy.

My Friday afternoon email and its organisational reverberation comprised a microcosm in which some of these questions might be resolved. US Senator Joseph McCarthy, the 1950s Commie Chaser, didn't hate communism, though he played that role. He shared the outrage of the unusually insightful (but unfortunately not prescient) woman who emerged from Miller's *Death of a Salesman* on opening night calling it "a time bomb under American capitalism". What drove McCarthy was his panic at the readiness of "communists" to say capitalist America wasn't perfect. That is the genre of Siobhan's driver, too. My Friday email said life, fate and the Department weren't perfect. For her and McCarthy their enveloping context had to be perfect. Living, and the psychological accommodation it required, were impossible without it. Siobhan, though not as capable of evil as McCarthy, nevertheless, "knew" life was perfect. Both realised that to ensure it remained so domination of the public image agenda was essential, as essential in the USA in the fifties as it was in Queensland in the noughties.

Australian ABC television and radio presenter Peter Thompson, delivering the 2005 Bruce Allen memorial lecture, explained an unusual feature of the strategy he adopted in the creation of his successful radio program focussing on international and national affairs.

He and his producer decided to cover politics, wherever possible, without politicians.

"Not a single listener complained about the lack of political talent [on the program]. ... [T]he warmth of feedback for the program exceeded anything I'd experienced before.

"...Why did we make that choice? Well, frankly, I don't think people want to listen to politicians any more. They don't answer questions. They're not straight with us. They're masters of spin. They won't engage in real dialogue. They always want to keep control. The bottom line is they don't earn our trust, just like the [public opinion] surveys say."[15]

Being clever at spin might be a legitimate boast (if such an oxymoronic concept may be tolerated) for those wishing to impress the selectors identifying who's to play cricket for Australia, but it appears a boast more and more successful in impressing those other selectors, the ones in our political parties choosing vote-winners who might run the country.

Spin doctoring, i.e., the distortion of reality for ulterior purposes (what we used to know as bullshit), is, significantly, the *modus operandi* of the biggest player in town, especially in its presentation of self to the rest of the world[16] (and, significantly, to its own citizens). Continuous reality repackaging is integral to the foreign policy façade of the United States of America.

Fast learners in many ways, the US One Percent have absorbed one particular lesson of history, the one that matters to its survival, and cut its cloth to suit. It is a truism that, as pre-eminent imperial states have always done, the US has chosen endless expansion as a means of staying economically and politically on top. What's new is that the One Percent is wise to the modern zeitgeist and knows that if it presents itself plainly as imperial it will be rejected by the domestic voters who give it its

---

[15] "Memorial lectures are worthy legacies", Errol Simper, *The Australian*, 20 October 2005.
[16] From *The Australian*, 2 December 2005, p. 11.

license to print money, both in the US and abroad. It knows that it must combat the growth of awareness in its citizens and subjects to stop the lethal build-up of resentment that could one day unseat it, as it has historically unseated its predecessors.

Fortunately the Orwell manual has clarified the remedy for this potential disaster, so the US can avoid sliding into the fatal groove which geo-dominant states have always slid into by describing each of its imperial acts as if it were its opposite. It must needs be seen to be an exporter of democracy, not of revolution like those dumb commies in the twentieth century, or of Frenchness like Napoleon in the one before. The US can and does support right wing dictators, and even left-wing dictators, abroad when their proxy local authority is required, but must spin such commitments into its overall web of bullshit about nurturing democracy.

The US's rhetoric about freedom and democracy must be loud, and constant enough to achieve saturation level. In this enterprise it must employ the talents – *buy* the talents, which is to say, prostitute the talents – of the best legerdemainists it can find. White House spokespersons with dancing tongues, actors who become Presidents and Presidents whose main job qualification is thespian are merely the emblematic figures who epitomise and model the function. The heavy duty, day to day, micro level, bulk propagandising is carried out not only by, as you would expect, private sector enthusiasts whose bottom lines benefit enormously from association with Brand America, but also by public servant after public servant (including military spokespersons doing PR for adventures on foreign soil, e.g., Afghanistan, Iraq, Cuba/Guantánamo) all the way down the hierarchical line, and in client nations of the US who know what's good for them as well. There are dozens of different head-kickers at points down the hierarchy, with a hundred ways of suborning and seducing the scores of public servants below them. One of these head-kickers is our friend Pollyanna/ Siobhan.

Since all of this mystification is in the cause of greater repatriated profit, identifying democracy with the free market goes without saying.  Identifying *as* democracy (or as the necessary lead up to democracy) whatever works for the One Percent, whether at home or abroad, is essential to the success of their strategy.  That strategy's prerequisite is globalisation.  So we have also had it explained to us that we must have a "globalised" economy.  What we haven't had explained to us is how we can have both democracy and a "globalised" economy at once.  Since a country can no longer decide how some very basic features of its society (education objectives, healthcare delivery, ownership of exploitable resources) will be arranged because "globalised" economics requires them to be otherwise, democracy in one country becomes as hollow and impossible an ambition as socialism in one country was a hundred years ago.

That leaves the One Percent in a bind.  Because exported democracy is as visibly phoney[17] as the free market economy is

---

[17] *Papers paid to run stories* WASHINGTON (REUTERS): The US military has secretly paid Iraqi newspapers to run dozens of pro-American articles written by a special military taskforce, the *Los Angeles Times* reported yesterday.  The newspaper also said the Information Operations Task Force in Baghdad had bought an Iraqi newspaper and taken control of a radio station, and was using them to disseminate pro-American views.  Spokesmen at the Pentagon and with the US military command in Iraq did not deny the report.  This is a military program within the Multi-National Force (the US military command in Iraq) to help get factual about ongoing operations into Iraqi news," said Lieutenant Colonel Barry Johnson, a senior US military spokesman in Iraq.  As recently as Tuesday, US Defence Secretary Donald Rumsfeld touted what he called the "free media" in Iraq and called it "a relief valve".  He said: "They're debating things and talking and arguing and discussing."  The *Times* reported that the program began this year and the articles were written in English, translated into Arabic and then given to Baghdad newspapers to print in return for money.  It said it based its story on interviews with US military officials who spoke on condition of anonymity and with Iraqi newspaper employees, as well as documents it obtained.  The Times said the stories were "basically factual" but omitted details that might not reflect well upon the US.

mythical,[18] the sell has to be twenty-four seven and ubiquitous; that means the ears of the punters soon reach saturation point, and what that produces in them (if they haven't despaired into nihilism, surrendered into materialism or succumbed to drugs) is rage. To neutralise that rage – it's so bad for business – the Machine must deny that its propaganda is a sell and instead feign ever more fulsome enthusiasm for democracy and freedom. But no matter what spin you put on your spinning, or how much you deny your denial, or pass your forked tongue fandango off as mere misspeaking, you are still a liar. More is not better. Laura Penny, in her book, *Your Call Is Important to Us: The Truth About Bullshit*, (Crown, 2005) observes of some example she has shown us: *"Like most bullshit, the more times you hear it, the bullshittier it gets. This is why bullshit is best served quickly, with many visuals, in mass quantities..."*

One might say that much of American public culture can be seen as the practice of bullshit for nefarious purposes, that public culture being both the unconscious model for and the instigator of Pollyanna behaviour like Siobhan's. The role of bullshit is crucial to the explanation of American culture. Something in American history, in the peculiar development of its demographic, some outfall from the clash of the original American "idea" with native Americans (such as the need to re-present that clash to the world and to themselves as good), perhaps, and, later, that idea's subsequent absorptions of, and contaminations of, its cultural rivals, the influencing back and forth between them, the compromises American history's idea of itself had to strike, the whole imbroglio, produced as emblem the Pollyanna myth and the Pollyanna posture.

---

[18] In his 2005 Nobel Prize acceptance speech Harold Pinter characterises the gap between American democracy rhetoric and the reality of its foreign policy this way: America, he says, "has exercised a quite clinical manipulation of power worldwide while masquerading as a force for universal good. It's a brilliant, even witty, highly successful act of hypnosis."

It is a posture perfect for its purpose. It provides a self-flattering persona so positive and hopeful none could contemn it without risking disapprobation all round, leaving America free to interpret silence as approval. Under such a canopy the works of the devil himself might proceed apace unnoticed and unknown *even to the perpetrators.*

To wit, see Marilyn French, *Beyond Power*, page 408ff, where she discusses the historical, philosophical and political origins of universal schooling and curriculum in nineteenth and early twentieth century United States. In particular, she points out that organised business early in the 1800s was hostile to the idea of universal education because it wanted to maintain a pool of uneducated labour it could *reasonably* pay low wages. To bring them around, urgers whom French labels the schoolmen, impressed upon them the usefulness of an education whose objective was congenial to their interests. Its objectives would be worker complacency. Convincing restive workforces that they were/are content with their lot, French argues, was the movement's deliberate objective, even if unconscious in some of its champions.

Eleanor Porter's *Pollyanna*, having come along in 1913, would have served to bolster this new approach that saw universal education as win/win for business and society as a whole. That new approach was catapulted into flight by the catalyst of America's shock at how generally poorly informed were the recruits for its First World War effort. It was a shock that resolved the conundrum of whether or not an educated workforce was a desirable thing.

The bind I have identified as the present predicament of the One Percent is, ironically, one of their own choosing. Not that, given their nature, they were ever likely to choose differently, yet we might pause to look at how things might have been for a moment, had they paid more respectful attention to one of their own gurus.

Back in 1948, flushed with the success of arms and gearing up to swap them for the not so obviously threatening brief case (the one with which the Godfather noted it is possible to make more with than a gun), the US One Percent were presented with the following *realpolitik* from George F. Kennan, an elder statesman recognised during his years at the State Department as the government's leading authority on the Soviet Union. Kennan, in a paper he wrote for planning staff at the State Department called "Policy Planning Study 23" told them:

> We have about 50% of the world's wealth, but only 6.3% of its population. ... In this situation, we cannot fail to be the object of envy and resentment. Our real task in the coming period is to devise a pattern of relationships which will permit us to maintain this position of disparity. ... To do so, we will have to dispense with all sentimentality and day-dreaming; and our attention will have to be concentrated everywhere on our immediate national objectives. ... We should cease to talk about vague and ... unreal objectives such as human rights, the raising of the living standards, and democratization. The day is not far off when we are going to have to deal in straight power concepts. The less we are then hampered by idealistic slogans, the better.[19]

By 1948 Pollyanna had already had thirty-five years to work her magic on the American mind. Kennan was no match for her. From then on, with the small, exceptional moment when The Project for the New American Century, a think tank[20] based in Washington from 1997 to 2006, spoke some plain, appalling talk, whatever was going out was going out in camouflage Kennan would have called vague, unreal and dreamy. Something called Democracy was on the march. Democracy it wasn't.

Unless, of course, exported democracy is exactly what the phrase suggests: a product that arrives on the wharves of the world in boxes, tamper-proof boxes, pure from the United States of America's top think tanks, with the following Customer Information Notice on the side:

DIRECTIONS

---

[20] http://en.wikipedia.org/wiki/Project_for_the_New_American_Century

Do not add water, especially the local water. Apply to problem area strictly as directed. If pain persists, consult only specially trained spin physician, or local accredited practitioner. Worldwide 1800 free call number for assistance can be provided. Send stamped, self-addressed envelope with cheque payable to Log Cabin Franchises.

(There is no customer complaints phone number on the boxes because that section was closed as a cost-cutting measure.) The notice continues:

CONSUMER ADVICE
Unfortunately, our complaints team has been re-assigned to Sales Enhancement. But, really, complaining is unproductive anyway. A focus on the successes and positive stories is far more productive. In fact, this is a good approach to take in respect of everything connected to the development of your local economy, especially if it is going to articulate smoothly with Ours. And it would help if the civil structures and regulatory agencies adopted this style as well; all singing from the same hymn book will result in a much more integrated chorus. In further fact, if your public service could be encouraged to see itself as another module of the business world it would move things along exponentially. After that it would be much simpler for its internal public sector discourses to align with the real engine of social progress, i.e., Capital, whom it exists, after all, to serve. A good aim to keep in mind, just as a way of keeping focus, would be to have the public sector think in terms of greater market share and to position itself ultimately for a public share float and stock exchange listing.

But what you must always, always insist on is positive focus.

The tip to foreign nations in the fictional sign on the crate about the crucial role played by their local public service found its way there to swing our focus back for a moment on to that body of operatives in whose company we sat when this journey began.

To be precise, from an original concern with a specific, identifiable infestation of pollyannaism in my little neck of the public service woods, we have arrived back at a high bluff overlooking that neck, along with much other forest. From up here it is clear the infestation is widespread. It is also clear that this way madness, or at least corruption, lies.

This has been known for a long time among those who have actually honoured the profession of public service. The longevity of Chinese cultural coherence has been achieved in the face of more than a few despotic and would-be despotic lunatics and their lunar ideologies of societal governance, ranging even within the last two hundred years from Hong Xiuquan, "little brother of Jesus," to Mao Zedong, little brother of Stalin, and this durability has been largely due to the rationality of its mandarins, who have managed the nation's administrative and social life for 2000 years. (Testament to their importance: the term mandarin[21], is now synonymous with influential public official, which he was about to become.) It is not without significance that Mandarins were forbidden to marry or to own property within the province for which they had responsibility and in which they might serve for not more than three years, and that, as observed by historian Justin Wintle, beginning prior to 1000 AD, before the Song dynasty, "the taboos that separated public service from mercantile activity"[22] were observed. Like many other Chinese wheels the West had to reinvent, this carefully designed approach, or artefact painstakingly evolved in the bio-cultural context of the peculiar Chinese kind of sanity, bespeaks wisdom about how to preserve integrity in public service.

The integrity of ours is threatened by the Trojan horse of mercantile corruption, subtly poisoning first the way public

---

[21] The term Mandarin itself does not come from the dialect spoken by that imperial Chinese corps of elite officials (a dialect that has become the official national speech of the country), but is derived from a sixteenth century Portuguese word, mandarim, which had travelled, via Malay, from the Hindi mantri, meaning "counsellor". The delicate irony of finding myself, etymologically, at so highly placed and venerable a level in this line of descent, a virtual antecedent of those who would abjure me, is reward enough for much discombobulation. [The word for a mandarin in the dialect they themselves spoke (i.e., in Mandarin) was guan (kuan).]

[22] The Rough Guide History of China, Rough Guides Ltd, London, 2002, p. 180.

servants are encouraged to use language, and later the way they think. Pollyannaism is the plume on the bridle of that horse. Fortunately, even in the face of the blurbspeak positivity of modern organisational (and therefore public service) life, that equine enormity and its favoured way of neighing attracted the attention of researchers in 2003. Their work indicates that the course followed by reality is sometimes refreshingly, shockingly unimpressed by popular fantasy.

Writing in the *Harvard Business Review*, an organ many of the principal offenders might regard as honour bound to boosterism, Dan Lovallo and Daniel Kahneman, respectively a business scholar and a psychologist, examined the phenomenon of monumental scale organisational and business failures, citing three examples from across the developed world with a combined price tag of cost overruns and share market losses of scores of billions of dollars and decades of completion timeframe blow-out.[23] They draw attention to some disturbing facts: "Most large capital investment projects come in late and over budget, never living up to expectations. More than 70% of new manufacturing plants in North America...close within their first decade of operation." The vast majority of efforts to enter new markets "end up being abandoned within a few years" (p. 58).

Lovallo and Kahneman reject the conventional wisdom explanations of such debacles in favour of seeing them as the result of flawed decision-making based on "delusional optimism". The three culprits the authors identify to account for these corporate failures are cognitive and social phenomena that magnify what they call "people's native optimism". The third of these is pertinent to my general thesis. They call it Organisational Pressure, an intra-organisational political behaviour that seeks to "emphasise the positive and downplay the negative":

---

[23] *Delusions of Success: How Optimism Undermines Executives' Decisions*, Harvard Business Review, July 2003. Their three main examples included a combined project mounted by the national governments of four European countries, with an original proposed budget of $20 billion.

> Organisations also actively discourage pessimism, which is often interpreted as disloyalty. The bearers of bad news tend to become pariahs, shunned and ignored by other employees. When pessimistic options are suppressed, while optimistic ones are rewarded, an organisation's ability to think critically is undermined. The optimistic biases of individual employees become mutually reinforcing, and unrealistic views of the future are validated by the group. (p. 60)

Thus, what happened, and from all reports still happens, in my old Department's mental life doesn't spring fully formed from the brow of Siobhan. Rather, her brow is formed by the warp and woof of the world's geopolitical intellectual context.

Why should we worry about this?

We should worry because there is a risk to something precious. A tree in the forest unobserved may fall and raise dusty philosophical riddles about whether the event occurred, but the subterranean connection between what we find precious, the profession of public service, and those agents that would suborn it is real with or without our attention.

What it may take Australia's public services yet some time to learn is that we cannot adopt only part of the mercantile system, e.g., in the interests of making ourselves more efficient take on the trappings and ideology of private enterprise – that is, ape it – because of its vaunted superiority in efficiency, any more than you can be only a bit pregnant, or half a gangster. The truth about mercantile activity is: I can only grow richer if you grow poorer; I can only become pre-eminent, if I make you de-eminent. There is a simple lockstep correspondence between harbouring that guilty knowledge in the mercantile heart and the need, for peace of mind's sake, to deny it. One cannot live in a naked state of guilt. Denial must wear clothes of ideology. Capital is capital for you. Buy it now! That it manifestly is not, and that one cannot consciously lie to oneself, sets the stage for the entry of Pollyanna.

If a society elevates profit-making to the status of national credo, then it must either live chronically in active denial or, if it hold to the only intellectually self-evident virtue, honesty, must admit that it has chosen greed.  It then must teach its young that "Greed is good," or lie to them.  But as soon as one says that greed is good, the social and economic landscape around one gives the lie.  Half one's compatriots in poverty and despair, and a threatened nest for all is not good.  This so forces itself upon one, that one must cease to pretend to goodness and hold to greed alone.  The pedagogy then becomes merely, "Greed is," which is less a pedagogy than a vicious and defiant expulsion of bad breath, equivalent to, Fuck you.

Australia has something to preserve, a culture of its own which is at risk from the political slavishness of the dominant sycophants hell bent on aping the socio-cultural, class and financial systems of the United States of America.  A clear vision of the difference between the two cultures touting for our future was achieved by the indefatigably Australian Germaine Greer when she visited Cuba in the seventies and attended a session of the Fourth Congress of the Federation of Cuban Women.  Cuba's President, the voluble Fidel Castro, also attended the session.  Describing that session's discussion, she writes,

> Sometimes when the head of state wagged his hand for recognition, the chairperson ignored him.  At other times, the delegates noisily disagreed with him, crying, "No, no!" some even booing.

She makes unfavourable comparisons with other heads of state of the time incapable of listening, especially to someone who disagreed.  Then she draws out a meaning from her observations of the absence of theatricality in the behaviour of Fidel and the others:

> People did not sell themselves as they do in consumer society. Life was not soap opera, but real. ... They spoke not to persuade

or bamboozle, but to explain. ... Life without gossip magazines
and advertising seemed wonderfully uncluttered.[24]

It is no accident that the unbullshit of what she saw in Cuba
attracted Greer's attention. This is a quality once prized in
Australia. It is often the subject of embarrassed debate here.
Oddly, one of the reasons our countrymen and women are
reluctant to assert, define and defend[25] Australian culture is an
awareness doing so dishonours what it would honour. On top of
that, we are aware that one's own partiality tends to invalidate
one's assessment and one has the healthy shame to desist, leaving
in place a paralysis preventing one from, honourably and
intellectually, going forward or back. Thus it is sometimes a circuit
breaker to have a detached outsider observe and report. Mark
Twain did it for the old world and before him de Tocqueville did it
for the very world that now so takes our fancy. Australia has had
its de Tocquevilles (Twain himself, and D.H. Lawrence), and
recently one that was a compatriot of the original of the species,
Catherine de Saint Phalle. She liked what she saw a little more
than her venerable predecessor did in America:

> Even as a very new inhabitant, I understood what Mark Latham
> meant when he spoke of Australian culture. The American belief
> in pushing individual ambition to the extreme is the opposite of
> the tall poppy syndrome. Somehow, 'being part of' is more
> important for Australians than driving themselves to compete.
> Australia has filled a delicate place in the world between
> America's ferocious individualism and Europe's tribal fear
> regime.[26]

---

[24] *Ourselves Among Others: cross-cultural readings for writers,* Carol J
Verburg, ed., St Martin's Press, NY, 1988, pp. 443-4.

[25] In late 2005 Australia *abstained* from a vote in the UN in which the first
international treaty to affirm the right of countries to "maintain, adopt and
implement policies and measures they deem appropriate for the protection and
promotion of the diversity of cultural expressions on their territory". 148
nations said yes. Two said no, the USA and Israel.

[26] "Flames old and new", *The Big Issue,* # 240, October-November, 2005.

If we must re-house the philosophy of our public service, as we seem determined to do, we could do worse than to give the naming rights over the new sandstone edifice to de Saint Phalle.

So, now, in reparative mode, let us ask, "What is to be done?" (I borrow Lenin's title in the superstitious hope that it will bring my words as rich consequence as it once brought his.)

Well, once one knows one is marked for drowning by the forces of marketing, aided by analogous forces which reside like a fifth column within, how does one then contrive to stay afloat, how resist? There are three ways for individuals to negate the effect of the US's and its idolatrous adulaters' marketing of the market ideology and useful postures to adopt towards one's internal saboteurs.

One is to understand market ideology's influence upon the body politic, how it captures and contaminates, buys and/or buries in media sludge any who oppose its relentless rewriting of history and redrawing of the philosophical, ethical and common-sense map. We can still, even after the (grey) flannelling we've copped, succeed at this task of plain seeing. For somewhere within each of us is an obdurate memory of freedom from before we were conscripted. From the point of view of the Machine, it is what needs eradicating, but defended it can be the nucleus of our rebellion.

A second is by resisting market ideology's minions in the individual's own walk of life, exposing them where possible. One must be prepared for the fact that its minions generally do not know whose shilling they are pocketing and won't know what you're on about. Or they will know in some half-intuitive way and will react to your resistance like Siobhan.

In these two ways one takes its exports back to its front door, rings the bell and goes. Just telling, in the face of the spin, the uncomplicated truth about one's world is resisting. Sometimes one does this instinctively – the market ideology hasn't completely destroyed our nose for bullshit – and one doesn't realise that that is what one is doing until the reptile's tail sweeps around and knocks one down, and suddenly there one is, looking into its glowering eyes as it reminds one just who runs things around here. Honest reaction is the only response that marketing can't tolerate, that jolts it into unseemly hostility and unpositiveness.

Before I come to the third way you can stay afloat, let me say a little about denial.

Denial of the truth, as opposed to the honest reaction above, is marketing's partner in crime. It is in this sense, in the opinion of Arthur Miller, as instinctive as self-interest for human beings to bullshit about things, to participate in the general denial, which may explain the insidious and subversive charm marketing appears to hold for us and the way otherwise reasonable people will sit patiently through TV advertisements, prime ministerial sound bites and CEO's mission speeches without demur.

They will attend a workshop which is designed to combat serious stress problems in the organisation and yet is absurdly titled, e.g., "People Working Together", as if it were a paean in praise of something else entirely or a lesson in what you already know, and they will attend without rising up and saying, "Where has our concern about stress and its roots in the bad behaviour of the organisation gone?" They will act as if their concerns about asbestos exposure in their children's schools are allayed when an Education Department spokesperson tells them it is only blue asbestos in the roof, not the far worse white asbestos. (They will act allayed, not be allayed.) They will cop it sweet when an official responds to a series of horrific cases of schoolyard bullying by announcing a program of activities to "celebrate bullying prevention measures in our schools," obediently marshalling facial muscles for smiling rather than shouting, "What do you fucks think will happen to us if we are allowed to stay for a minute longer than you could tolerate with an unpleasant insight or observation about our world?"

To understand how the third way of fighting back works, consider this.

... In standing absolutely still in the midst of our conflicted, conceptual world, we may discover the explosion of unity, of love, that is the bare actuality of life.

Here is the challenge. Stop. Look. Listen

Nothing is in the way.

Spontaneously, life is bursting forth[27].

These lines from Steven Harrison are about faith. Prince Charles, asked if, when he became the King of England and head of the Church of England, he would use the title, Defender of the Faith, replied, "Not the Faith. Faith." A supplicant father approached Jesus for help, despairing at his son's diabolical condition, a challenge which had defeated, because of their lack of faith, the best efforts of Jesus' disciples. Exasperated, the usually sanguine Jesus cried out,

"O faithless generation, how long shall I be with you? How long shall I suffer you?" (Mark, 9:19)

Then Jesus confronted the foul ugliness, named it and exorcised it. He called it dumb and deaf, identifying the features which accounted at once for its potency and its stupidity. Clearly, these characteristics attributed to an entity with no corporeality were fictive and pedagogically chosen faults. The catechesis is plain: it's dumb to choose to be dumb, refusing to name and refusing to hear. Do, and you will continue possessed, not by that Walt Disney devil evangelists on TV warn us about, but by the one who has the TV evangelists in his pay. But they're telling us something we instinctively know as babies. Curiosity is OK. Look at things and know things. If you don't paralyse yourself with fear, you will know what to do when knowledge happens to you. We

---

[27] Quoted in Josh Baran, *365 nirvana here and now: living every moment in enlightenment*. Element, Hammersmith, London, 2003, p.362.

may simply have faith in our capacity, and that of other human beings, to handle the truth. We may. We don't have to be afraid of the dark, and we certainly don't have to parlay fear of the dark into a way of life like Siobhan.

When I emailed Marley just after 1:00pm on the Monday following my fateful Friday broadside to say that my conscious intention had been to darken the picture HR operatives have of our fellow worker's lives, I had in mind the fecund dark of Rembrandt, that ultimately enlightening foil whose end is to collect and focus attention and thus to bathe in light the inward life of those it surrounds. I was thinking of the darkness in that secret, suggestive matrix of light and shade which the eye sweeps across, tacitly accumulating the unresolved and complex, the half-seen, the ominous, the guilty, the shameful, the deeply dissonant and integrating those qualities into the formless and powerful understanding of things that lies beyond the reach of words, nay thought, and then, from within that cloud of unknowing, distils understanding like the very intimacy of God, forms it and focuses it upon those faces that inhabit the painting's regions of light, investing them with meaning, pity, identity and psychological complexity beyond the power of mere physical wattage to illuminate or elicit.

What I loosed instead were the night terrors that provoke the somnambulists, somniloquists, sleeping beauties, brain disordered encephalitics, gargoyles and all the other capricious Goyan fiends which the sleep of reason produces who would take to the canvas with a knife or douse its pain with bright pink paint. Meanies and monsters amok with pollyanna pencils.

If light consists of extremely fast oscillations of an electromagnetic field in a particular range of frequencies that can be detected by the human eye, then darkness may comprise and conceal those things that can, if fear not deflect, be detected by the human heart. For it is at last the spectator's own heart which the caressing or accursed, frightful or fecund dark illumines.

Michael O'Neill

It's tempting and thus traditional to exploit the fear of the scary dark, though. Generations of parents in many cultures have used it in its bogeyman form as an easy way to dominate their kids, making use of a ready-made motivator/scarer the surrender to which is forgivable in children. Not so in parents, however, is the expedient deployment of that fear. That is, their lazy, didactic shortcut may have consequences (e.g., creating in juvenile minds a predilection for avoiding darkness) which last a lifetime, in fact many lifetimes, and become established under the guise of a world view of optimism, or pollyannaism, and go on to assume respectability in the intellectual life of the species, a self-replicating virus continually mutating and regenerating. Iconoclasts have their work cut out.

The actual people whom my fantasised fuck-shouters challenged, the Machine's minions in the individual's own walk of life, are our fellow citizens, in many cases our friends. Heaven forbid, even those contaminated parts of ourselves. Let me speak of a case close to me, my own; because, if we are trying to observe what inveigles people into this spin of spin and keeps them going round, I can supply a communiqué from the front, from my intimate encounters with a couple of practitioners, one recruited to this devil's employ, but disguised, including from herself, as one in the employ of Devil's nemesis. Her name was Sister Boniface. The second was Max. Max came 10 years after the good Sister, but I hadn't learned much in the meantime and I was still susceptible.

Sister Mary Boniface reigned over a classroom in which I spent my seventh and eighth years of life. Boniface once had a real name, but abandoned it when she became a novice in Ireland while still very young. Now, in her forties perhaps (the habit made it hard to tell), she was serving God by educating us children of Australian working class Catholics in every kind of moral living, and using a four-foot bamboo cane to paste the message into our palms. My parents either didn't know or didn't care that I spent six hours a day playing a bit role in a very early version of the war on terror. As a victim. As far as they, and the world, were concerned, what Mary Boniface was doing in the privacy of that schoolroom was an unalloyed good thing.  That she was a reverse agent or dupe of the culture prevailing outside the school, outside the suburb, outside the town, outside the state, outside the nation occurred to no one, including Sister Mary Boniface.  But that of course is what she was.

Her alternating savagery, frustration and spiritualised self-absorption – uncannily prefiguring Siobhan's traits – fitted her for the function she performed, one mandated by the sub-Machine[28],

---

[28] Sub-machine it may have been in the 1940s, but things were reversed in the 1490s. Then it <u>was</u> the Machine. When avaricious European eyes first fixed their gaze upon the Americas it was the Pope who, on the 4th of May 1493, issued papal bulls assigning the zones of influence and exploitation, and, of course, salvation of souls, often misread as enslavement of bodies, to Spain and Portugal, respectively. No-one seems to have thought this odd. Indeed, it was routine.

Hubert Bancroft, who gives May 2nd as the date of those papal bulls, makes the *realpolitik* plain in *History of Central America*. Vol. I. 1501-1530. (San Francisco: A. L. Bancroft & co Mr. Any, publishers. 1882.)

What Spain required now was a title such as the neighbouring nations of Europe should recognize as valid. So far as the doctrine was concerned, of appropriating to themselves the possessions of others, they were all equally sound in it. Europe with her steel and saltpetre and magnetic needle was stronger than naked barbarians, whose possessions were there upon seized as fast as found. The right to such robbery has been held sacred since the earliest records of the human race; and it was by this time legalized by the civilized nations. Savagism had no rights; the world belonged to civilization, to Christianity if Christ were stronger than Mahomet, to whatever idea, principle, or power that could take it. In none of their pretended principles, in none of their codes of honor or ethics, was there any other ultimate appeal than brute force; their deity they made to fit the occasion, whatever that might be. This they did not know, however. They thought themselves patterns of justice and fair morality; and all that troubled them was in what attitude they would stand i.e., the Church, to do the bidding of the Machine in the formation of little Michael and his helpless classmates (as in so much else). For even behind such cloistered insulation as Mary Boniface enjoyed, member of a then socially unloved religion, celibately free of the usual need to impress and to seem up to date and modern, committed to a Way that eschewed the World, her *Weltanschauung* was, I believe, no less influenced by the million stick-and-carrot mechanisms of manipulation which typify the Machine's modus operandi. No less influenced than Siobhan, than I.

---

toward each other with regard to their several discoveries and conquests. The recognized theory of Christendom was that the earth belonged to the Lord who made it, and the children of the Lord were alone entitled to inherit it. The unconverted were the sons of Belial, the enemies of God, and as such should be exterminated. The Almighty ruled not this world in person, but through the pope at Rome, whose captain and vicegerent he was, and whom all princes even must obey. The first right, as they chose to call their claim, was that of discovery. To the finder belonged the spoils, but always in the name of God, the creator, the owner. God and Mahomet, or God and Christ, Mahomet or Christ, whichsoever was the stronger, in his name should the thievery be done. Thus it was that the Spanish sovereigns, being Christian, applied for a confirmation of title to Alexander VI., then sovereign pontiff of Christendom, at the same time insinuating, in a somewhat worldly fashion, that learned men regarded the rights of their Catholic Majesties secure enough even without such confirmation. No valid objections before the holy tribunal could be raised against Christian princes powerful enough to sustain their pretensions to ownership while propagating the true faith in heathen lands;...

Come back and have another look at this note when you've read Gibney's comment in Toolkit Item 7, below, about the power of organisation, *qua* organisation, to homogenise.

Boniface was determined the Devil would not have me. She had the wrong devil in mind. Which, as it happens, is where he lived. Hers and other minds like it, which were legion, were, ironically enough, almost the only places he could live. Boniface could only see him when he was holidaying between my legs. And all the while I was falling into the clutches of a devil who did exist, the one taking up residence between my ears and doing great work there. Against that great Satan and the actual outside world I had no defence, and Mary Boniface didn't offer me one.

Coinciding with my burgeoning awareness of it post-Boniface and eighteen, that world, my world – local, Australian, mid-century – which had not long since hosted its greatest single, if temporary, immigration of foreigners, led by the Corncob Douglas MacArthur Himself, continued its ever-accelerating, enthusiastic surrender to the Great Satan.[29]

This surrender to the Great Satan in the fifties had become inevitable when he sent the Cob here to save himself and us from Nippon. For our gratitude lived on, encouraging my love of Americanism when I succumbed to it so happily at the end of the Fifties. I sported a completely bogus trace of American accent and achieved the acme of career aspiration by finagling a job in the advertising business, an eighteen-year-old "Account Executive" doing layout and copy. Look down upon me, Jesus. I didn't know what an executive was, and up to then I thought an account was something my ignorance of provoked Father Connelly – he might have been Boniface's bog brother, since they had one and the same corporal attitude to pedagogy – to give me the cuts in book-keeping period. Sister Mary Boniface might have failed in what she thought of as her main object, but her name itself prevailed over my soul. I set out to prove I could put as good a face on anything Myer wanted to shift as anybody else. I seemed still to live in a homely southern suburb of Brisbane, but my heart moved,

---

[29] Ironically, yet another present day group struggling not to surrender to his influence and with no sense of irony baptise him the Great Satan, sensing correctly the danger he embodies, but misattributing its source.

in line with the affectation of the late fifties and early sixties, to Madison Avenue, a street in the centre of that part of what Paul Goodman called the Empire City in which this dark art's practitioners held cabal. It may have been one of the first streets in history to furcate with such fecundity, emigrate so enthusiastically and be received so rapturously. We had one here. It wasn't in the street directory, but it was in the uber city of our minds.

But despite Madison Avenue's rabid rabbit ubiquity, it is, at last, even in New York where it seems so concrete, a made up land, like Homer's island of Aeaea, where Odysseus fell so foul of Circe. Made up, it may be, but it felt nevertheless real to me as I wandered through it entranced until I was ejected at the other side.[30] I had been welcomed into Circe's luxurious bosom as a trainee adept and throve there, my rudder as fouled by infatuation as Odysseus's; but eventually my visa was deemed unrenewable on grounds of disaffection. (I had begun to wake.) Max, a wonderful name for an advertising department head, realised one day that I was no longer the right type. Acquiring disaffection – the beginning of wisdom – there, where falsity was so patent and so admired, had been, in hindsight, easy[31]. Falsity's prominence made it hard to miss, and its being so admired among that company eventually made it an irresistible target for the Irish/Lebanese Catholic boy with an unresting heart, living like a refugee in a Protestant land under his Frank Sinatra patina. When the time was right.

For a long time, of course, the time was wrong. Thriving is one of those practices that send you blind, and in this case, deaf. I was

[30] My erstwhile colleagues on Madison would not agree. They thought and think it real enough. Its walls are solid to their fingertips and they cannot pass through them.

[31] Ah, Falsity! A made-up land should produce made-up product. It is only right. Remember this in a few minutes when I tell you some more about the work of Laura the bullshit explorer. I'll provide a footnote there in which she identifies for a radio interviewer exactly what Madison Avenue's one and only product is. Don't miss it.

deaf as Tarquin to my conscience's Eurylochian misgivings and kept my snout in Circe's trough, while she kept her hand on my balls. Though the money was just OK, the glamour was priceless.

But, alas, even worms can be satiated and glamour is ultimately no match for the viscerally volcanic nostrum of moral disgust. I came to see the phenomenon I once had gloried in and called persuasion from a different angle and was chagrined to recognise it as inveiglement. This inward disaffection must have showed in the loosened grip upon me of the sartorial imperative – I began wearing cotton slacks and leaving my necktie at home some days – for, even as this interior pot was coming to the boil, Max intervened and sacked me and I split; and ever after was, and am, allergic to falsity's presence.

## 10
## Come In Spinner

FAST forward to the 2000s: nowadays, spin generally is close to perfect, and the poison of it has penetrated surreptitiously and ubiquitously into the mode of civic thought. This new improved falsity pervades the Machine entire, not just its private sector lair where I first encountered it, but also reigns throughout its sub-Machines. The public service is a sub-Machine. It has not been immune from the present virulent strain, though it had been from earlier, weaker strains. (The years I spent in it before my starburst advertising career provide me a benchmark.)

Today, we are all endangered, more so the less we are aware. For my part, I have long been protected by my positivity, intolerance and the jaundice acquired in button-down collar days. Against traditional forms of bullshit this has worked, but Pollyanna is smart, smarter than Max, and much smarter than Mary Boniface. Falsity is now integrated into what appears normal behaviour, even – perhaps especially – into the faddish phenomena designated "best practice" (a certification none of its dispensers can specify). In the public sector, for example, we don't have planning any more, we have business planning. Even in jails, including those still publicly owned and operated. Surrounded by these new toxins in the atmosphere, I could only hope my inoculation would last. It did, as this book may show, but I didn't.

My disgust with duplicity never abated, but my body wearied. When I wrote the first draft of this book I was still employed in the public service, an affront to the laws of probability even then, and the previous paragraph ended

"...I can only hope my inoculation will last and I can remain and continue to make trouble. Since there is no Max[32] here to

---

[32] As it turned out no Max was needed. Some breathtaking, but simple strategy adopted by the bad guys eventually put paid to me. The story of that totally predictable demise is the third part of this book.

summarily dispose of me – unfair dismissal is still a valid concept in the public sector – I might be able to hang on for a while." [33]

That was then.

However, as spin spun faster, something else about the world, no doubt to the greater glory of Herr Hegel's alleged trifecta, changed as well, though ever a beat behind. Ever more observant social criticism is closing the gap between the moment of onset of new forms of idiocy and corruption, bread and circuses, and the moment of public articulation of their insane pretension. The little boy now runs along almost at the same point of advance as the naked emperor's equipage.

For all that, the world, as Laura Penny declared[34], is still drowning in bullshit. In her book, *Your Call Is Important to Us: The Truth About Bullshit*, she writes:

> "Your call is important to us" has been chosen from a very deep reservoir of bullshit phrases for the title of this book because it best exemplifies the properties native to bullshit. It tries to slather some nice on the result of a simple ratio: your time versus

---

[33] And, again predictably, when I re-wrote the paragraph, not only was I out of the public service, but so also were 14 000 others freshly out; and outed at one fell swoop. It was 2012 and Queensland had a new premier and a new shade of government, and unfair dismissal was looking like a Dead Sea scroll.

[34] Penny was interviewed on ABC Radio National, Wednesday, 31 August 2005, and 2 September 2005 about her book (Crown, 2005). On 2 September interviewer Steve Austin editorialised:

Laura Penny says phoniness "not only alienates us from each other but degrades public discourse, breeds apathy, and makes us just plain stupid". She says the sheer volume of commercial communication and the technological advances that spread it has (sic) led to an explosion in bullshit. "Advertising and PR make one thing and one thing only, and that is shit up. Making shit up is not to be confused with outright lying, although lying is sometimes involved. Making shit up is more like painting the lawn green when the Queen comes to town. The grass may be green to start with, but it ain't that green," she argues.

some company's dough. Like most bullshit, the more times you hear it, the bullshittier it gets. This is why bullshit is best served quickly, with many visuals, in mass quantities, with no questions from the floor.

Undoing Mary Boniface's successes, and those of her legion of successors, and making good what their diligence deprived me of, was and is and will be a long and painful process of scale removal and organ transplant.

Well, who are the spinners? Who chooses to get into this line of work? The answer to this question is us. We almost all have a part-time job spinning. We are all capable enough of compartmentalizing our minds/selves to the degree required. The same man who tells the White House or Prime Ministerial lie to a press gallery or doorstop gaggle day after day can go home at close of business, turn on the TV, and laugh sardonically at thin rationalisation and false spin put out by a politician from a different country, different jurisdiction, different state. What enables the sustenance of such duality in a person or in a social echelon?

Enter Pollyanna. Or rather, let us say, the principle of Pollyanna in each of us, who aids and abets us in keeping this cognitive dissonance going, supporting and reinforcing the pretty picture while distracting us from the sight of ugly things which would disfigure it. We are prepared to pay her handsomely for this deeply psychological service, not much differently from the way a sexually-starved man will pay a prostitute to help him avoid masturbation, something he needs to avoid because it undoes his idea of himself and confronts him with evidence of his threadbare life. Likewise, it is our need for a counteractive façade that keeps Pollyanna in work.

But what does being in demand do for those of us who work full-time as Pollyanna? What keeps Siobhan at the loom?

Let's ask the question of an analogous profession. What keeps the advertising man and woman in their grey flannel suits even though they know, and not always unconsciously, that they are in the deceit trade? I think what rewards is confirmation of their power to influence and the gratification of their artistic impulse that comes with every successful visual or literary incitation of the punters to part with their money. Where in another age we honoured and respected linguistically and graphically gifted schoolchildren as potential poets and artists, today we arrange to let them work it out in advertising and its spawn. Marketing rules, OK. Sit up now, kids. Here, catch this can. Campbell, you design a creative promotion. Warhol, you mock up an ad campaign, do a nice label. Monroe! Pay attention here and sit up straight, shoulders back. You do a PR plan. If you make me want to buy it, you can have the soup for lunch.

Influence and gratification, can these also explain Siobhan? Perhaps. But what less obvious reward (of even greater power) is hers in return for the positive focus she relentlessly supplies? It is the keeping at bay of her fear of the dark, behind a firebreak she must maintain. That back burning is at once essential to her survival and an eminently saleable skill. This is lucky for her. If she didn't transmute that fear into something we can make use of, something that screens it from view, we'd have to scorn her for a wimp and couldn't continue her clientele. To us she is the optimist's optimist. Within, however, and most likely unconsciously, she is ferociously treading water over the abyss.

Let us leave poor Polly in the pool for a while and turn to the victim of the particular ministration of hers that gave rise to this book. Not me, but the institutional victim, the EAP. We begin by asking what is an EAP's social and organisational mandate?

It takes years to bounce back from such a dismissive backhander as Siobhan delivered the EAP operative (i.e., me) in her email and its sequelae, and that means it also takes years for the institution to bounce back. And while I have crystallised some wisdom from it in the process, years have gone into licking the wounds sufficiently to perceive even the outright lies, the patent denial, let alone the subtler destructiveness, the damage to the corporate morale, the let to the overarching project of social amelioration inherent in HR's role, and in particular, the EAP's role, in the organisation. That role is its very raison d'etre.

This bleak prognosis, implying as it does that recovery takes so long, should provide a lesson to Power: Do not defensively abuse your authority, knee jerk, for the purpose of preserving your ego, your image, your official worldview. Allow that trouble-makers may be making something more than trouble. [35] Listen harder for the self-serving tones in your battle hymn as you rush to the crenellations to defend the way things are. If you don't, your complacent neglect will one day redound upon the very image you are so desperate to manage and your defence will be for nought. You kill your friend.

Sadly, one of the very things that, from the perspective of organisations, make an EAP worth having, i.e., its gadfly potential for holding up a mirror to their decision-makers and tone-setters, is the seed of its own potential destruction when they don't want to know. Wilde said each man kills the thing he loves. Perhaps it is also true that each man kills the thing that loves him. For we are working hard to kill the public discourse, that great conversation (as historian Manning Clark describes it) of humankind which obtains in so many disciplines and sub-divisions of life, and is our decent love for each other, our serious socialness, made visible. We are dealing it the death of a thousand cuts. Laura Penny has observed this and draws attention to our obfuscation compulsion, our devotion to pretty falsehoods which degrades the public discourse that should conjoin us all on almost every topic it touches.

Tony Fitzgerald, reporting in 1989 upon what his commission of inquiry had revealed to him about Queensland's public service, identified an example of this degradation of great relevance to my central thesis:

---

[35] What a good EAP Counsellor does, particularly an in-house counsellor, can often look just like trouble when viewed from senior management level. Facilitation of a claim for Workers Compensation for the ill-effects of "legitimate" management action can be seen as disloyalty or biting the hand that feeds. This is especially so when the claim succeeds. *A Subversive's Toolkit* presents a case in point.

A system which provides the Executive Government with control over the careers of public officials adds enormously to the pressures upon those who are even moderately ambitious. Merit can be ignored, perceived disloyalty punished, and personal or political loyalties rewarded. Once there are signs that a government prefers its favourites (or that a particular minister does so) when vacancies occur, or other opportunities arise, the pressure upon those within the system becomes immense. More junior public servants rapidly become aware of the need to please politicians and senior officials who can help or damage their careers, and *not to provoke displeasure by making embarrassing disclosures*...One of the first casualties in such circumstances is the general quality of public administration. (*My italics*) [36]

That an EAP, one worthy of the name, survives at all in any organisation is a miracle of human insight into, and discipline of, self on the part of an organisation's decision-makers, and of the delicate umpiring of internecine forces. Those decision-makers' magnanimity has to outweigh their immediate ego needs; or, to define the miracle less pollyannaishly, when such senior managers are discomfited by the gadfly's bite they need to have already learned that ego supplies delayed are non-perishable, that a reputation for generosity of spirit is money in the bank.

There is somewhere in all authorities, albeit often dim, an awareness of the value of taking such a miraculous position, of "being big about it". Siobhan herself was not untouched by it. At the HR network retreat which began with our drubbing at the hands of Jody Laden, and perhaps unlocked by the shock of that public comeuppance, it found daylight. As a group, we limped, nursing our wounds, through the two and a half days remaining. The planned agenda was obviously in tatters, jettisoned. In that milieu, buoyed by Jody's unlooked for, tacit vindication of my perennial plaint, I had driven home my advantage, ever and again reminding my colleagues we had been put on notice, that

---

[36] Commission of Inquiry into Possible Illegal Activities and Associated Police Misconduct, GE Fitzgerald, July 1989, page 130.

something had to change, and I knew what. Siobhan, the ranking officer present once Jody swept out, recognised from the podium late on day three my persistence in the unpopular task of keeping them all honest throughout the retreat and insisting they re-focus every time hurt pride and special pleading tried to rationalise our network's past failures. Her accolade was as sweet as it was rare; unique, in fact. It was also veiled acknowledgement that this had been my function over the long years to then, even encompassing the period of the Friday afternoon email. It was an accolade never to take a curtain call, of course.

Why then and no other time? I think the main reason is that then, at that singular moment, Siobhan could afford to indulge me. I no longer mattered. Within weeks, I and my position would be gone to the SSP and out of her hair. True, I would still see the same clients (staff of the Department), still be exposed to and able to itemise the dysfunctions of the organisation, may even continue to speak the same truth, but I would be an outsider. That xenophobic bobcat would remove the ground from under any future moralistic posture I might adopt; so this plaudit was absolutely cost-free, would commit her to nothing and gave a priceless boost to her reputation for big-heartedness. For her settled view of me was no secret.

A second reason was that even for Siobhan it was too hard not to acknowledge, especially so soon after Jody Laden's scathing remarks, the rightness of my analysis. I really had known what.

Conflict of obligations within far-flung operatives always resolves in favour of the local boss, who can easily make life hard for an uncooperative HR advisor. There was another, subtler reason such bias would always be shown: if the provincial HR advisor took a principled stand to gainsay the satrapy, line management's corner-cutting and non-observance of staff rights and industrial protocols – all antithetical to good HR practice – would be laid bare in controversial circumstances and this would trigger local unniceness. Taboo.

By the time the retreat ended Siobhan had accepted my argument and promised reform. However, from close of business on day three that promise was quietly shelved; and many months later, when a very expensive consultant opined as I had about whom the provincials should report to, his recommendation was rejected, the only one rejected of scores he made. But I was long gone and could only smile bitterly from afar.

The dilemma for organisations which try to hold in fruitful tension, on the one, hand self-interest and their now *de rigueur* self-congratulation and, on the other hand, an insider who pricks their consciences and bites the hand that feeds him/her was observed by Elizabeth Hutchison in 1989. Writing about another organisational setting in which social workers (my own discipline), by attempting to fulfil their professional ethic, stir conflict with people implementing other functions, she said,

> The social work profession has difficulty coming to terms with the reality that society employs social workers as agents of social stability and seldom as agents of social change. The profession should struggle, honestly, with the nature of its societal mandate.[37]

Clearly, it is not just the social worker, counsellor or other worker attempting to ameliorate social relations who must struggle honestly. Conflicts like the one which blew up around my fateful Friday afternoon email are inevitable in this line of work. Some human beings are not interested in social change, if it disturbs their comfortable grip on reality. They, also, believe in their usual way of doing things, and with equal passion.

A rule of thumb many counsellors working within organisations would subscribe to is, if you are not getting into serious strife with someone senior in the organisation at least once a year, you're not doing the job. The struggle can take forms other than mine took. One colleague who faced a struggle to hold fast to his professional obligation to advocate for his clients in the face of a boss whose worldview (not to mention her personal convenience)

---

37 Elizabeth D. Hutchison 1989 "Use of authority in direct social work practice with mandated clients", *Social Service Review*, vol. 61, no. 4, pp. 581-598.

was offended by his actions presented his circumstances to his employer this way:

> The problem for the Department is that while it may, from an administrative perspective, legally delineate my "duties" as a Counsellor, it may not, from the broader societal perspective, delineate with any authority (other than that of a corporate or societal citizen offering an opinion) the content of the sociological status, Counsellor. It is simply not the Department's, or even the government's, prerogative. Rather, it is the helping professions which, in the aggregate and/or by individual profession, assign meaning to and define the status, Counsellor. In turn, every Counsellor, via the strictures and ethics of her or his individual discipline or profession – in my case Social Work – maintains allegiance to a set of ideas and actions thus constellated that delineate what's included and what's not included in the practice of counselling. The professional and social legitimacy or otherwise of advocacy's place in that constellation is decided thus, not by administrative fiat[38].

For him, advocacy and its legitimate role in his work were the particular sticking point. For me it was the permission to tell my HR colleagues the truth about what our frontline public servant clients were really facing in their working day.

Just about any local action in one's immediate context will resonate among the music of the spheres and turn out to be, simultaneously, a temporally local variant of a parent theme of timeless ancestry. My impulse that Friday afternoon to enlighten my network colleagues transformed itself into a goad to unseat authority's official worldview. Loosed from my computer, it took up an independent life not only to foment unrest among those

---

[38] A reinforcement of this perspective on settling the relationship between managerial and professional authority can be found in another legal judgement, by Wilcox, J, which canvasses pertinent arguments, esp. paragraph 36. See Geoffrey Preston v L Carmody, J Cauchi and J Mcauliffe and Chief Executive Officer of the Family Court of Australia [1993] FCA 377; (1993) 44 FCR 1 (1993) 31 ALD 309 (Extract). (12 August 1993).

two warring camps into which our group split, but also to echo an ancient theme of civil strife.

That is, when my email deployed its partisans on one side and Siobhan's on the other it gave contemporary form to an age-old contention.

Conceive of that model as having first been manifest in the societal outworking of the dispute between freedom and unfreedom, an oscillation easiest studied in the relations of kings and subjects before one tracks it to its battleground within the human heart.

Athens at its democratic flowering revelled in the new Greek opt for openness and light. The republican Romans, though early bathed in those Hellenic rays, fell victim at last, perhaps doomed by temperament, to bathos and scurried back to that same basileus the even-eyed Greeks had shed like a chrysalis. Caesar, symbolically almost astride BC/AD line, born of one, bent toward the other, left us, in his wake and through his heir the very paradigm of authority and administrative excellence: A civilisation freed of doubt by taking up deference, and by deferring freedom finding effectiveness – for some a satisfactory trade. Rome, solidifying into empire under her oligarchs and emperors, learned that light meted out to the citizens must be calibrated, dosed and metered to maintain the status quo. It is a lesson we have not forgotten.

This oscillation discernible in the life of Greece and mirrored in reverse order in the life of Rome, reappears in the lives of nations emergent from their marriage, not least the USA. Early Thomas Jefferson, speaking of the press, knew and wrote that freedom cannot be limited without being lost – The Queensland newspaper the *Courier-Mail* no longer flies this on her mast, but in the lightsome sixties did, a micro oscillation of its own – and by that meant as well that the light a free press depends on likewise cannot be controlled without being lost.[39] After Jefferson the wheel began to wobble again. Fear of freedom, nostalgia and timidity panicked sensitive souls yearning for the lost certainty that goes with blind obedience to authority, to basileus. That panic was exploited by and coupled to the grasping and controlling motivations of the less sensitive, who desire above all things power and market control. Banishing debilitating doubt was necessary to their ends.

The wobble of the wheel during the generation that followed Jefferson would not be the last in America. We (if you will pardon the first person plural here; when they catch cold on Wall Street, we all sneeze) have gone slippery dip and back on your feet again a few times from Jefferson to Obama[40], sure, but we know who's with us and who's against, and we know what to think. And if we forget which picture of the world is the real one, commercial TV is always there to help us remember.

Our wonderfully unusual Australian SBS Television showed a program (16 August 2005) detailing the Pentagon's strategy for control of the image of the Iraq war. The thinkers in the Pentagon, where folklore is that "Vietnam" was lost in America's sitting rooms, not in the jungle, know that the view of the war held by US voters needs to produce no niggling doubt in them. The imperative is to keep them lulled and patriotic, exactly as Rome's citizens were

---

[39] Queensland, as many other jurisdictions, first installed Freedom of Information legislation following a public inquiry into a scandalous cover-up corruption in the body politic, and at once began to hedge it around with let and hindrance so that it became freedom *from* information legislation. The next scandal will reinvent the wheel and at first it will have no wobble.

[40] For example, when the United States reeled to the left under the impetus of the Great Depression in the thirties "Communists gained an unprecedented respectability, working closely with church, academic and civil rights groups... Earl Browder, the party's leader, even appeared on the cover of *Time*". [Foner, Eric, *The story of American freedom*, Papermac (Macmillan Publishers Ltd) London 2000, page 212.] Foner's book makes the wobble very clear. It's an antidote for the despair contemplation of the US sometimes produces.

kept amused with bread and circuses. Rome's masses, though militarily powerless by comparison with Emperor's commanding Legions, were then, as US voters are now, the key to high office. Retention of their frontmen in high office allows the One Percent to seamlessly continue practising high theft and exploitation of the vast income-producing potential of an empire, its vast reaches of conquered and/or dependent client states and cultures. That Halliburton made a killing in Iraq, and only US companies got a look in in the rebuilding of the oil rich country's infrastructure after the US military had destroyed it, are merely the latest items in a long tradition.

Hypnosis of the voters is achieved through fair means (TV shows, scripted news, embedded "journalists", and for the Roman One Percent, *circenses*) or foul (dissent is undermined, reviled, misinformed, disinformed, or terminated – in the present Iraq theatre, over a two-year period, thirty, non-embedded, independent, Western and other war correspondents have been killed, e.g., shot dead when their cameras were "mistaken" for rocket launchers; others have survived having their living quarters shelled by US tanks responding to "sniper fire from the building" or found their bedrooms had mysteriously occupied the coordinates for a missile attack).[41]

The response from officialdom which my Friday afternoon email evoked suggests the Machine's approach to image management is universal and timeless: White House spokesmen, Directors HR and Nero, all pedlars of such stuff as dreams are made on.

Yet it is necessary to remain conscious that it is not just They who wobble, but We; not just in the life of nations and the boardroom deliberations of newspaper proprietors, this wobble. The tension between freedom and unfreedom is internalised within us all, and may even have started there. Oedipus, as man

---

[41] Journalist Steve Weissman presents information about his profession's links to the military at:
http://www.veteransforcommonsense.org/?Page=Article&ID=2900.

and king, examples for us all its wild careen. First he is basileus, secure and bold and in denial. Then he abandons denial and embraces truth. That brings him crisis and change, but ultimately resolution. Yet the wish not to know the truth is powerful: we can ignore the exhortation to see even when Zoroaster, Sophocles, Christ and Freud are chanting on the cheer squad that truth will make us free (or at least free of all but the ordinary misery of daily life). Perhaps we ignore them because freedom is the last thing we want.

The closing lyrics of Bob Dylan's 1962 song, *Blowin' in the Wind*, penned a decade before our *New Yorker* journalist prosaically presented us with the insight that gave rise to my long reverie:

> Yes 'n' how many times can a man turn his head
> Pretending he just doesn't see?
> The answer my friend, is blowin in the wind,
> The answer is blowin in the wind.

Thirty years after Dylan's wistful query about denial, in a climactic courtroom scene from *A few good men*, Jack Nicholson's character, Colonel Jessup, the crusty and unsympathetic Commander from the US military base in Cuba, takes the stand. He replies to a question from Tom Cruise's young lawyer, Kaffee:

Col. Jessup: You want answers?
Kaffee: I think I'm entitled.
Col. Jessup: You want answers?
Kaffee: I want the truth!
Col. Jessup: You can't handle the truth!

Much as one might revile the way Jessup superciliously stakes out the moral high ground (or the *immoral*, ugly, but *necessary* high ground) and reject his disdain for our brittle naivety, there is that in his sneering contempt for people afraid of the dark which speaks to us, to our awareness of how many of us deserve his riposte.

And yet Colonel Jessup's tormentor, Kaffee, was right about one thing. We are entitled to the truth. Jessup would withhold that truth from us because life has taught him we cannot be trusted to wear it stoically, as they must who, like him, are charged to wield the sword on our behalf. In this he differs not in motivation, but style only from others who would adopt the same condescension towards us. For all her fog of asphyxiating maternal benefaction, we observe in Siobhan's approach to image control a purpose no less steely.

Freud, no stranger to polemic, would take the stand himself, but, having always admired not scientists and psychologists, but artists and writers as his most influential intellectual forebears, will instead don the wig and call to the stand a witness of that stripe. In fact, it is one whose good graces he has once already called upon. For when our learned Counsel Freud had earlier stood ready to disturb the sleep of humanity – he was about to present the world with his insight into the long-obscured psychological truth of human infancy – he reached back over two millennia to borrow from this Greek dramatist of whose testimony he was confident a name to conjure with. He knew that this same insight – the child's desire to annihilate one parent and possess the other – was camouflaged artistically in Sophocles' play.[42] For Freud's own experience had already taught him the value to one's well-being of camouflaging such truths. What they both knew, artist and scientist, was the unpredictability of human reaction when the defence of denial is ripped away by unwelcome exposure to plain insight.

Sophocles is likely the earliest secular writer to deal with denial and its consequences, so let us not ask him to testify, but simply look over his shoulder as he goes about the writer's business. Let us fancy that as he approached his creative work he realised he needed two characters to personify the oscillation between freedom and unfreedom, between truth and denial. He chose Teiresias because of his unbeatable back-story. Olympian

---

[42] Freud, in a letter to Wilhelm Fliess, called this insight the source of the "gripping power" of *Oedipus Rex*. October 15, 1897, Letter 71. [Cited in Patrick Lee Miller's "*Oedipus Rex* Revisited", presented to the North Carolina Psychoanalytic Society, Cary, NC, April 2, 2004.

Zeus and Hera, his wife, had argued about whether man or woman enjoyed sexual relations more, each claiming the other sex did. Wise Teiresias was consulted. Having been a woman and a man, Teiresias's opinion carried weight. He agreed with Zeus. This earned him blindness from Hera as a reprisal. But Teiresias's crime was only to tell it how he saw it, so Zeus immediately compensated him, not by reversing Hera's decree, but balancing it with a gift of sight of a different kind: prophecy, an ability far more comprehensive than mere fortune-telling.

Thus Teiresias, the cultural artefact, had exactly the credentials Sophocles was seeking and the playwright recruited him to the *dramatis personae* of a story in which he would examine the role of denial in the oscillating interplay of dangerous knowledge and obstinate, willed ignorance born of arrogant certainty. For Teiresias's dramatic antagonist and counter-weight in *Oedipus Rex* he chose Oedipus, proud, knowing, self-willed.

At a pivotal point Sophocles has Oedipus recklessly hector Teiresias to cough up the dangerous truth. He prevails over Teiresias's reluctance. Then he doesn't like what he hears. He abuses Teiresias without mercy or justice (providing us with the template for shooting the messenger).

Oddly unable, despite his seeming self-confidence, to let it go, Oedipus pursues the matter further – something he could have done years earlier and had avoided – learning the truth at last by allowing witnesses to the events now decades past to speak *their* truth, much as we are doing now. He is magisterially mortified and, reprising Hera's spiteful use of Teirisias, pronounces a sentence of blindness upon himself. For he finally realises what he has wrought with his earlier wilful ignorance and arrogant certainty (i.e., his denial). Oedipus's blindness, however, differs from Teiresias's. The blinding of himself by Oedipus is his own first and still wilful over-reaction when he sees the results of his own handiwork. He reacts hysterically, being as yet unused to facing and accepting the darker side of life (and thus of himself). It's been a Pollyanna world for the king, and it crashes around him.

Dangerous knowledge resolutely ignored wreaks a terrible vengeance.

Something about Colonel Jessup's face as Nicholson portrays him just hangs on to me. Truth could have a more congenial champion, I suppose. He's so ugly compared with Cruise's Kaffee. But he values the truth. And even though he thinks he owns it by right of unsentimentality, would withhold it from pantywaists like us, and can't really disentangle it from his penchant for staring into the abyss, he nevertheless honours it.

Sages have light to shine, your sovereign poet's more sublime. I'll end as I should've begun. Wisdom's fine; poetry's fun:

In truth, an 'twere mine,
I would thee e'en adjure,
Accept not less than all revealed.

What yet denial close,
Demand be op'd,
What's hid, said.

For this dissembler,
Who fain at first, not fell, appears,
Nor strict seems in's arrest,
Still is the sergeant's cousin,
Inevitable and elephantine yet
In's unforgetting, and
Once in the room, leaves not.

For comes it all at last to this one light,
He will undo thee when the time is right,
Insouciant, and Oedipus, that fleeing his fate
Flew to it, he'll have you, mate

## 11

## The Paradigm of Ending: Farce follows tragedy in the usual way; first Karl, then Groucho.

> In this time of transition, many people are the victims of deep structural change. Some have their concepts of reality overturned, others cling to former notions of sanity and order, while others succumb to depressive illness when they see through the lie of the modern world.
>
> David Tacey, *The spirituality revolution*

WELL, the real story is over, but to wind down, read this tale. It's pure Greek. Start with this diary note I made on my second last day in the public service, about seven years after the Friday email hit the stands:

> They just had a morning tea/send-off for me here and I made a speech in which I mentioned the Nagel article my intellectual colleague in Main Roads, sent me. The bit about reticence and the social usefulness sometimes of keeping your mouth shut so social interaction can continue to be possible. I also mentioned to them that my wife had urged me this morning to "be gracious" at the morning tea. Thus, I was not going to go into detail about the involuntary nature of my voluntary early retirement. And I didn't, though I could feel the pull of it.
>
> Instead I told them a story of 51 years ago, about to do my last two and a half hour exam before leaving high school and writing in numerals "two and a half" with chalk on every lamp post I passed on my way to the school, and how railway security threatened to arrest me that morning for writing two and half on all the trains. Only I forgot to mention that the exam was two and a half hours long until Rose asked me what the two and a half meant. They must have been polite. Well, the old are forgiven much.
>
> Now I am sitting in my denuded office – nearly every movable thing has been secreted home in small amounts (like the M*A*S*H guy's motorbike) over the last several weeks, files, records, evidence – and my colleagues have all gone back to their desks and rooms to resume working with the sort of concentration possible only when the horizon that one day ends

it all is too far to see. Lying open on my desk beside its gold envelope is the card they just gave me, with $50 bookshop voucher taped to the back of it. I detached the voucher and pocketed it. The card I half wish to leave lying around so the people who were away today can sign it tomorrow, my last day, and write on it more little messages of thanks and goodwill.

I look at it, the open card with its slantwise inscriptions like disorganised paw-prints left by a St Bernard who danced on it with crowded feet, and realise how archetypal it is. "Lucky bastard," 61-year-old Bruce's paw-print says, though noting it may not be appropriate. Lito, a young man whom I have not bothered to get near in the year he's been here, has surprised me with "it was a pleasure working with you. I've really appreciated the experiences you have shared." He may refer to Levina, the case study I circulated for comment, or the stories I have told in a desultory way at team meetings. And Jeff, a man whom I did bother with – he had a career in the hard end of mining before going back to uni to get a Business degree in human resources management – wrote, "I have really appreciated some of the insights you have provided to me since I joined the SSA." Jeff and I had a conversation one day in which I pointed out to him how the client department was using its consultation with him and feigning interest in what they had asked him to do to assuage their guilt about being totally uninterested in such an unprofitable enterprise which government regulation forced upon them. The rest are all the bests for your futures.

I think it's the little island of silence that surrounds me and my card that has yanked me into this indictment, saying capture this, capture this, this is epochal and haloed in gold. This is the paradigm of ending.

If you've been paying attention, you will remember that after the forces of righteousness in the Department triumphed, my job and I went from there to a shared service provider, where I served a five-year sentence, at the end of which I wrote the farewell note you just read. During that time I continued to provide counselling to the staff of the Department I came from, much to the annoyance of its senior managers, who couldn't prevent me, but bided their time.

A shared service provider is a number of bodies of people congregated, each body drawn from within (in our case) a government department in which it had been employed keeping it running, paying its staff, minding its HR obligations, and other administrative house-keeping, now reassembled with similar bodies from other departments as one unit to provide exactly the same services to the same people, but to do it from "outside". The newly formed unit, i.e., the shared service provider, has all the departments from which its own people are drawn for clients. One of these newly formed units was the land of my exile.

The land of my exile, however, was itself unquiet. There were tensions between it and the public service departments who were its clientele that were the consequence of fundamental flaws in the theory and therefore the structure set up to give form to the government's vision, a vision dependent upon the fantasy that economies of scale applied to corporate services delivery just because they are, roughly speaking, replicated in each of the departments who contributed staff. Somebody, the guilty party is never likely to confess now, looked at the Queensland Public Service and the subparts of it, its Departments, and saw them as theoretically subparts of one organisation. In reality, of course, the mother ship is itself a conglomeration and each subpart a huge assemblage of people traditionally dedicated to one pursuit with which they feel strongly identified. Theorising that when you gathered those corporate service deliverers from all the subparts together in one place their combined strength could be applied more efficiently was rank fantasy. Perhaps if they'd been blocks of wood . . .

As well, if more were needed, what the originators of this project refused to contemplate was that the service so delivered was a lowest common denominator sort of service. They then were, of course, surprised to find that client departments (subparts) were furious to now see corporate services delivered back to their remaining staff with an alienated yawn. The originators of the project were also surprised when the operatives plucked out of their erstwhile nests, within which they had enjoyed honour and effectiveness, and therefore good repute, within which, in other words, they had taken pride and been accorded respect as HR workers, were less than keen. People at high levels in the now client subparts may have been discreetly and silently concerned about this diminution in usefulness of the HR help they were getting while attending reverently at councils of the mighty, where lip service to the originator's grand vision prevailed. But not elsewhere.

We had to learn for our laborious selves – you may remember my footnote about Queensland's disdain for the warnings from over the border – that you cannot take a model that works for widget production and impose it upon the "production" of services requiring subtle intimacy with the served and expect it to succeed.[43] The inapplicability of such an approach, for example, to counselling work which is delivered as much to the organisation as to its individual members, is clear. If that work is done right, its client catchment becomes, in effect, a parish. Done wrong, it's not worth doing, and it's costly. A parish priest is part of the parish. He/she is not outside it. That seemed obvious, at last and with a stiff dose of hindsight, to New South Wales.

It was also obvious to me; and I had learned nothing about keeping my mouth shut.

I had volubly refused to participate in my new agency's system of constantly tallying up the bestowal of our staff person-hours on each of our client departments. Upon that tally the agency based its billing of those departments. For me that meant keeping a note of which of our client departments were receiving service from me. We were playing at being private enterprise practitioners.

My old Department was, of course, one of those client departments, and I served it exclusively, that being the condition upon which my position had transitioned here. ("Transition" had

---

[43] This act of policy insanity has been incisively laid bare with surgical detachment in an academic paper produced by my intellectual colleague in SSA, subsequently escaped to Main Roads and from thence to oblivion along with 14,000 others cut from the public service by the new Premier of Queensland in early 2012. Like me, he had been conscripted from the Department to work in the agency, his exile providing him the vantage point from which to dissect. I will seek the author's permission to release it.

come into vogue as the favoured epithet to describe what used to be known as being transferred.) So record keeping in my case was pointless. Only my old Department could be invoiced, since it was my sole "customer". Theoretically, the whole cost of me could be recovered from my old Department. In the general malaise, it wasn't noticed for a while that I turned in no tally sheets.

My new employer's title was CorporateLink, at least in the beginning, with the modish capital letter stuck in the middle of its name. After the inevitable restructures it morphed into Shared Service Agency. We called it by its initials: SSA. All of my new SSA colleagues consented not only to the tallying, but also to the overall commercialised approach, if silence really does mean consent. But to my mind it was utterly at odds with everything I believed public service work was.

Keeping records of whom I had done what for – they called it TimeCapture – would have articulated my work output to SSA's overall "product" (a new name for intellectual services provided which is used by people who fear their work won't be taken seriously by Mr Money), like a wagon to a prime mover. We were living out a commercial fantasy, one part of the Crown paying another part of the Crown for services to itself. And if we fell into dispute over money, another part of the Crown arbitrated.

When I questioned any co-worker engaged in this practice, they would stay shtum or admit it was ridiculous; but the emperor wore what he wanted him to wear, or at least what the guru of the moment wanted him to want, and no one laughed. However, I found it all not only ridiculous, but also unethical, and had already identified from our everyday practices four examples of unethical actions (other than using TimeCapture) we took as an agency which were purely motivated by the profit motive. Profit. I kid you not. But I should explain, just so you don't think mass psychosis had taken root, that although nearly everyone pretended to this talk, behind our hand many still groaned. And occasionally did things that didn't turn a profit, but were merely sensible.

Nevertheless, the charade was embarrassing. Official talk in the place was of bottom lines and threats to our existence, if we didn't get sufficiently fiscal to "make money". For all our posturing, we were merely a unit of public administration with a tenured, or as good as tenured, staff, who were on salaries paid by the taxpayers and not at risk of losing our jobs. The worst that could happen would be the shared service agency, and/or its commercialised mode of operation might be judged a mistake, and we would all be reassigned to other parts of the mainstream public service. There would be humiliation at senior levels, where the rhetorical trappings of private enterprise had taken hold, but no one would have to pull their children out of private schools; and there would be relief among lower ranks, who could then unclench that set of facial muscles which defends ideology from unhelpful facts.

I shouldn't have been surprised when the senior people to whom I addressed my concerns over the ethics of participating in the morally corrosive commercial modality resisted the logic of my position as if I was speaking a foreign tongue. But, naively, I was surprised. I watched, fascinated and furious by turns, as the matter of my moral delicacy was escalated like a hot spud to chief executive officer level as a result of the keystone cop flailing of management at each successive hierarchical level between me and him. I think their various ineptitudes owed a lot to the off-handed approach they took to me, an approach resulting as much from their inability to conceive that critique of the ethics of our day-to-day practice was a legitimate activity as from their being unused to observing due process and natural justice in their dealings with subordinate staff. The foot inside the stamping, uniformed boot is not evil, just unthinking.

Thus I was eventually given the opportunity (and the time) to spell out the logic of my conscientious objection for the Chief Executive Officer at his reluctant invitation. So I wrote an opus for his consideration.[44]

At the time I was unaware of another possible reason the advent of my moral outrage might have wrong-footed senior

---

[44] The paper is included in *The Subversive's Toolkit*.

people. Looking back a few years after the event, this suggests itself: Their whole project, i.e., the shared services project, was not going so well. Even then, self-referring and gun-shy as I had become, I had to notice that the disquiet in the agency wasn't localised to my immediate vicinity, and that even there not all the disgrunt emanated from me.

My personal situation was merely emblematic. The commercialised approach was as inapplicable to a host of other like functions to which it was being forcibly applied. The senior people in the shared service agency determined to make it work were living in a fool's paradise, but at some deep place in their psyches were aware of the contradictions their project so precariously held in tension. It was only a matter of time before the crack of this inevitable doom, awareness of which they were managing to *re*press in themselves and trying, unsuccessfully to *sup*press in others. In the end the contradiction undid them, naturally, and their (partial, anyway) demise came about in a way no one expected, a way authored by the very government whose will these senior people thought they were implementing.

The natural history of this process could have been mercifully telescoped had anyone up top listened to lower ranks' corridor talk. It was, however, out of their earshot, especially ideological earshot. Fools' paradise has soundproofing.

So the demise took a good five years, and in the meantime, here's this pest of a counsellor laying bare for them the micro pathologies that were its harbinger and wanting to rub their noses in it. Had they known my history better, they would have formed a support group for themselves and invited Siobhan as guest speaker.

I must acknowledge that my hindsight about the unspoken concerns senior management of the agency harboured, beside which I was a pimple, was largely bestowed upon me by that unexpected action the government itself took (to solve a different political problem), the action which had the welcome but unlooked for side effect. That act was to announce a review of the shared services agency.

To what degree this decision to review was also motivated by awareness at high levels of the tension between the agency and its client departments is unclear. There was enough discontent out there to be audible to government, but it is unlikely they had ears or stomach for it. The Shared Services miracle solution was ultimately, after all, their baby and they had pursued it in the face of warnings from the south. And east and west and north. For public consumption the Premier proffered as a reason, perhaps sincerely, that the review was merely part of the complete overhaul of expenditure across all departments and government agencies to find savings to throw into the hole called the Health Department. Ailing and politically disastrous, the Health Department, whose expensive bungling continued coming to light in the press as sequelae to the inept and deadly surgery at Bundaberg Hospital, had become government's albatross. For all I know, that might have been the Premier's whole motivation. What I ended up being grateful for, however, was that public submissions were called for by the panel undertaking the review of the little bit of the whole public service where I was, the shared service agency. I made a submission.

I titled my submission, *Nobody Here Speaks Elephant*. In it I canvassed many matters illustrating the mismatch between the shared service agency concept and public service, one facet of which was its inevitable elevation of unethical behaviour to standard operating procedure. It was to illustrate this facet that I identified and described the four examples of unethical action I later elaborated in the conscientious objection paper to my CEO. By the time I submitted *Nobody Here Speaks Elephant* I had spent almost a year composing it. It was one of the five private submissions the review panel received and I was eventually sent a bound copy of the findings. That was when I learned that more than twenty departments, along with the major union which had public service coverage, had also made submissions. The review may have been set up to find savings by identifying waste – indeed, *Elephant* was offered as identifying the shared service miracle as squandering the public service's skill capital[45], trashing inter-agency goodwill and integrity – but it moved quickly beyond that, as if it had been in fact set up because the reports of the shared service initiative's failings became so constant it was impossible to ignore them any longer.

I was in a very good place to blow the whistle, having been conscripted to shared services from day one, and thus reporting from the belly of the beast. There was much to tell. With attachments, my submission ran to 23 pages.

---

[45] Skill capital, an analogue conceptually of the notion of social capital, I defined in the submission as that body of expertise and knowledge possessed in the aggregate by public servants and at the disposal of the government. I added that there was capital of that sort laid up aplenty in the Queensland public service, but our continued possession of it was at risk.

## 12
## Finale

THE review took a long time to come to its conclusions, but they were uncompromising when finally published. My own was among those functions it declared were not being suitably managed and ought be immediately repatriated to the Departments which had been forced to surrender them.[46]

When it sank in that I had convinced them, or at least been among those whose evidence convinced them, my delight was considerable. From then it was, I thought, only a matter of time. A fairly long time, of course. The public service churns slowly, and this particular revolve bid fair to yank a few senior noses out of joint, so ways had to be found to save the faces those noses belonged on. One favourite way to do that is by delaying the date with the firing squad. If public service bureaucracies are reliably skilled at anything, it is face-saving; and a way for the Machine to supply salve to these high level egos lay to hand.

The top nose-bearing-face belonged to the naked emperor spirit's physical and organisational embodiment, the same whose arrival on the scene I anticipated early in this tale when I suggested that the shared services initiative, then on the horizon, would produce its mini-empire. This face now required humouring, along with those of its retinue. Those worthies were, of course, loath to see their empire crumble, and produced the inevitable counter-offensive debunking the Commission's findings. That counter-offensive had to be accorded a level of apparently serious consideration suitable to the altitude of the eminence who signed it. It took the form of a counter submission, a doomed enterprise, given the length and complexity of the examination the Commission had undertaken and the care it took constructing its own proposals of remedy. That everyone knew the emperor's counter proposal was thus foredoomed was not a problem. If fact, it simplified matters, removing risk from appearing to pay grave

---

[46] The Review's report used to be on a state government website, but had been removed by 2012.

attention to his last ditch stand, and stretching out pre-execution time nicely. And so it was done. This was right and proper and in accord with the actual values obtaining, as I set them out earlier. You may not remember them word perfect, but the foundational belief – remember this for the test – is: Since the superior pulchritude attributed to senior face is never to be gainsaid, at least not in public, none will object to its high heritage listing. If there is face to be saved, this is the face.

But at last the senior rank of the shared services agency had to accept that twenty-five per cent of their underlings were to be returned to their Departments, me among them. I was all but home. Not a little of the satisfaction I felt could have been labelled vindication, of a sort. Having survived the exile arranged by the triumvirate, I would now, to their great chagrin, return.

Alas, it was not to be.

I had been originally engineered out of my Department, spent just over five years in public service Siberia, been delivered from evil at last by the review and was waiting with packed bag for the train home. I was in turn engineered out of that homecoming as well. For by then the number of senior people back in the Department whom I had discountenanced had hit critical mass. The Department's response to the review findings, which had the government's endorsement, was one that up to then I had thought unthinkable. It refused the government's instruction to take me back. Huhh? Departments don't say no. To the Parliament. Do they? The situation became a stand-off.

And then, suddenly, old *deus ex machina* descended.

The *deus*, appropriately, ominously, was an engineer who had gained the Premier's favour and was out of the blue appointed new boss of the Department, its erstwhile boss having been advised he would be sent off to boss elsewhere. I went to see this boss-elect. I told him the Department was refusing to take me back. He was outraged. He wanted us to stay in touch. He gave me his phone number. He told his secretary. I went back to my cell chuffed. Justice loomed. Three days later he assumed office. Suddenly he needed the high level people there, my offendees, more than he needed me, which they made clear to him was like a hole in the head. From that moment he was so busy his secretary couldn't find a space in his diary for me "until at least October". That is not an actual October.

Now I had been – the word is advised – engineered out of the public service altogether. My new home (the one I had been exiled to) was sold out from under me and my old home, the Department, was closed for the holidays. I fought it, of course, for almost a year, but eventually grew weary. I belonged nowhere. Bowed, I accepted the exit note. And on my second last day wrote the diary note.

And so there had crested and broken over me the second wave of defeat. The first, ironically, had been my banishment to the shared services agency, a long delayed *dénouement* of the Friday afternoon email affair; the second was my banishment from that place of exile to nowhere.

Once I sagely declared to a younger friend that a man should study poetry in his youth, for the day will come when he holds in his arms his firstborn and how else will he release the glory inside him. Well, as well might he study the buried lineaments of life made so luminescent in the drama of the ancient Greeks, for a day will also come when he holds in his arms less pleasant ballast.

It began to build outside my line of sight, that second wave of defeat, and just as I tasted the sweetness of influencing the review's findings, it crashed on the sand around me like checkmate. I had in spite of myself to admire its classic lines. One is rarely so personally and consciously present at such a clear outworking of *ŭbris,* or sees it writ upon one's own body so plain. It appealed to the philosopher in me that victory could so seamlessly produce defeat.

# BOOK TWO

# A Subversive's Toolkit

*A collection of dissident texts useful for derailing organisational bullies*

# Introduction

IT was years after the event that I began trying, via the keyboard, to make sense of the whole experience of the Friday Afternoon Email. However, responses to less emotionally paralysing depredations by the organisation, including some that occurred outside of the Email adventure, were easier to make. Things, more or less awful, would happen and I would think about them. Whether these injustices or acts of bureaucratic uncaring were visited upon me or fell upon my clients, they triggered a reflexive anger which I eventually learned to turn to account.

Remember the once eminent Dr Scott, the ex-Deputy Director-General of Health whom we met undergoing interrogation at the Bundaberg Hospital malpractice inquiry? He admitted there he could recall issues that needed addressing, but weren't addressed because they were not attractive politically. With me it was the opposite. I had the advantage, of course. I was not a rung or two down from that ceiling which is also the floor of the capital P political sauna. So, let me misquote Dr Scott: "I was probably more of an activist for the *common public servant* than perhaps I should have been."

Organisations generally like to keep their oppression of staff from the public eye because that enables them to use weaponry better confined to the backroom, where it is easier to ignore the values enshrined in wall mottoes. Staff would come often to my office because what happened in that backroom was upsetting. They talked to me about the issues underlying their struggles. Unlike Dr Scott's issues, these I found politically quite attractive. They frequently lay among those at the heart of the organisation's dysfunction. I could rarely let them go, and routinely worried them into the shape of a piece of writing of one kind or another. As a result I have accumulated a cardboard box full of incendiary devices designed to blow struggles between the organisation and its victims into a larger, more public arena.

I have raided the cardboard box for what follows.

# TOOLKIT ITEM 1
## Hiring out bits of yourself for nothing

THERE are skills and abilities, parts of yourself, which you can put at the disposal of a client. Your mental acuity, another word for rat cunning, is one. Any skill you have that your client doesn't, for that matter. I think of it as evening the match between your client and the Machine.

I should acknowledge now that some, perhaps even you, Reader, find this improper and have an objection similar to Shipwoman's in *Cloud Atlas* when Zachary's dying sister needed her intervention. One must help people, certainly, but not *do* for them. They must self-determine. Watching relentless management mistreatment of workers wore out my devotion to that rubric. So did time's winged chariot bring me ever nearer to this realisation. St Peter is not going to wave me in because I abstained scrupulously and watched clients swirl down the drain for lack of, say, the literary skill, to set down in writing my suggested approach to redress of their industrial oppression and place it before Power's baleful eye. St Peter and his Principal probably don't care about scruples like that, nor do they disdain such acts as spoon-feeding that thwarts clients' developing self-efficacy. Like Shipwoman, I got over it. (Of course, it's possible I never grasped guru Biestek properly, in the first place.)

At any event, here is an example – which you are free to plagiarize – of a ghost-written plea. I will give you the context.

Government sometimes looks in the till and finds no money. One way to fix this is to cut resources to those agencies which provide services. If someone other than the staff providing the service notices, it says with evident regret that cuts have to be made everywhere due to budget restrictions. Since the economy is god, people wear it. If an agency is providing an essential service, like licensing drivers or maintaining ambulances, it must continue to do so whether resourced fully or not. The innocent phrase "resourced fully" translates to chronically over-worked staff. Over-work plays havoc with many things, including the immune system. Workers succumb, some sooner, some later. A customer service centre learns to adapt to chronic absences and disappearing staff. Even workers with strong commitment to service finally succumb. Garrison camaraderie grows in the agency and may include the manager in its embrace, especially a manager who empathises with the staff and attempts, unsuccessfully, to secure more money to relieve the situation. This atmosphere can be seductive to staff and heighten the determination to carry on at any cost. That cost, sooner or later, is the collapse of someone's health, mental, emotional or physical, or all three. That someone will not be the last.

Now reason tells us that the resultant unfitness for work, certified by a sick staff member's doctor, is an injury suffered in the course of his or her employment. History, on the other hand, tells us that the (equally over-worked) decision-makers in the workers compensation agencies, routinely reject a claim for compensation based upon such circumstances. We learn to accept this as inevitable and cease to base compo claims upon that logic.

One day I had in my office in tears a woman I will call Elizabeth Windsor. Elizabeth was not the first of her line to visit me, merely the latest inheritor of the thorny crown of over-work. Elizabeth was a product of one of the scenarios above. In this scenario the bad black hat guy is the Crown, a fond name we ex-British colonies continue to use as shorthand for government. Elizabeth's case was so clearly a manifestation of the trickle down from government miserliness to a worker's illness, that the prospect of her time off being debited to her sick leave allowance of ten days per year and after that called sick leave without pay was insupportable.

On her good days Elizabeth might have the ability to put all this on paper, but it was clear she didn't have that ability at the time we met. I drafted the claim. She signed it. Some claims for compo fail at first, but then are won on appeal. Elizabeth's claim was accepted[47] without going through the second hoop.

### WorkCover Statement
By Elizabeth Windsor, Customer Services Officer,
Mt Pleasant Customer Service Centre
[...Date...]

Events leading up to my becoming unfit for work

I arrived at work in Mt Pleasant on [a specified date] at 8:15am. I noticed there was only one other CSO present, being Julianna Frobisher. Mary-Louise de Witt (Sen. CSO) approached me, put her arm around my waist and led me to Counter B. She told me we were two short already and that I would not be working on Switch. Instead I would be serving on Counter.

I suggested that I do Counter H as it is both an early shift and a special services counter which we otherwise wouldn't have covered until a new Casual arrived at 9:00am. I was on automatic pilot going to the safe collecting my cash tin, setting up on counter; I felt totally overwhelmed and burst into tears. I knew I could not "step it up" any more than I had already been doing.

The telephone rang again and we were now three staff short. The missing staff are very experienced and timely workers. The workers who were present consisted of (a) three new Casuals who started seven weeks prior, had three weeks training and four weeks experience, (b) one of whom was a Casual with approximately 12 months experience, and (c) one of whom was a staff member on a temporary agreement, and (d) one long term staff member working from 10:00 am until 3:00 pm.

---

[47] The gods have my own mental health close to their hearts, and they are particularly attentive to hubris. I presented this story to my colleagues in the HR unit of the Shared Service Provider I worked in as a strategic victory for common sense, a template for future use. It went down like a lead balloon.

I could not stop crying but started serving customers and continued to do so until I was removed from counter at approximately 9:45 am.

The previous day at customer free time we were told that the next four weeks were going to be just as tough as what we had been doing it, as Mt Pleasant needed 22 shifts to cover holidays and flextime days. This was only allowing 2 people to be on holidays at one time over the school holidays. One permanent staff member would be returning to work, after being on sick leave, for three hours per day for two days per week to see how she goes. We were told other centres were doing it tougher than us and we just had to step it up and work harder.

The Circumstances of working in this Customer Service Centre

The extra workload has been increasing over the last few months with staff going on sick leave (obviously at short notice) and there being no casual staff available to cover these shifts. All long term Casuals are currently in temporary agreements which reduce the amount of available Casuals to backfill positions. This also puts a lot more pressure on the experienced staff and employees who can do transactions such as special services and certifications.

Two new Casuals were trained by Mt Pleasant staff over the last seven weeks. They had three weeks training which was conducted at Mingoolba. Mt Pleasant lost a very experienced operator to conduct the training. Once again we were being stretched. Our office has been so short-staffed the new casuals have been required to do the counter alone from very early in their training. Even though this puts a body in the chair they obviously have lots of questions and need a lot of assistance.

The staff have been asked to surrender planned flextime days due to the shortage of staff and then on the other hand been told that they are not allowed to accrue more than two days.

Staff are put under a lot of pressure in their daily work by having to not only serve the customer they have called but to also assist new staff, keep an eye on the queue for both certifications and special. We have two staff on specials and they are assisted by the other counter staff if their waiting time is unacceptable. The reason we have been given to give them priority is that people coming to do their specials have only allocated a small amount of time, for example their lunch hour, whereas the person coming to do certifications should have expected to wait. Specials also takes priority as Mt Pleasant office only has a small car park and by turning these customers over quickly we are able to provide more car parking and in that way prevent complaints about the inadequate car parking. So you can't just settle down and concentrate on serving the line of customers in front of you. You have to keep an eye on the specials line and take someone from there if it is blowing out. The customers who are not in the specials line notice that people are being served out of turn and get annoyed. When you eventually serve them they take that out on you. Asking me to participate in this practice is, I believe, an improper use to put me to. It is a politically motivated and/or public relations-oriented practice designed to disguise an inadequacy in the infrastructure of Mt Pleasant's service delivery system (i.e., inadequate parking) and places an improper pressure on me. It is an unreasonable management action, in my view. It also asks for my cooperation while at the same time my need for a reasonably arranged workplace is ignored. The sense of injustice this creates is quite strong.

Performance and Practice Reviews (PPRs) are conducted as per policy and staff are asked to give feedback on fellow staff members. Over the last couple of weeks extra pressure has been applied to complete this feedback. It is very difficult to write feedback at the counter when you have customers lined up out the door, so I have had to complete the feedback at home. Other staff choose not to take their work home, but once again the team member undergoing PPR is disadvantaged as they don't get the opportunity to receive the positive and constructive feedback from their team mates.

I recognize PPRs are important and policy needs to be adhered to, but under our conditions of understaffing, having them done means more pressure is put on the remaining counter staff to cover for the staff member having their PPR and the Sen. CSOs attending the session.

Properly attending to a customer's situation means staying up to date on the latest regulations. It may not be ignored. A policy may change at any time. Being thorough with each customer is therefore necessary. However, it is time-consuming, so doing the job properly takes time and, in turn, creates longer waiting times for the customers waiting in line, and that eventually increases the level of frustration which they and we have to deal with when they get to the head of the queue.

Important information to consider:

The reader/investigator might say of this statement that it is just a tale of understaffing and inadequate resources, and then sadly but resignedly pass over it as just the way things are, reluctantly admitting that nothing can be done about it and concluding that no unreasonable management action has contributed to my illness. But that would be wrong. Understaffing and inadequately resourcing a workplace is a political choice by management (i.e., by the employer).

"Management" in the context of this application refers not only to local Mt Pleasant Customer Service Centre management and/or State East Area management. It is not their inability or refusal to command or assign the resources needed to stop the understaffing which caused my illness.

Management here means the whole tiered structure all the way up to the state government, my actual employer. It is my employer whose actions have to be shown, under the terms of the workers compensation legislation to constitute unreasonable management action to establish my claim to compensation and it is therefore proper to show that my employer chooses to allow this situation in Mt Pleasant to persist. Whether that is achieved by senior management reading what is implicit in the Government's attitude to the Department when it seeks more resources and therefore not asking, or by the Government clearly saying no to the Department when it presents its requirements, is beside the point. The end result is Mt Pleasant CSC is understaffed, everyone working there comes under pressure and the situation made me sick.

Resources can be assigned to meet the public's demand for our Department's services <u>prior</u> to staff collapsing under pressure (i.e., in the form of adequate staffing levels) or <u>after</u> they collapse, in the form of costs of sick leave, Casuals recruited at the last minute and thrust into the gaps, workers compensation costs, damaged staff morale and staff disaffection – all less visible and less politically damaging than a hefty, sufficient increase upfront in base staffing level. (While it is uncertain which of the two approaches ends up costing more, I, as a person made ill under the second approach, would prefer the first.) However, that my employer chooses to stick to staffing and resourcing policies that allow staff to collapse, whatever its motivation, is not an action for which it can disclaim responsibility simply because it fails to recognise the connection.

The fact that local Mt Pleasant CSC management acts with patience, sympathy and understanding (e.g., the Sen. CSO "approached me, put her arm around my waist and led me to Counter B", and "I was removed from the counter at approximately 9:45am") is admirable and I appreciate it immensely, but it does not alter what they are doing, reluctant as they might be to do so. Unable to get from the upper levels of management the resources necessary to meet the public demand for our Department's services, local managers resort to urging us to "step it up" more and more and to showing sympathy for our plight. (It is their plight, too, of course.)

There is obviously a limit to a staff member's capacity to increase output without a proper pattern of recuperation (for example, flextime days secure from last minute cancellation, reasonable and fair access to recreation leave) built into his/her working arrangements and it is clearly dangerous to push a person beyond that limit, no matter how nicely. It just means the inevitable rest comes about not in a planned way but haphazardly via sick leave or even resignation.

### RESPONSIBILITY AND BLAME

I do not identify anyone as being to blame. But, in my view, the responsibility for my becoming sick lies with those at high levels who made choices to use public resources in the ways that resulted in understaffing of Mt Pleasant CSC. That such choices at those levels are made, motivated in the way I suggest, is borne out by the evidence presented at the Inquiry held under Commissioner Geoff Davies, QC, into practices at the Bundaberg Hospital and in the Queensland Health Department.

Dr John Scott, who was until very recently the Deputy Director-General of that Department testified on September 13 2005, "I was probably more of an activist for the Government and the minister than perhaps I should have been." He spoke of issues that needed addressing, but were "not attractive politically". Dr Scott said, "It was and is the case that more money is required to produce an optimal service." He was talking about the Health Department. In my view, his comment applies equally to my Department.

# TOOLKIT ITEM 2
## Conscience, its uses and its discontents

THE agency I was working in when the axe finally fell was the Shared Service Agency. It had been set up to act like a commercial entity. It took as its model the commercial entities that surround us. Many staff dragooned to this Agency, as you will have gathered, had little more philosophical rapport with it's *raison d'etre* than I. I had none. My discontent was visceral and automatic, and at last I found the opportunity to transform it into something I could nail to the Cathedral door.

In *Michael, we really have to talk...*, I gave a brief account of the genesis of that something nailed and said my employer had given me a generous amount of time to compose it, a formally stated objection to participating in TimeCapture. TimeCapture supplied the data upon which was calculated the dollar amount a client Department "owed" the Shared Service Agency for my counselling services. When I look back I see that I was lucky. Claude was the high-ranking executive who proposed this indulgence of paid time in which to write, and my luck consisted in his desire to act or appear statesman-like in dealing with this oddly venerable-looking old pain in the arse with the slightly unsettling superior demeanour and intimidating, over educated manner of speech. He put a magnanimous face on SSA's reluctant recognition of its statutory obligation to accommodate my delicate conscience. This posture meshed with my own unconscious, but deliberate, strategy. (Claude's act of grace in the crucial meeting may also have been influenced by the articulate and unafraid union official who accompanied me.)

The formal conscientious objection stand I took here came some years after the matter that is the subject of TOOLKIT ITEM 5. In that matter I had manoeuvred myself into the position of being under threat of formal discipline for non-cooperation with the demands of the legal section of the Department. At that time I had a strategic reason for such an ostensibly self-destructive move of which I was fully conscious. Here, in the conscientious objection situation, I was following a similar strategy, purposely making myself a target for discipline, without being conscious of the reprise. The ultimate similarity of the two strategies lay in my expectation of making strategic use of my employer's response to my obstinacy; back then, after a seemingly inevitable arraignment for my non-compliance, here and now, after an equally inevitable failure of my employer to comply with common sense. The way I expected the strategy to pay off in the TOOLKIT ITEM 5 story, I will leave until then. The way I expected it to pay off in the conscientious objection matter was to provide me a pulpit from which to articulate and publicise the morally deleterious trading methods being implemented by the Agency, which I would do by spelling them out in the conscientious objection document itself and then reiterating in the Public Service Board tribunal which would hear my appeal against the inevitable failure of the CEO to decide in my favour. I had no doubt that, failing divine intervention, the CEO would decide against my objection. I might have been Martin Luther himself and been equally assured of rejection. My antagonists were not seeking truth, but glory and triumph.

Thus, the better the statement of objection was, the more glaringly unreasonable would be its failure.

To get the play as high as Claude had required that I repeatedly refuse, placidly and politely, to join in the Agency's commercialised practices as each successively higher-ranked officer carpeted me and insisted I comply. Eventually Claude, the CEO's Dick Cheney, sat across the table from me. When he decreed I was to put my objections in writing, a briar patch of some magnetism for me, I mentally prepared to devote my nights and the coming weekend to that task. When he went on to say I may have one week only of work time free of other duties in which to do it, I nodded and gravely accepted his ruling. So, ahead of you now is the quotient of that week's work. You, Citizen, paid for it. Please read it.

I cannot tell a lie. I enjoyed writing it immensely. It was the perfect opportunity to think through and set down everything that had bugged me for years about the decayed public service culture

I lived in, and to take moral inventory of myself and the beliefs and ethics that sustained me.

My writings were addressed to the CEO, who told me when we met to exchange compliments and my 95 theses that my statement would be examined by a retired public servant with credentials for the task. Before that examiner made his recommendations to the CEO, he asked for a meeting with me. We talked a long time. He thought my case successfully made. This was welcome news, but something recalcitrant in me stayed celebration. Case made or no, the CEO faced an impossible choice. If he didn't uphold my conscientious objection, he would go against his own expert. If he upheld my objection, no one in the Agency who disliked behaving like a huckster would continue to do so. Worse, the entire edifice would begin to look like what it was: a house of cards. The CEO knew that I knew what his expert thought. This, I thought, is truly a rock and a hard place. He also knew that, if he didn't decide in my favour, I would appeal his decision to a tribunal at the Public Service Board. He didn't, and I did.

CORPORATELINK
6 DECEMBER 2006

Mr Barry Martin
Managing Director
Shared Service Agency
Level 9, Capital Hill
85 George Street
Brisbane

**CONSCIENTIOUS OBJECTION TO A LAWFUL DIRECTION**

Dear Barry

Following an invitation from Claude Conte, Executive Director, CorporateLink, on November 28 to submit to you in relation to a direction issued me on August 30 by Lola Sandford and a follow-up direction issued to me on November 14 by Claude, I respectfully present the following submission for your consideration. The submission is divided into two parts. The first outlines the basis of my objection and the second presents supporting argument, evidence, comment and relevant documents.

I would be grateful if you would note that I first suggested to my manager, Ms Sandford, in a memo of August 31, that the issue of my conscientious objection be raised at a higher level in the organisation in compliance with the obligation laid upon us, as I saw it, by Section 3 Principle 1 of the Code of Conduct of Queensland Treasury. I indicated my willingness to elaborate my objection several times, but did not receive the invitation to submit for nearly three months, a trying wait. I would, nevertheless, like to put it on the record that I am grateful to Claude for granting me the time to compose my thoughts free of other obligations.

The Direction

Lola Sandford wrote to me as follows:

> You are hereby directed to fill out your time capture, consistent with Agency requirements for both the months of July and August 2006. You are directed to have completed your time capture for the months of July and August 2006 by midday 1 September 2006.

Claude Conte wrote a follow-up direction as follows:

> You are ... directed to complete all entries from 1 July 2006 to the present and to continue to enter those records in the future in accordance with required timelines. You are directed to have the outstanding entries since 1 July 2006 to the present time completed by close of business on Tuesday 21 November 2006.

As well as reiterating the direction, Claude, in his 14 November letter, presents some argument about what he perceived to be my conscientious objection, some implications regarding its quality, etc. Although his determination was premature, in that I had not at that stage been given the opportunity to present my conscientious objection, his letter nevertheless represents official response to my position.

Whilst this is the first formal opportunity I have been afforded to elaborate on my conscientious objection, I have previously indicated my position to my supervisors on a number of occasions. Indeed on two occasions I have indicated that position in writing. (Attachments 2 & 3)

### What I Object To

I object to the direction to fill out TimeCapture for two reasons:

> 1. TimeCapture connects my work directly to a commercial model of operation, rendering me a participant in a mode of operation which I believe undermines and interferes with the HR work we are charged with; further, it erodes the integrity of otherwise ethical public servants because they are forced to behave unethically to sustain this mode of operation.
> 2. The commercialised fee-for-service mode of operation runs counter to my conscience and I have deliberately chosen to work in environments not based on commercial values.

It is not, of course, the physical action of keying time periods into the pro-forma on the screen, but the purpose for which one is asked to enter those time periods, i.e., it is the meaning of the act, over which my conscience misgives.

The adoption of commercialised practice is sometimes defended as achieving greater efficiency and accountability. If I thought this model was actually serving this purpose, and not at the same time causing detriment, I would be more inclined to try to accept its validity.

While I endorse efforts to find ways the agency can improve efficiency and accountability, I believe adopting the fee-for-service model actually runs counter to those aims. Indeed, in my experience it not only reduces service efficiency and effectiveness, but also displays the hallmarks of being ultimately more expensive. And whilst I recognise that this model has enjoyed widespread recognition as a way of reaping efficiencies in the public sector, it is clear that in relation to higher level HR services delivery it just doesn't work.

### Explanation of Reason 1:

TimeCapture connects my work directly to a commercial model of operation, rendering me a participant in a mode of operation which I believe undermines and interferes with the HR work we are charged with; further, it erodes the integrity of otherwise ethical public servants because they are forced to behave unethically to sustain this mode of operation.

The fee-for-service model in our case endeavours to fit the day-to-day activities of delivering higher level human resources services to our client agencies into a model they do not suit. Because the model is not a good fit it causes otherwise ethical public servants to behave without due regard for public service ethics, that is, it causes good people to act badly.

Below I present four examples of this damaging effect upon our ethical behaviour, and then five items to illustrate the inappropriateness of the model to the work:

### Example 1

The Branch had been approached by a client agency about the possibility of its providing the Harassment Referral Officer Network for that unit of public administration. This fact was reported at a meeting of Senior Staff within the Branch and was greeted with enthusiasm on the basis of the revenue it promised. There was no consideration given to whether or not it was appropriate for this service to be provided by the branch. Given that the whole reason for having a Harassment Referral Officer Network is to minimize the occurrence of workplace harassment and in so doing fulfill the employer's legislative and other obligations to protect their employees, the primary interest of our client agency was to gain protection from this risk/exposure. It was therefore, in my view, incumbent upon us to consider whether the outsourcing of this traditionally internally provided Harassment Referral Officer Network would still afford the agency that protection. It was incumbent upon us to protect our client agency first and foremost. At the least a check with the appropriate oversight agencies such as the Anti-Discrimination Commission, Human Rights and Equal Opportunity Commission, OPSC, Industrial Relations Commission and even CMC to gauge their view about the validity of an externally provided Harassment Referral Officer Network was required. However this did not happen. I contend that it did not happen because our enthusiasm for the revenue the job would attract (our own interests) clouded our ability to focus on the interests of our client.

Alarmingly to me, our knowledge of and expertise in these more sophisticated HR areas was not sufficient to counter the influence of the promise of generous revenue for undertaking the task. Any HR expert who considered this proposition rationally, without the overlay of the need for business and revenue, would have considered whether it would be proper to outsource such a service.

I queried the propriety of the Branch's taking on this job but the query was unpopular, acting as it did as a drag on the consensus satisfaction. The reaction to my expression of doubt about this new commission was one of blank incomprehension and genuine puzzlement. I have found that a common reaction from fellow workers to my reminders of what I suspect we all regard as fundamental good HR principles in the face of these pressures is discomfort with facing up to the contradictions.

Not only was there a reluctance by the majority of fellow workers to contemplate the loss of the lucrative commission, but any reference to my query about the possible impropriety of our accepting the job was absent in the Minutes of the meeting that were subsequently circulated. I drew this absence to the attention of the group at the following meeting and requested that the minutes be amended to more accurately reflect the actual conversation that occurred. This again caused anguish and

Michael O'Neill

although after some discussion it was agreed that the Minutes would be amended to reflect the actual discussion, the amended minutes were never presented. In addition the Director announced that minutes would no longer be kept of the meetings. In fact one meeting later a decision was taken to stop having the meetings altogether. These meetings had been standard operating procedure since the SSP began.

I suspect that my request for the amending of the minutes created discomfort as a consequence of my colleagues' perception of themselves as doing nothing wrong. Unfortunately for me and people such as me who persist in questioning in the face of resistance, this discomfort with questioning of the issues can often manifest as discomfort with the questioner.

All teams tend to develop unexamined, and usually unexaminable, shared ideological assumptions of which they are mostly unaware and which collectivise and compel their assent to things they might, as separate individuals, repudiate. The problem is not that our groupthink is more intense than most, but that it tends to elevate a consensus intrinsically pernicious, as well as being unsuited to proper public service. The motto that any income is good income (or, the customer is always right) has been contradicted only once in my experience of the Branch's meetings, by an officer who announced he had rejected a commission because it was not right to accept it.

### Example 2

At the same meeting of the Group on 28th August discussion also occurred about the fact that a non-CorporateLink person was responsible for undertaking some work that CorporateLink would charge for as if one of our own staff had undertaken the work. Significantly however, a decision was taken that this fact would not be disclosed to the client agency. Indeed the decision was that this fact would be concealed from the client agency.

This discussion was fixed in my mind for a couple of reasons. Firstly because of my sense of its importance and secondly by the brief conversation I had immediately following the meeting with

170

another attendee at the hand basins in the toilet. In that conversation he asked how I was. I indicated, involuntarily, that I felt sick at heart. I said I had just witnessed an agreement to engage in what amounted to deception for which the motivation had been commercial and that we had all been implicitly invited to collude added to the distress. We mused on this for some time. The corrupting influence of the tendency to disguise the truth in the merchant purchaser relationship has long troubled ethicists.

Thomas Aquinas the 13th Century Philosopher "devotes an entire article to condemn cheating and using deceit to sell things for more than they are worth. (ST 2-2 77). For justice to prevail in commercial transactions, one must maintain an equality and balance between what a commodity or service is worth and the price paid (ST 2-2, 77, 1) Contrary to what many believe today, Aquinas believes that the seller has to state known defects in items offered for sale (ST 2-2, 77, 3)." *Dwyer 943b]*

In my request to amend the draft minutes of this meeting to more accurately record the discussion, I also drew attention to the fact that this concealment was not mentioned in the minutes. In my view, the decision to conceal and the subsequent decisions about the minutes of meetings and meetings altogether were motivated by the commercial imperative in the following way. Staying afloat in the marketplace depended upon maintaining a reputation for fair dealing. A decision to deceive the "customer" was clearly not in the best interests of the customer and obviously not something one would like the customer to know about. Keeping this knowledge from the customer requires smudging of the truth, selective accountability and covering of one's tracks.

These sets of practices, both the fundamental adoption of untruthfulness and the thwarting of exposure, are indicative of eroded integrity, but are not perpetrated in the full knowledge that they are wrong. They are able to be justified by the belief that they are the right thing to do. My point is precisely this. Otherwise decent public servants are suborned by the instinctive demands of the commercialised system. Acts committed seem necessary to preserve the consultancy's marketability. The deeper implications of such actions are not understood. A government in the western democratic tradition is supposed to be accountable. Transparency in decision-making is required for accountability. That presupposes honest records. For a public service which implements the decisions of, and shares the values of, a western democratic government, honest records are accurate minutes of meetings. This truth cannot be allowed to become opaque to people operating in an environment that also requires upholding of the public interest.

Example 3

A further example of concealment was provided at the eventful meeting of the 28th August. At that meeting an announcement was made that Consultancy Services Branch's TimeCapture (record of person/hours we can charge other agencies for) for July was 150, 000 dollars in the red. (This covered a period for which my involvement in TimeCapture was not in dispute, by the way.) The reporting of this fact was not recorded in the draft minutes of the meeting nor the redrafted minutes, even though I had requested that it be included.

Initially this may not appear to be surprising. Obviously, a business would try to hide from outsiders that its revenue was not amounting to a figure equal to its costs. And in the hothouse atmosphere generated by the pretence of living in the business world it actually requires an effort of will to remind oneself that Consultancy Services Branch is a unit of public administration. Many of the parties from whom we are keeping information are also units of public administration. Real, do-or-die businesses, the ones whose owners' children, if the business fails, will have to be pulled out of private schools, may be entitled to that instinctive obfuscation and forgiven for exiling Cassandras like me; but, aside from a brief and ill-starred masquerade by the Bundaberg Hospital, units of public administration are not businesses and therefore have higher order obligations in relation to ethical behaviour, accountability and transparency in decision making. In addition we are also all owned by the same shareholder so our deceit ultimately injures our own shareholder rather than protecting it.

Example *4*

At a meeting in early August of the senior members (AO6, PO4, AO8) of Consultancy Services Branch's HRM team there was discussion of the imminent departure of three AO6-level staff from the team. These were merely the latest in a long line of staff losses which have continued since as well. The inevitable effect of our increasingly denuded state upon our capacity to meet our obligations to our clients was discussed. One of the AO6s proposed that the only sensible course was to admit the truth to our client departments: we did not have enough staff to meet their needs at the moment. The manager clearly rejected this proposal and articulated a different form of response to the clients, one which made no such admissions. This response can only have been motivated, in my view, by the commercial imperative. That is, because admission of incapacity would lead to loss of face and shrivelling of the incoming work, both death to the consultancy's hopes, it was to be abstained from.

Back in the 13th Century Saint Thomas Aquinas had pondered the nature of ethical practice in the exchange between merchant and purchaser.

Judgment cannot be pronounced save on what is manifest: for "a man judges of what he knows." Hence if the defects of the goods offered for sale be hidden, judgment of them is not sufficiently left with the buyer unless such defects be made known to him. The case would be different if the defects were manifest. (Summa Theologica, 2-2, 77, 3.)

The sensible course proposed by the AO6 at the meeting would have made the defect manifest.

These four examples illustrate, in my view, the way the imposition of a structure or mode of operation can, as Marx believed, induce altered behaviour in those subject to it. In his biography of Abraham Lincoln, Carl Sandburg relates Lincoln's belief along the same lines: It doesn't matter what sort of man the winner of the election is when he assumes the Presidency, it is The

White House that shapes him. It is likewise, in my view, for ethical public servants who have a commercialised model imposed upon them.

There is, I believe, something of great significance in this to be legitimately concerned about. The public service has special expertise and the peculiar capacity to defend the public interest. It is ultimately the task of the public service in one or other of its manifestations to regulate the behaviour, especially when that behaviour is deficient in integrity, of the commercial world.

However, the more we (the public service) are indifferent to ethical standards, the more we engage in commercial behaviour and thus, as Marx and Lincoln would predict, take on its coloration, the more the line is blurred.

Why bring this style into play, with Departments charging Departments for services like the ones we perform in Consultancy Services Branch? Why the rush to use a fee-for-service model? For we *will* succumb – I believe we already have to an alarming degree – since we are not intrinsically better people than those who succumb in the commercial world, whose sad tales assail us any day we care to open a newspaper. We are made of the same stuff.

In fact, the more likely scenario, I believe, is that we will survive the danger even less well than people do in the genuine commercial world. Public servants precipitated into a commercial milieu, with their corporate armamentarium devoid of the learnings of real apprenticeship in that world, with no gradual acclimatisation process behind them, with no built-up immunity to the temptations to take moral shortcuts like deception to get to business goals; such naifs will have a *harder* time with ethical challenges, not an easier. The problem with this sink or swim approach is that the public sector, indeed government, cannot afford the risk, cannot afford the gamble.

The process of bringing that end to fruition and conducting our affairs to sustain it on a continuous basis has, I believe, a deleterious effect upon the ethical radar of the public servants who engage in it. Knowingly to participate in that process is, to my conscience, wrong. I object to it.

The following points illustrate five ways in which the model can be seen to be inappropriate for our purposes:

1. Because we have, as it were, thrown our lot in with fee-for-service, there is a significant amount of resources devoted to supporting that mode of operation and much profitless busywork. Extensive resources have been devoted to "branding" activities and all the resultant expenses, including expenses on such things as stationery, logos and IT systems.

One of the areas of endeavour is the seemingly endless pursuit of a perfect system of measuring our consultants' "earnings". An unconscionable proportion of our human resources, i.e., of our work time and energy, periodically goes into meetings, planning, discussion, training and experimentation concerning such arcana as hurdle rates, revenue streams, billing styles, accounting systems and charging protocols; and getting right the important ratio of billable hours to non-billable hours, or, in other words, getting the balance perfect between time allocated to administration and supervisory duty and other "down" time and time that can bought by our clients and thus turned into "money" for the improvement of our "bottom line". Furthermore, this is a ratio that must be perfected differentially, i.e., for each level in the hierarchy. Such complex calibration, though diverting, is not easy. The ratio has to be determined, then revisited regularly and determined all over again. One of the reasons it takes so long is that the model doesn't fit the actuality of the work day to day. So systems are trialled, adapted, abandoned and retried.

If we were not obliged to pretend we need "revenue" to keep our jobs (in other words, if we were allowed to simply admit we are on the government payroll), that energy could be diverted to actual service of our client departments. Maintaining a façade few genuinely believe in saps morale and requires the living of a lie.

2. An intellectual technology spawned by the commercialisation ideology is the (now in widespread use) tag "commercial-in-confidence", a device enthusiastically adopted in Consultancy Services discussions. Interactions among commercialised entities default to concealment, as anti-collusion

legislation attests. Concealment is, by definition, antithetical to the public service values of transparency and openness. But commercial-in-confidence is nevertheless a first resort and one unashamedly adopted among us now without any thought given to the way it detours around our ethical obligation to transparency. Commercial-in-confidence is equal to saying, yes we are required to be transparent, but in this case (or that case, or whichever case we choose) we will not be transparent because it may damage our commercial chances.

Self-promotion (Points 3 and 4)

(i) A consequence of Consultancy Services' adoption of the commercialised modality is a requirement and a readiness to engage in self-promotion. This is a practice utterly endemic to the commercial world and, since the commercial world systematically influences, via a pervasive media, the cultural atmosphere that contains us all the way the sea contains fish, we are all always at risk of being contaminated by that practice. This means, I believe, that when the officers of Consultancy Services pick up the implicit instruction to adopt the practice of self-promotion officially the predisposition already present meshes easily with it. As a consequence, engaging in frank self-promotion does not even appear to embarrass us now. (Once boasters were reviled by conventional morality. No more.)

(ii) A difficulty arises also with the people in the client agencies who form the audience for our self-promotion. While we are proof against it, it does embarrass them. If those embarrassed persons are among those whose actual experience as clients of ours has soured their view of our skills and capability (and these are legion), it embarrasses severely. And irritates. We put ourselves intentionally in the same category as toothpaste hucksters who ambush them on their lounge chairs every night with slick, 30-second TV ads. We invite our target punters to revile us for presuming to treat them like fools.

Even if it weren't true that many of our targets are aware of how far short of our claimed expertise we fall, our self-promotion would still be counter-productive. Our targets expect to be bombarded day in day out by self-congratulatory, over-hyped and deceitful messages from promoters trying to sell them soap, sausage and ski trips, but they resent it when it comes from public service units whose claims, which they know to be exaggerated, are presented with a straight face and the expectation of being taken at face value. The parties on both sides of these promotional transactions know that demur (or laughing out loud), though demanded by rationality, is prohibited in such situations because no one could bear the loss of face. But whatever face might be saved by the dependable devotion to decorum which we can count on in all parties, what is not saved is social capital, or the goodwill that exists between departments and lubricates much of the productive interaction between them. This represents a tension in the way units of public administration regard each other, where soon a layered state obtains in which formal relations belie what lies below. That state is the direct result of adopting practices which take as their model behaviours *de rigueur* in the commercial world, such as self-promotion and image-management.[48]

4. Commercialisation of the relations between units of public administration also has an effect which has to be understood sociologically. SSPs' fee-for-service based interactions with client departments contribute over time to a wrench in the fundamental structure and conception of a public service agency. Its form moves away from the traditional, organic, cohesive whole that embodies a human, integrated way of being that enables the agency to tend to its own needs safely and well and as a result know itself, towards a form constructed on values alien and Capitalist and streamlined for greater profit. This new form is the inevitable consequence of the alienation and wariness that is part and parcel

---

[48] This same enthralment to the ideals of the commercial world can also produce *in*action, "Account of a managerial process outcome dictated by market considerations", where the motivator is not image creation, as above, but image management. [*ed.* 2013: This footnote appeared in the original document as footnote 1.]

of the way entities joined by a commercialised nexus relate to each other. Transactions must become standardised. The problem is that not all of life's subtleties *can* be packaged like corn flakes in square boxes that fit better into delivery trucks and hit the shelves cheaper.

Unfortunately, however, an SSP which is obliged to "make a profit" will always be pushing towards the corn flakes aisle to stack its wares for sale. It will promote its services as "just right for you", dear Customer, but in reality must respond to the constant pressure towards providing lowest common denominator services to keep costs down. Leaning always towards this kind of uniformity exerts pressure to commodify and standardise human interactions, attend to the generic and not the peculiar and individual.

Anticipating the need for us SSPs to be like this, the designers of the shared services initiative, consciously or instinctively, began very early to acclimatise us to it by promulgating the analogy of the two car models, Volkswagen as opposed to Statesman, to characterise standards of service we might deliver. We had it explained to us at seminar and workshop pre-SSP that client agencies and we would simply have to get used to it: we'd be delivering Volkswagens, not Statesmans. The lower standard of service was the key to the riches to be had from economies of scale. Client agencies would soon accept the diminution in service quality. That such services are not worth purchasing, however, experienced practitioners in client departments are quite ready to say, privately, if not publicly, because they know that economies of scale in other than robot-like functions are false economies. They wonder out loud: if the Statesmen used to be available, why should we ride in a Volkswagen.

### Explanation of Reason 2:

The commercialised fee-for-service mode of operation runs counter to my conscience and I have deliberately chosen to work in environments not based on commercial values.

I haven't worked in the commercial world since 1962, when I scuttled my job as an advertising account executive with Myer. My conscience had become offended by the realisation that behind the glamour lay organised deceit. Increasingly alienated, I was yet too unfamiliar with the implacable nature of the moral imperative to accept that I had to leave. I baulked at the inevitable. My creative fire was at last smothered by the impasse and my usefulness to Myer declined. They let me go. It was a relief. I made a conscientious decision to work in non-commercial environments from then on. Yet at the stroke of a pen in 2003, my employer (the Crown) moved me forcibly back into such a world – to a shared service provider. That set the clock ticking towards the moment when I would have to engage in commercialised practices: my salary quarantining would end in June 2006 (later extended to 2007). During this hiatus I twice made it clear to CorporateLink, in 2004 and in 2005 that I was seriously at odds with the commercialised modality. The 2005 submission was explicit about my "conscientious objection".

I was not consulted about the move to an SSP. If I had been offered an option, I would have declined to move – an in-house staff counsellor who isn't in the house is not good sense anyway – and if I had known as well that the SSP would practice fee-for-service, I would have declined double, if it hadn't been an offer one couldn't refuse.

On July 1 of this year I was instructed to commence cooperating with the year of notional billing by filling out TimeCapture. This amounts to my being forced into a violation of conscience. I object to it.

My view is that silent compliance with the commercialised model in the face of the evidence now available does not fulfil my obligations as a public servant, one of which is to be cognisant of the public interest and on that basis to provide to government, via the proper media, plainspoken advice about issues of public concern. I believe the proper media include the Service Delivery and Performance Commission, to whom I have made a submission, and the procedures pursuant to the provision in

Treasury's Code of Conduct for conscientious objection, which include the present submission. Government is entitled to be advised that this model for delivering higher level HR services is not a good way of doing things. In my view, if I don't do my bit to tell them, I am negligent.

Uncomfortable as it is for me personally, and inconvenient as it no doubt is for you, I am conscious of the obligation laid upon me to speak out. For example, the *Public Sector Ethics Act 1994* places clear impost upon every public servant to take conscientious action despite their bosses' expectations of compliance with an unconscientious course. The *Act* also respects *customariness* of a process of a public official's work as a legitimate countervailing force to a contrary instruction, and the responsibility this can place upon the official to act independently of an instruction.

This legislation indicates that speaking out, for example under the impetus of a conscientious objection, is reasonable and lawful when considered from a higher perspective than one normally employs in one's day-to-day work-life activities

All of these indicate that speaking out, for example under the impetus of a conscientious objection, is reasonable and lawful when considered from a higher perspective than one normally employs in one's day-to-day worklife activities.

In this connection, it is ironic that one reason the commercialised ethos's adoption by public servants goes unprotested is the alertness public servants now have to their obligation under another section of the *Public Sector Ethics Act 1994* to respect the system of government, uphold the laws of the State and carry out official public sector decisions and policies faithfully and impartially. That is, to do what they're told.

CONSCIENCE IS NOT THE EXCLUSIVE PRESERVE OF RELIGION

The response to date by CorporateLink to my conscientious objection has been to question the legitimacy of it because it hasn't a religious basis; i.e., my conscientious objection is not on religious grounds. I believe this response to be incorrect on two scores.

One, conscience is not the exclusive preserve of religionists, as even the writings of religionists themselves attest. Two, my objection, while it does not depend upon this similarity for legitimacy, finds itself congruent with much religious concern over the ethics of untrammelled commercialisation, as shown above, where Example two of the deleterious effect of commercialisation is discussed, and St Thomas Aquinas's work referred to.

While it is clear that conscience is not the exclusive preserve of religion, there is another excuse for those who conflate the two. Persons involved in religious activity and religious thought are at risk of thinking about conscience and discussing it. The two, religious concerns and conscience concerns, become identified with each other. Indeed, much of the writing of theologians concerns conscience and acknowledges its primacy even against the religious authorities. Some of this theological writing has been influential for me, for example, this passage Vatican II's *Pastoral Constitution on the Church in the Modern World, Gaudium Et Spes*:

> In the depths of his conscience, man detects a law which he does not impose upon himself, but which holds him to obedience. ...For man has in his heart a law written by God; ...Conscience is the most secret core and sanctuary of a man. There he is alone with God . . . In fidelity to conscience, Christians are joined with the rest of men in the search for truth . . . (Article 16.)

Conscience is not seen here as Christian or Catholic conscience, but as mere conscience. Indeed, in Article 26 of the *Gaudium Et Spes*, we find these words:

> Therefore, there must be made available to all men ...the right to ... activity *in accord with the upright norm of one's own conscience*, to ...rightful freedom *even in matters of religion.* (my emphasis)

And at section 41,

> For this Gospel announces and proclaims the freedom of the sons of God, and repudiates all the bondage ....[I]t has a sacred reverence for the dignity of *conscience and its freedom of choice*... (my emphasis)

Indeed, it is religiously-inspired regard for the primacy of conscience which allowed and encouraged the development of the Western secular tradition and, through that, the separation of church and state. We are its beneficiaries; and thus the existence in Queensland (and elsewhere) of a legislated requirement to respect conscience, and thus conscientious objections such as mine, ultimately derives at once from the religious tradition and from something prior to religion, a feature of the human condition which allowed for the rise of both religion and secularism.

It is easy to see how one might misconstrue this confusion and conclude that provision is being made for the protection of religious freedom, rather than conscience in these instruments. That it is conscience and not merely religious observance that provision is being made for is clear from the word I have underlined in the following passage from the Grievance Resolution Directive:

> *"Issue of conscience" refers to a conflict between a religious or other similar <u>belief</u>, and the performance of a specific authorised work activity.*

The provision is being made for conscience, pure and simple.

Since this document is a formal, written defence of my opinions with a legitimate focus on the formation of my conscience in this matter, I will identify some of the places and contexts in which teachings pertinent to it were inculcated in me.

These include: my primary and secondary education at Catholic schools under the control of Good Samaritan Nuns and Augustinian Friars, respectively , my presidency of the Coorparoo Catholic Youth Club in my late teenage years, my responsibility for the editorial content of the parish's youth magazine *Inter Nos*, my engagement at the University of Queensland (after spending some years in the moral wasteland of the advertising industry deceiving for a living) in studying for a degree in literature and then, years later, in social work and, finally, my involvement in political activism over many years confronting the oppressive Bjelke-Petersen government.

A central step in building an understanding of my conscience formation, or sense of the good, is to appreciate the influence upon me of the work of Saint Thomas Aquinas, and the way his cultural heritage, permeating the thought and literature of the centuries since he wrote and taught, has come down to me. The legacy of Aquinas has been an influence on me in a direct way, via teaching in which my educators reported his writings directly to me, and in an indirect way, by virtue of the ideas in his writings having in turn informed the cultural productions of the secular world. This happens in the same way as Shakespeare's aphorisms pepper the discourse of people who have never heard of him and think they are merely using folk wisdom and proverb.

It was an influence I absorbed second-hand and indirectly long before I experienced it directly. For example, as I described above, many years ago I won a job in the advertising business, becoming an account executive, designing layout and writing copy. I set out enthusiastically at the beginning, but eventually came to see I was contravening (what I would later learn were Aquinas's) strictures against using deceit to sell things. It was an experience I came out the other side of with a slowly forming realisation that that work amounted to deception and lacked integrity. That realisation solidified into a firm understanding that left me aghast and determined not to go into that place again.

Thus, inexorably, I have arrived at the position of formally presenting to you the reasons for my conscientious objection to completing TimeCapture, along with some idea of the nature of my conscience.

Should you wish to discuss this further or seek clarification on any of the matters I have raised, please contact me on 3834 2544.

Yours sincerely, etc.

**Attachment 1** (to Conscientious Objection statement)

Response to Issues Raised in Claude's 14 November Letter
**1.** In his letter Claude states that I "may have a personal and sincere objection" to our commercialised mode of operation. He goes on to say that the thing I am objecting to (i.e., "accounting for

my time") is not in the serious categories represented by assisting in lawful terminations and profaning religious holidays by working on them. I do not agree with this.

I am not objecting to "accounting for my time", but to the ill effects produced by achieving the end which accounting for my time is a means to (i.e., the end of gaining "income" from other units of public administration). Therefore, it is that ill effect to which lawful termination exercises and profaning religious holidays must be compared. It is my view that collaborating in producing a deleterious moral effect upon public servants falls somewhere between profaning a religious holiday and assisting in lawful terminations.

In relation to whether or not one must honour one's conscience, it is pointless to give scores out of ten to the matter which my conscience occupies itself with as against the matter which some other person's conscience occupies itself with. If a person herself assesses her conscientious position in regard to an issue as significant enough to demand her obedience to conscience, it is of little consequence whether I or anyone else contradict her. If my conscience tells me that collaborating in producing a deleterious moral effect upon myself and my fellow public servants is an issue significant enough to demand my obedience to conscience, the case is likewise.

In the second, the follower of religion is declining to allow a spiritual event to occur in his mind. My conscientious objection is like that of the nurse, in that I, too, am objecting to helping us bring about any more real events (like the ones I illustrated above) that I *regard as evil*.

**2.** Claude points out that

> ... it is important to consider what you may actually be objecting to, that is, the accounting system itself which is called TimeCapture, or what it may symbolise for you such as the Shared Service initiative.

He appears here to be on the verge of drawing a conclusion about which of his two possibles it is, but does not go on to determine that explicitly. He merely goes on to say TimeCapture is like Alloc8, only with more detail. That is, Alloc8 and TimeCapture are simply alternative time recording systems. The question of what TimeCapture "symbolises" is dropped from his letter. He does go on, however, a little inconsequentially, I thought, to say that accounting for my time is not in the category of performing lawful terminations or being asked to work on religious holidays (demolishing an argument I had not put[49]), but is a standard work process. Shorn of its symbolism, Claude's words imply, the physical act of tapping the keyboard to place numbers in the time period slots on the screen is of no moral consequence. This is hard to rebut, of course, but also hardly the point. The suggestion that an act can be shorn of its symbolism by anyone other than the person for whom the act is symbolic makes no sense. Another may put argument or set example that influences me to abandon the belief that the thing in question symbolises what I thought it symbolised, but it will be I who decide that. Claude's dissection of my objection into concrete act (fingers on keyboard) and symbolism (he wrongly identifies "the Shared Service initiative" as the thing symbolised for me) does not, of course, dissolve my objection for me, since it does not influence me sufficiently to shear the symbolism from the act for me.

I find Claude's implied logic that means and ends, i.e., completing TimeCapture at the keyboard and the reason for which the captured information is required, can be morally separated unconvincing. I do not believe I am alone in taking that position. By introducing the distinction between means and end, Claude here has, I think, reached for a quick rebuttal of my position, and,

---

[49] I had alluded in my letter to Claude of October 3 to the Catholic nurse scenario because I thought the then OPSM&E's August 2003 Directive on Grievance Resolution which includes it signalled the correct way of conceiving of and responding to the tension between compliance and conscience in a public service context.

without saying it, offered me an out. That is, if I merely focus attention on the physical act of entering times and disconnect that act from its end or meaning, I will have no dilemma. However, well-meant as it undoubtedly was, I could not take up his offer.

Claude's distinction, which implies means and ends, can be morally separated, failed to convince me and I could not take comfort from it. Claude thought I might be able to just do the act of keying the information into TimeCapture, like a horse wearing blinkers perhaps, and not think about what the information would be used for by someone else.

It is Aquinas, in his *Summa Theologica*, who is the spoilsport again:

> Although the end is not part of the substance of the act, yet it is the most important cause of the act, since it moves the agent to act. Therefore the moral act is specified chiefly by the end. (*ST*, 2, II, Q7)

> ...volition, properly speaking, is of the end itself. On the other hand, the means are good and willed not for themselves, but as related to the end. Therefore the will is directed to them only in so far as it is directed to the end, so that what it wills in them is the end. (*ST*, 2, II, Q8)

> ...according to the Philosopher,[50] "where one thing is on account of another there is only one." But will does not will the means save on account of the end. (*ST*, 2, II, Q9)

And, referring to the above, Aquinas goes on to say,

> This argument holds in respect of the will being moved to the end as the reason for willing the means. (*ST*, 2, II, Q9)

---

[50] Aquinas is referring to Aristotle's *Topics*, III, 2.

**Attachment 2** *(to Conscientious Objection statement)*

<u>Note December 2006</u>: The following report was written and submitted in 2004 after I attended, at management request, the workshop it describes. I include it as an attachment to my submission to indicate that my thinking about the general concept of a commercialised public sector agency then was consistent with my thinking now.

### Rendering the invisible visible:

A Comment on Champs Unlimited
Professional Service Excellence for Managers Pilot Workshop

I attended the pilot workshop above on 24 and 25 March 2004. Jessica Nash presented the sessions with the assistance of another Champs staff member, Carolyn Richards. Subsequently I reported some observations and reflections upon it at Paul Turner's fortnightly meeting on 31 March. This written Comment is an expanded account of my report to the meeting.

Jessica Nash's qualifications for the design and delivery of the workshop are very impressive. Her experience in media and in recruitment has been gained at various levels, including senior management level and she has clearly reflected upon it and understood in great detail and at depth the principles that lie behind her success in those fields. Her grasp of these matters is not merely academic: she has been able to translate that understanding into useful educational experiences designed to allow adults to comfortably participate. The modules of the workshop she provided for us to work through taught us exactly, in my opinion, what they were intended to teach us, and achieved that end by involving our minds and our emotions and even to some extent our motor skills, and did all of this in an appropriately interactive social mode. She seemed to me to have a good sensitivity to the threshold of toleration of the various participants and kept a close enough eye on them to adjust the intensity of what was happening. Her judgement seemed good. Promises of follow up distribution of material used (PowerPoints, etc) were kept.

Michael O'Neill

Jessica also informed us, as part of our two day process, about the parallel workshop (its contents and learning experiences) Champs was providing to non-manager CorporateLink staff. My impression was that the other workshop process was as well designed and executed as ours, and by all accounts equally successful and well received.

One way to describe the subject matter of the workshops is: the personal interactions which surround and in fact form the basis of the process of delivering to our fellow public servants (i.e., our clients) in the cluster agencies the services we are employed to provide. Accordingly, close attention is paid in the workshop to the form and style of the interpersonal exchanges which are the mechanisms of those service interactions, and the workshop activities and videos shown tended to elucidate the underlying structures of those things and familiarise us with them.

As an attempt at achieving the intended objective one would have to assess the workshop a brilliant success, with effects both subtle and powerful. And that is where my difficulty begins.

Training such as the Professional Service Excellence workshops inculcates in people a way of being in the world and a way of interacting with others which implies an ethos or worldview, but doesn't always state it outright. Most often, in fact, the existence of the implied ethos is not referred to or even known about by the facilitator or trainees. Nevertheless, the ethos lies behind the façade or below the surface of the recommended way of being and interacting and is as much a part of what is being taught as the trade secrets of persuasion and other devices that appear to be the content of the training. It is part of the intended objective, even if unconscious.

My difficulty is with that ethos part of the intended objective. I have a doubt about the appropriateness of the ethos that lies behind the approach taken by the workshop. When I talk here about the concept of ethos I am not discussing the presence or absence of morally correct behaviour but rather the spirit, beliefs and values characteristic of an individual, a community or a social grouping. I stress carefully here that my Comment does not take issue with Champs Unlimited (or with Jessica Nash in particular) over its (or her) ethics. There was nothing to suggest unethical practice on the part of the designers or the presenter of the workshop. Quite the contrary, in fact. Jessica was very open about the exact nature of the skills she was teaching us and straightforward about their intended effect upon persons we might practise them on. For her it was not ethically problematic. It may however be ethically problematic for someone dedicated to a different ethos to practise those skills. So there is a tension between two ways of being in the world here. In what follows I will explore that tension.

Professional service excellence (which translates in our CorporateLink setting as giving genuinely good service to our client agencies) will require several things of us. One is the capacity to innovate as we respond to requests for help. Innovation arises out of and depends upon individuals' freedom to do things creatively. Creativity, in turn, needs to be uninhibited by any sense of obligation to behave in a corporately designed style. Such service also requires us to be as other-centred as we can be within our over-arching obligation as public servants, which is, when succinctly and generically put, to implement legislation. Genuinely other-centred public service activity, therefore, must figure out or intuit what room to move there is within our overall obligation and take advantage of it inventively. It also requires us to recognise that implementing legislation is different from promoting ephemeral political spin such as Smart State rhetoric, for example, or genuflecting before buzz slogans like working smarter not harder. A good public service is the instrument of government (government generically understood) but independent of a particular Government (say, the Beattie Government or the Borbidge Government). Responsiveness to the government of the day does not mean that with each election everything in the house of the public service is hosed out, including the values that define it as an Australian institution. Were it to be interpreted that way, there would be no durability to an institution whose contribution is vital to the continuity of our culture. (If it

Michael O'Neill

seems odd that making choices among different workshop styles should lead into a discussion of Australian culture, that sense of oddness is resolved by following out the implications of the choices we are making.)

Genuinely other-centred public service does not include self-promotion. While it is traditionally anathema to the Australian style to big note, distaste for the practice is a feature of our ethos coming under more and more threat as our culture is increasingly pressured to adopt the least ethical and most commercial elements of Americanisation. Seeing marketing as a value neutral or even acceptable practice rather than recognising it as a sophisticated form of deceit is one such unwelcome element.

The encroachment of the marketing way of being in the world is ubiquitous, spreading outwards from the commercial activities which spawned it to influence the style of all societal activity. Over many years now it has made itself seem like the only game in town. The Media accept it unthinkingly (TV, newspapers, and so on). Practices of self-aggrandisement once derided as boasting are now (under the more agreeable label self-promotion) commonplace, even required, *de rigueur*. In sport, for example, failure to self-promote raises eyebrows and suspicions of lack of seriousness about winning. (That sport is about something other than winning has long since been lost to the popular imagination.) The self-effacing person couldn't possibly be a trier. And the media, which is now highly commercialised in style, even public broadcasters like the ABC and SBS, being the dominant societal meaning-bestower across Australian culture, sets the self-promotional tone, and virtually ensures the predominance of the new ethic of a thoroughly marketed life.

Real consequences flow from such ideological takeovers. If they didn't, the interests of those who devote such enormous resources to seeding these social makeovers would not be served and would reap no rewards. One such real consequence is the unnoticed acceptance of marketing principles as OK things to found a society upon.

The danger of adopting practices which embody such principles can be exemplified by considering a common phenomenon and imagining its possible consequences: If we all wear CorporateLink logos on our shirts and blouses we may enjoy the sense of solidarity it engenders and feel some esprit de corps, it may resolve the dilemma of what to wear every day, and it may have tax advantages and other benefits for our personal finances as well as. This last benefit sounds a warning bell; for the prospect of financial gain, here as everywhere, tends to undermine adherence to principle. The way it works here, in relation to wearing uniform dress, is that it tends to clone us in ways other than just image and appearance. It may reinforce the idea that our individual thinking has to align with some fictional CorporateLink position (the "party line") on a range of intangibles and attitudinal characteristics, producing a uniformity of thought which is anathema to genuinely Other-centred service performed with integrity. True public service accountability is achieved from within the individual worker and arises out of his or her conversation with his/her own conscience, which in practice is the final yardstick. We should do nothing that limits or puts a straitjacket around that internal dialogue with the self. Cloning our thinking limits that dialogue. Dressing the staff in uniform is trademark behaviour for modern, marketing-driven organisations in which uniformity of attitude is sought after.

Now the public service is not McDonalds yet, so when public servants adopt the uniform dress practice there still can be a watch kept to guard against the simultaneous adoption of uniformity of thought with its anti-creative consequences. It requires constant vigilance but is possible, partly because uniformity of dress is so visible and hard to miss and thus alerts us to the danger. However, where the uniformity adopted is more subtle, for example where it results from training people in linguistic devices and persuasive but covert stratagems for winning personal interactions based upon the principles of marketing, the dangers are greater.

The principles of marketing are not the principles of good governance, of justice, of truth, of public service, or of democracy.

Michael O'Neill

They are not OK things to found a society upon. I will say some more below on the tension between the two sets of broad principles and the values each implies, but here let me acknowledge, if it is not yet obvious, that the apprehension of things I am expounding and the recommended behaviour I am implicitly espousing in this Comment rest unambiguously upon a value stance.

There is no less a value stance behind the Professional Service Excellence workshop, whether or not it is stated openly or its existence even suspected by the designers of the course or those in CorporateLink who chose it from among the various consultants' designs and commissioned its execution.

I do not mean to suggest that there was conscious intent to prefer a style of workshop that moved us towards, or purposely introduced the influence of, an inappropriate ethos for CorporateLink. The seductions of the marketing ethos are subtle and pervasive and there is no reason to imagine that those succumbing to them must be choosing in full awareness. Marketing as a worldview and style of thought has achieved near perfect saturation of society. It seems as natural as breathing. After all, the locations in which departments interface with the public look enough like shopfronts to call them Customer Service Centres so it seems inevitable that we should so label them. But there is an underlying conceptual contradiction at work here. One can see it laid bare when one considers, for example, the spectacle of staff of Corrective Services – the word services in the name of this particular department is itself evidence of the ideological seepage – trying to emulate the elegant customer service provided to inmates by its privately run competitors and generally twist the reality they see before them into shapes that match marketing's reduction of life to trade arrangements.

If the rise in water temperature is imperceptible, the frog in the bucket does not notice until the change in its state is a *fait accompli*.

## Some philosophical tensions

Marketing principles developed as attempts to understand how best to fall in with the underlying mechanisms of the market, how to anticipate the purchasing behaviour of human beings whose self-interest, conscious and unconscious, directed their actions. The objective is to exploit that mechanism to advance the interests of the party controlling the marketing. Marketing's modus operandi is to first implant in the subject a desire for something, e.g., product, sweater, politician, lifestyle, guru, car, VCR, philosophy, cooked chook, and then exploit that desire to the profit of whoever is paying the marketer. The misgivings such a practice generates in us are usually "allayed" by reassurance that the marketers' ethics will make certain that only desires for good things will be implanted (as if that were the point.) Marketing is amorally content to gain its ends using manipulative processes, for it must use such processes. It has no interest in a moral discussion about the matter.

However, good governance, fair play and justice as exemplified within the tradition of decent public service is not content to gain its ends that way. A personal interaction style more in keeping with that tradition is one that speaks plainly to the "customer". Nor does it choose a word like customer to designate a departmental <u>client</u> or a <u>citizen</u>. Of the three c words, the latter two are fitter to describe those persons we are meant to serve and/or to regulate the actions of. The debate about the choice of description or designation is not without relevance, in spite of the way the word "customer", a label that has its roots squarely in the values of the market, appears to have completely colonised the mental space in which we conceptualise and evaluate service provision.

Such a personal interaction style – you might call it the Westminster style for lack of better name, associating it with the Westminster mode of government – accepts that the Other has a perfect right to know what you know and to make choices the real consequences of which are spelled out plainly, has a right not to be conned, has a right not to be condescended to or patronised (don't you worry your pretty little head about it), has a right not to have the service provider's aims camouflaged by the use of linguistic tricks and conversational stratagems that subliminally limit his/her range of responses to the one the service providers (such as we at CorporateLink, for example) have pre-ordained. This is true when the Other we are talking of is a member of the public whom the public servant serves. It is even truer (if truth can have degree) when the Other is a fellow public servant with obligations just like ours in a client department. We do not have several lines of sweaters to sell, one of which gives us secretly the greater profit margin and is therefore the one we want the customer to desire.

To adopt this style of service provision includes being willing to live with the possibility that the client may be seeking an objective contrary to the one we have in mind for him or her, and accepts the legitimacy of that without trying to outflank him or her in secretive ways. (Putting plainly in front of the client what bad outcomes may result from his or her pursuits is quite a different act.) Contention over which pathways to choose is not a crime, nor even is disagreement over the final choice. It is not necessary to right behaviour to pre-empt all uncomfortable outcomes.

The Westminster, or British civil service style is distinguished by a number of hallmarks. Some of those are: the practice of offering frank and fearless advice (to facilitate which traditional ideas of tenured employment were important), respect for the dignity of the individual you are dealing with and his or her right to decide his/her own actions, the entitlement of citizens to know the truth and, by extension, the right of our fellow public servants to know it too. Recommending this style of operation to CorporateLink, as I am doing, is taking a value stance. I know the value stance ultimately adopted by an agency with 700+ staff will be the result of a complex process influenced by factors beyond what staff may think is preferable. Nevertheless, this Comment is my one seven hundredth part of the input of staff to that process.

I opened this comment by describing the technical quality of the Champs Unlimited pilot workshop in glowing terms and I was fair dinkum in that assessment. Some of those technical qualities are value neutral, or close enough to value neutral, and genuinely admirable. The difficulty for me, clearly, is that exemplified in Jessica Nash's approach were some qualities that derive from principles inappropriate to our purposes.

It is two thousand years since the Roman imperium realised the totalitarian value of blurring the distinction between Church (in the broadest sense of religion) and State for controlling the opinions of the citizenry. As a result each new Emperor deified the one recently deceased. (Some didn't even wait and did it before they died.) It worked a treat. The subterfuge persisted until the Enlightenment of the 18th Century gradually unravelled it by showing the advantages to good governance of keeping Church and State separate. The contemporary form of that subterfuge is the blurring of the distinction between Market and State. We do not have to wait centuries this time to undo it.

Michael O'Neill
27 April 2004

**Attachment 3** (to Conscientious Objection statement)

**To:** "[name of my immediate boss at CorporateLink –suppressed]@ CorporateLink"
**cc:** [name of my boss's boss – suppressed]@corporatelink.qld.gov.au>
**From:** Michael P O'Neill/cp1/qdot/au
**Date:** 19/12/2005 02:55:10 PM

Subject: tender

Dear Dxxxxx

Michael O'Neill

Thanks for the voicemails Friday and today asking me to help write the [Department's] tender response. Your request brings a serious problem which we are all facing into sharp focus for me, and I will try here to make a start on explaining it, not only to you but to myself as well. I will cc this reply to Sxxxxx and Bxxxxx because the whole issue is very important to us all, it seems to me.

I think that a worrying trend developing in the public service is illustrated by The Department's tender process, and particularly by their neglecting to proactively ensure we were at least welcome tenderers.

When the government chose two and half years ago to implement shared service provision in the public service clustered agencies were intended to accept the services being provided back to them. Alleged economies of scale, believable perhaps in relation to some unsophisticated HR functions, made sense on that basis. Then some clustered agencies arrogated the right to NOT take services from their SSPS.

These agencies put, and are putting, the work out to tender. (I, at least, haven't heard of any policy reverse by government that justifies this.) The result is that the public sector is being turned into a buyers' market in which an agency can shop around for private consultancies to do their work for them, in the process nurturing and husbanding the expertise of private sector consultants with taxpayers' money, while simultaneously facilitating the deterioration of the same kind of expertise in the public service and allowing it to atrophy. Unfortunately, however, the lure of being seen to behave like the free-wheeling private sector, exercising ruthless choice and rejecting those whose capacities we, in our pursuit of excellence, judge second rate, is seductive.

As far as I can see, this all runs counter to the public statement of Premier Beattie about reversing the trend towards outsourcing public service work to consultants and dumbing down the public sector. As well, I suspect it has policy implications for this and successive governments, which, to my knowledge, are not being discussed frankly with government, or sanctioned by government.

The responsibility to alert government to debilitating trends which our vantage point in operational work makes us intimate with is not central agencies' exclusively.

Departments are flouting the principles espoused by the Premier, in my view, and this creates a Toni Hoffman [*ed. then famous public service whistleblower*] situation for us. I think we are in danger if we simply collude, or, worse, participate enthusiastically in the delusion, all the while telling ourselves we will somehow "go out of business" - a concept that makes sense in private enterprise only - if we don't get in step. The danger is that we will be seen in retrospect to have been complicit when a Geoff Davies-type inquiry occurs. One might pooh-hooh the idea that such a widely accepted practice could ever be seen in a different light than that which it presently is seen in. One might say, everyone is doing it, what can go wrong? Drs Buckland, Scott and Keating and Mr Nuttall and Ms Edmond and Mr Leck certainly thought that way. [*ed. These were parliamentarians or government officers caught up in the scandal*] But if the emperor is naked, it will out.

The apparent impropriety of action such as The Department's in seeking tenders for HR services rather than accepting that CorporateLink has the commission ought not, in my view, to be tolerated and humoured.

For my part, I used to be in the advertising and marketing industry in the private sector, where my job was to engage in bullshit. I gave it away as an immoral occupation and began to practice the vocation of public service. Touting for business, with the smudging of the truth it entails, and the implicit acceptance that such practices in the public service are ethical, is, I'm afraid, beyond my moral boundary. I conscientiously object and may not do it.

In fact, it's my opinion that none of us should. We should rather challenge and confront it formally, as an agency. The word on the street is that departments served by other SSPs wish we were their partner because CorporateLink is seen as the leading SSP. Whatever virtues brought us that reputation, I think it can't hurt to add more integrity and courage.

Michael O'Neill

Regards
Michael O'Neill

*Attachment 4*  (to Conscientious Objection statement)

*Higher level human resources services*

For the purpose of establishing some common understanding I offer a catalogue of what I see as "higher level Human Resources (HR) services", as distinct from such services as delivery of payroll systems and (some) information management systems.  They are as follows:

> managing diminished work performance, workplace rehab, employee assistance of the "internally" located variety (e.g., the services of a Staff Counsellor) and coordination of the externally located variety,  workplace health and safety compliance advice and support, grievance resolution, investigations, dispute resolution, career transition advice, mediation and conflict resolution, disciplinary advice, HR consultancy and HR policy development advice, project management, diagnostic safety audits, WHSO training, WH&S helpdesk facilities, development of award conditions, site specific agreements, tribunal representation, industrial dispute negotiation, employee relations policy development, consultation and coaching for managers and supervisors in morale preservation, organisational reviews, business process reviews, change management strategies, job design and redesign and analysis and evaluation, policy development, research on business trends, facilitation, including workshop facilitation, training services, business and strategic planning, project management and business improvement processes.

***Attachment 5*** (to Conscientious Objection statement)

## Account of a managerial process outcome dictated by market considerations

1. Over a period of more than a year a situation involving chronic staff dissatisfaction and distress obtained within a unit of Consultancy Services Branch. The Manager was a redeployee and not yet confirmed in the job. She was seen by at least one of her senior subordinates as micromanaging to an unreasonable degree. Their working relationship deteriorated steadily and the subordinate's doctor eventually insisted she get away from the situation. The subordinate at last accepted the inevitability of such a move and took a secondment, declaring she would not return to what she now was convinced was a toxic industrial environment.

However, before she reached the end of her tether she made a number of attempts to engage the support of her Director, the officer to whom her Manager reported. In my conversations with the subordinate (these were not counselling sessions but peer to peer discussions) I heard her account of the Director's comment that although she (the Director) did not dispute the account of the relationship between the subordinate and the Manager, she declared herself powerless to intervene. The Director's reported words were, "Well, what can I do? I can't sack her." This is, of course, nonsense. Supervisors in the public service have open to them proper procedures for managing diminished work performance, a possible outcome of which is dismissal. The will to use them is all that is required.

The subordinate departed on the secondment. In her absence the Manager's managerial style continued to affect others in a similar manner, and had affected a number of now separated staff also, I later learned when I conversed with a number of them. Having worked under this Manager and seeing no prospect of improvement, they had left, they told me (I was a total stranger), to escape the ill effects of being managed by her.

One of the staff affected by this Manager's behaviour subsequent to the first subordinate's departure on secondment was the officer who was recruited to fill the vacancy. It was when I, for the second time, found this colleague in tears after yet another encounter with the Manager that I decided not to merely stand by and see another person join the procession of departees.

After holding discussions with my peers, two of whom were willing to join with me in confronting the Manager (who managed all three of us) about her managerial style, which we all found unacceptable, I presented the plan to the CEO on March 8th 2005. [I had carefully decided not to take the matter to the Director, who had failed to take any of several opportunities to fix things.] The CEO, after informing me she had herself heard comments about the difficulties the Manager's operational style had caused, endorsed our plan and asked me to report back to her after it had been implemented. I made it clear to the CEO that I had had conversations, as I indicated above, with staff who had left the unit to escape the ill effects of working under this Manager, and that some of those still carried unresolved emotional pain from their time in the unit.

I then asked the Manager to meet with me and my two peers. These two were the most senior of the remaining group of staff, and they represented the views of many of the staff junior to them who had similar reactions to the Manager's style. The Manager at first refused to meet with the three of us, then agreed. I had suggested she have someone with her at our coming meeting and she chose to have her manager, the Director, present at the meeting. The five of us met in the Director's office on March 18, 2005.

My two colleagues and I each gave a very comprehensive account of the deficits in the Manager's operating style and explained the consequences for ourselves and other staff. We left in the hands of the Director and the Manager what needed to be done to correct the situation.

I met again with the CEO about two and a half weeks later, on April 5 and updated her on progress.

2. Some time after the Director had made the comment about being unable to sack this Manager, she confirmed the Manager's redeployment. At a later point the Director confirmed the Manager as the successful applicant for a new AO8 Manager position she had created. In my discussions with the CEO I had raised the question, why did the Director, if she knew there were performance problems with the Manager, first confirm the secondment and then promote her? The CEO said that the Director was aware but had intended to "develop" the Manager once she was promoted to the new AO8 position.

3. The Manager was left in place by the Director after the five-person meeting of March 18, 2005. [The Manager left of her own accord over a year later, in June 2006, on a six month secondment]. As far as we three senior members of her team were able to see, no action resulted from our March 18 meeting other than the Director's attendance as an observer at the next regular fortnightly meeting the Manager held with us. (The Director explained her presence at the meeting as merely the beginning of a new regime in which she, the Director, was going to sit in on all her subordinate Managers' team meetings. It never happened again.)

The Manager's operating style remained unchanged. At last it generated a second round of action from the subordinate group, by this time (May 9, 2006) composed of quite a few new people. This round of action was different from the one the CEO had endorsed over a year earlier. This action arose spontaneously among the Manager's subordinates and took the form of an *ultra vires* group which met weekly until June 30. Titled "HR Recovery Group", the group was attempting to respond to a bad situation proactively and constructively, and at its height included eleven of 15 staff members, a significant majority of the staff body. It was engaged in developing a reform-oriented document to be presented to the new Director, who was expected to take up duty on July 1. The HR Recovery Group's intention was to focus Director-level attention yet again on to this chronic problem and the unacceptable consequences it was having for morale, productivity and staff and skill retention. However, the Manager's surprise, voluntary departure on secondment at the end of June 2006 changed everything.

The situation had been building to a climax and the July 1 handing in of the HR Recovery Group's submission would have precipitated a crisis in the Branch, had the Manager's sudden departure not produced bathos instead. The situation, it is important to make clear, was not brought to term by proactive steps taken by the organisation, but by chance. (Unless the fortuitous secondment was organised behind the scenes with the staff purposely kept in ignorance.)

4. The first point to be made in drawing a tentative conclusion about how to interpret this chain of events is this: It is clear from the above account that the extent, seriousness and consequences of this Manager's diminished performance were known to the organisation. What needs to be answered is the question, "Why was no effective action taken to discharge the organisation's duty of care to the cohort of subordinates of this Manager who faced such a threat, realised in some cases, to their workplace health and safety?"

It is my submission that the over-arching inhibiting factor capable of staying the hand of senior management in the face of a clear duty to take action was an awareness of how much face in the marketplace would be lost – and hence how much business – if a diminished performance action had been commenced. A consultancy holding itself out as competent to advise departments about "excellent" HR practice would have become a scandal had right action been taken. We didn't steer a course by the stars, we positioned ourselves according to the expectations and prejudice of our fantastic marketplace, for the Manager was one of the chief salespersons, a very public face of the consultancy as far as the "customers" were concerned.

**Attachment 6** (to Conscientious Objection statement)

### My Conscience

Like everyone, I have been formed by the culture I grew up in. The whole set of influences include those mediated by tradition and those which are contemporary. Sometimes, perhaps always, these are in conflict. Sometimes the conflict is stark: as I grew up in the forties and fifties, boastfulness was reviled as a moral failing. At present it is rather seen as a characteristic necessary to full participation in our competitive society. Moreover, the competitive nature of society is now accepted as if it were a good thing, whereas, at an earlier time, at least in Australia, a more socialised view that held cooperative endeavour to be a good thing was the accepted view.

My moral formation, or idea of the good, which is the legacy of the particular period of time and the particular place (provincial Australia, for example, rather than Paris or Peking) I grew up in, continues in me but is continually exposed to influences that would undermine it and influences that would alter it in some other way. That personal moral formation is the result, if I take a larger view, of the Western tradition. That tradition begins, to my mind, substantially with the democratically atheistic/agnostic heritage of the Greeks, and flows from there to now. On the way, it passes through and is temporarily submerged by, the Christian influence – one pertinent to me in both a proximate and remote way – and is retrieved into the story in the Middle Ages, particularly via thirteenth century monastic scholarship (the time of St Thomas Aquinas, a seminal formulator of ethical thought). Over the last few centuries the tradition has produced a strand of secularism, made possible, unpredictably perhaps, by the very nature of Christian thought, with its commitment to the primacy of conscience, a commitment genuine enough to nurture an outgrowth of itself by which it was dislodged from the dominance it had enjoyed for a thousand years. Secularism, now joined to the tradition of Greek thought, continues to reject, enjoy the benefits of and live by those gifts it received during its long imprisonment in the Christian.

The relevance of this potted intellectual history for this submission is that I have been the beneficiary, I believe, of this resulting double-stranded tension. I was raised a Roman Catholic, devout and scholarly in the Church's lore, until age 24, and after that I came under the influence of the political activism and cultural lore of the sixties and beyond. My personal moral development, as far as conscience is concerned in particular, repeats in microcosm the last two thousand years of the western tradition: Christian first, then living with the permanent tension of a creative if unsettled secularism that was spawned and tolerated by the very core values of the Christian education I received. One sign of this twin inheritance is the confluence in me of the Christian tradition of giving witness to a deeper truth than is seen by the upholders of the status quo (exemplified by the tradition of Christian martyrs) and of the activist political tradition of speaking truth to power (exemplified by the protesters outside the venues where the G8 meets).

**Attachment 7** (to Conscientious Objection statement)

### What in the social environment brings about such casual indifference to ethical standards?

One possible answer to this question is as follows. The deterioration in their integrity results when there has been unreflective, and hence amoral, adoption of behaviours by public servants which they would not countenance were they not enveloped ideologically in the commercialised ethos, an ethos which fatally, and, it is important to state, unawares, distorts their ethical perspective. This enveloping wrong-headedness resists correction even when confronted because it has been brazenly promulgated as if someone else had already done the thinking about whether or not it was appropriate to our vocation, and that promulgation has resulted in its unthinking adoption.

## Bibliography

*The New Dictionary of Catholic Social Thought,* Judith Dwyer (ed.):The Liturgical Press. Minnesota 1994.

*Vatican Council II: The Conciliar and Post Conciliar Documents,* Ed Austin Flannery, O.P. The Vatican Collection Volume 1 Costello Publishing Company New York 1988

*The Summa Theologica of Saint Thomas Aquinas,* trans. Fathers of the English Dominican Province, revised Daniel J Sullivan. Great Books of the Western World. Ed. Robert Maynard Hutchins. 1952

*Rerum novarum,* encyclical of Pope Leo XIII 1891

# TOOLKIT ITEM 3
## When they are dumb enough to ask for it: Using the Machine's Own "Best Practice" to Put It on Notice

THAT sub-heading might as easily have put other terms in quotes. Modernity, Political Correctness, Transparency, Openness... They are all drawn from what Laura Penny calls a deep reservoir of bullshit phrases. What they all purport is the readiness of the organisation to listen and respond to input from outsiders. (Outsiders is itself is a term with a moveable border.)

I chose best practice, which I have admired above for its total flexibility[51]. Now, whatever the label given, it is the Machine's earnestness in posing as a listener we are talking about. There are other of its poses simple human occupants of the Machine who are in good faith can take tactical advantage of. (You will nose them as you mount the stairs. Have your rapier ready.) But here let me attend to the phenomenon of the Survey.

Surveying staff (or consumers) sends many PR messages even before the results are in. If you think of the advantages of responding to a survey, especially one focussed on how everyone liked the latest of the Machine's impositions, as a way to increase the likelihood of a one-eighty by the organisation's decision-makers, you are missing the point – and likely to be disappointed. As far as the Machine is concerned, commissioning the survey was the PR point, full stop.

No, the usefulness of the survey, at least the qualitative type, from the subversive's point of view is the chance to articulate.

What follows is an example of advantage-taking of that kind. It is a comment I contributed to the survey sent around by SSA (the Shared Service Provider, to which a great swathe of several Departments' staff were compulsorily moved). It sought our

---

[51] Flexibility is another candidate for the quotes in the sub-heading. Are you beginning to feel how slippery the ground is, and how deceptive is the seeming stability of the paving stones of language here? This difficulty we have now taking language and discourse seriously is a consequence of that anti-Chardinesque chosen deterioration I drew your attention to earlier.

reactions to the mass migration that had just occurred. To press the advantage home, one has to make use of the tacit permission, since the comment was officially asked for, to circulate it widely:

> The staff who were dragooned into shared services in 2003 were public servants. That is, they were people whose working life and predilections had led them into the public sector. They had, by and large, if demographics mean anything at all, non-commercial instincts and philosophical postures tending towards the social, not the individualistic. What they found when they woke up on July 1 as victims of the SSP pressgang was an official set of beliefs they were obliged to endorse which was anathema. None might say so openly, for the contradiction was early declared a nondiscussable. In truth, it became a non-fact. Some knew what had happened to them, but kept silent. Others knew not.

What happened to that second group here in SSP land recalls the observation of Orwell's lead character in *1984* about his co-sleepwalkers:

> ...he realised how easy it was to present an appearance of orthodoxy while having no grasp whatever of what orthodoxy meant. In a way, the world-view of the party imposed itself most successfully on people incapable of understanding it. They could be made to accept the most flagrant violations of reality, because they never fully grasped the enormity of what was demanded of them, and were not sufficiently interested in public events to notice what was happening. By lack of understanding they remained sane.

While many, perhaps most, of the newly created entrepreneurs of the brave new SSP world were thus able to defend themselves psychologically, as Orwell's creations did, and keep from awareness the tension produced in them by their plunge into commercialisation, its spoilage invaded the heart regardless. This it did for those aware and those unaware.

The standard line about economies of scale may even be true when it comes to such services as delivery of payroll systems, but it is not true of much else we are trying to do. I wrote about this in a submission to the Service Delivery and Performance

Commission which attempted to outline what an error of judgement the government had made when it allowed itself to be convinced by snake-oilers that higher level HR services could be standardised in the pursuit of efficiencies. I will include a passage from that submission here, one which shows, incidentally, that it was not just the hearts of us conscripts that were invaded, but those of our clients as well:

> One IR practitioner still in a client Department, reflecting upon the interpolation of clumsy SSP involvement in the Department's industrial life, says that he feels 'despair for the Department I once knew. Its heart is gone'. What's actually gone, to be plain spoken, is the sense of connectedness between practitioner and object of practice. SSPs represent a wrenched shift in the fundamental conception of a public service agency from organic, cohesive whole that embodies our way (as humans) of being a social species to one constructed on values alien and Capitalist and mechanised for greater profit. Not all of life's subtleties can be packaged like corn flakes in square boxes that fit better into delivery trucks and hit the shelves cheaper. The impost does not fit, fortunately, and in the long term cannot work; but the cost of learning this and then admitting it will be high, and in the end a face-saving lie will be required to get away from it. The sooner we begin the better.

> Note to the researchers: Thanks for running this survey. It provides one of the very few (perhaps the only) chance to say to our fellows what needs to be said. It means those among us afraid to speak, and each afraid they are the only one who wants to speak, can breathe easier and lose that debilitating feeling that all one's co-workers have morally expired.

When taking advantage of their sticking out their chin like this, my advice is to shuck modesty about the untypical (sadly) nature of your moral world view and give them both barrels. It's what we're here for. As well, one is often surprised at how easily other people's moral indignation can be stirred into life by example and permission.

# TOOLKIT ITEM 4
## When they are *worried* enough to ask for it...

I MENTIONED the quandary the State government found itself in when the hubbub of discontent with the SSA initiative became too loud to ignore, a quandary it resolved at last by setting up, slightly deceptively, The Service Delivery and Performance Commission, under the chairmanship of Dr Leo Keliher. Ironically or, perhaps, karmically, Dr Keliher was widely believed to be presiding genius of the shared services initiative. His Commission called for public submissions. As I told you, I made one, with moderately satisfying success.

The Commission's brief was known from speeches in the Parliament to be identification and eradication of waste. A concern with alleged waste in the public service was both electorally useful and administratively useful, the political placenta of the Shared Services push. I wrote my submission to refract through that glass. Ultimately, however, the concern with financial waste, real or not, on the part of the government, dovetailed with my concern over another, more spiritual and philosophical kind of waste.

The value that is unique to making a submission to a commission of this kind, from the subversive perspective, is that it circumvents gate-keeping by the egos of senior people in one's own organisation. The Commissioners have egos, too, of course, but part of their official self-image is flail for the government. That's what dilutes their normal human/organisational tendency to circle the wagons. The postures they are rewarded for can sometimes mesh well with the long-suppressed mutter of discontent from the ground floor. Notwithstanding, I made sure every page carried a formal Whistleblower stipulation in the footer.

**Submission to the Service Delivery and Performance Commission**

# Nobody
# Here
# Speaks
# Elephant

Michael O'Neill
November 2006
Michael O'Neill
CorporateLink
November 2006

Dr Leo Keliher
Chairman
Service Delivery and
Performance Commission
Floor 5 Executive Building
100 George Street, Brisbane
Queensland 4000 Australia

Dear Dr Keliher

I write to bring to your attention some practices of the Consultancy Services Branch of the shared service provider CorporateLink and some practices generic to shared service provision, in particular the adoption of the fee-for-service modality. It is my submission that the Commission should consider these practices, and the ideologies upon which many found their adoption of them, to assess how much waste, duplication and inefficiency they produce, how much of the public service's reserves of skill capital and inter-agency goodwill they squander, and how deleterious is their effect upon the integrity of the public servants who engage in them. It is my submission that examination of these aspects of our current public service practice coincides with the Service Delivery and Performance Commission's purpose of identifying public service problems before they become systemic, develop and needlessly claim energy and resources.

### Genesis of this submission

The original impetus for this submission was my submission to my own agency, CorporateLink, in December 2005, set out in an email to all levels of management above me. That email was a response to a request made of me to engage in a process that I found counter to good sense. In it I suggested CorporateLink formally challenge and confront a practice being engaged in by our client departments. My own agency's nil response then and since has convinced me that the matter ought be drawn to your attention. Since December several other matters have crystallised and I join them in this submission to the original issue of concern[52].

### A note on the concept of skill capital

In this submission I have used the term "skill capital". I mean it to point to that body of expertise and knowledge possessed in the aggregate by public servants and at the disposal of the government. There is capital of that sort laid up aplenty in the Queensland public service, but I think our continued possession of it is at risk. How it is at risk is in part my subject, but the reason I draw this risk to your attention is to provide sufficient cause for the Commission to inspect some of the practices now becoming common in the service and being perpetuated by otherwise ethical and conscientious public servants who do not see the wood for the trees.

---

[52] My first contact with the SDPC was prompted by the lack of response to my concerns from my superiors. Michelle Hartog of your office left me a voicemail in response on January 3rd of this year. By the time I heard Michelle's invitation to contact her I had realised a more comprehensive submission was required.

Issues of concern

The issues this submission will canvass are:

    1. Depletion of our skill capital (public service expertise and knowledge)

    2. Erosion of integrity standards resulting from adherence to commercialised modalities

    3. Diminution of intra-public service goodwill (social capital)

    4. Practical difficulties arising out of Queensland's Shared Service Provider (SSP) model:

        (i)  An under-utilised consultant cohort on life support: how it turns productivity into busywork

        (ii)  Condonement of agencies' misrepresentation of the purposes of recruitment (growback)

        (iii) Consequences of an organisational self-concept removed from reality

        (iv) The inbuilt obstacle for SSPs offering consultancy to Departments

    5. Myths and reality concerning accountability and efficiency

**Issue 1**

Depletion of our skill capital (public service expertise and knowledge)

Agencies fall into two groups in their methods of securing the higher level HR services they require. The first group appear to act on the assumption that they are free to purchase these services not only from outside their shared service providers, but also from sources outside the public service. It is the consequences of their behaviour that form the subject of this section. (The second group's way of securing this kind of service is discussed under Issue 4ii.)

The assumption made by agencies in the first group permits shopping forays into the consultancy marketplace and, as a corollary, causes deterioration in internal public service expertise. It is hard to believe that the untoward effect of this was not anticipated, given the Premier's statements on the matter and the

Public Service Commissioner's published guideline (www.opsme.qld.gov.au/directives/contracting.htm. Under this regime the skill capital of the public service goes to waste and tends to fall into disuse. As a consequence agencies become more dependent upon bought-in skill and the damaging myth of private sector superiority grows. This was a focus of the submission I emailed to my own management hierarchy in December, critiquing our cooperation with and implied approval of the practice of buying it in. My submission drew attention to the anomaly of taxpayers' money being used to buy in expertise while simultaneously facilitating the deterioration of the same kind of expertise in the public service and allowing it to atrophy.

That submission provided comment on the depleting effect the buying-it-in practice has upon public service reserves of skill in these fields. It was generated in the context of CorporateLink's hasty contrivance of a tender to be submitted to one of its own cluster agency clients. The client department was establishing a list of "approved providers" of higher level HR expertise, vetted by its own still resident HR experts and intended as a menu from which its line managers could choose when buying in talent to carry out an HR task in their local situation.

The great majority of approved providers on such lists are, by and large, from the private sector, and all on the list are, by definition, competitors with CorporateLink. This means CorporateLink's awareness of the ever-present threat that the client agency might take the work to someone else on the panel next time has clear effects upon the CorporateLink operatives. Apologists for competitive and commercialised practice usually point to the increased keenness on the part of the provider to excel as a beneficial effect of such a threat. However, the effects are not all beneficial. Another, for example, is never remarked upon, but occurs when the SSP supervisor "tones down" an element of honest feedback about an agency's managerial failings which her or his subordinate has included in a report on a grievance. The client's ignorance of its own organisational failings is perpetuated. No one intends that result, but it is nevertheless real.

**Issue 2**
Erosion of integrity standards resulting from adherence to commercialised modalities

Arguably the worst waste of all is that of our integrity reserves, even though this deterioration does not arise wilfully and intentionally, but rather carelessly.

Here are four examples from personal observation:

(i) The Consultancy Services Management Team met on 28 August 2006. When the minutes were circulated prior to the next meeting they failed to reflect three matters that appeared in my own contemporaneous notes, handwritten in my diary during the meeting. The first matter was a decision arrived at with no demurral to conceal from the client department the fact that a non-CorporateLink person was responsible for doing some work that CorporateLink would be charging the client for. I came prepared to the subsequent meeting with drafts of what I saw as more truthful re-writes of the three parts of the draft minutes which I thought deficient. An honest account of that choice to deceive was one of them. My dissent at this subsequent meeting from the minutes as circulated proved controversial. At last, however, the Director undertook to re-draft the minutes. When his re-draft was circulated some days later his treatment of that decision to deceive was unacceptable to me, falling short of the whole truth, in my view.

At the next meeting there was no opportunity to protest since the re-drafted minutes were never presented for acceptance. Instead, a decision to ban any further minuting of the meetings was announced. A bastardised form of minuting of this meeting did occur, however, and its product was presented at the next meeting. It could not stand comparison with real minutes. Soon the comparison itself became academic: one meeting later a decision was taken to stop having the meetings. These meetings had been standard operating procedure since the SSP began.

In my view, the original consensus decision on 28 August to practice a deception, the failure of the original draft of the minutes of the 28 August meeting to reflect this, the inadequacy of the Director's re-draft, the absence of any opportunity to dispute the accuracy of his re-draft, the decision to no longer minute the meetings and ultimately the abolition of the meetings themselves were motivated by the commercial imperative. Staying afloat in the marketplace depended upon maintaining a reputation for fair dealing. A decision to deceive the "customer" was clearly not in the best interests of the customer and obviously not something one would like the customer to know about. A government in the western democratic tradition is supposed to be accountable. Transparency in decision-making is required for accountability. That presupposes honest records. For a public service which implements the decisions of, and shares the values of, a western democratic government, honest records are accurate minutes of meetings. This truth is opaque to people operating in a commercialised mode and its opacity leads inevitably to debasement.

(ii) The second matter from the minutes of the 28 August meeting that concerned the announcement on 28 August that Consultancy Services Branch's TimeCapture (record of person/hours we can charge other agencies for) for July was 150,000 dollars in the red. I asked at the subsequent meeting that this clear statement, which I had a contemporaneous record of, be properly reflected in the minutes. The proposed re-draft of the minutes by the Director failed to include it. Why be surprised by that, one might say. Obviously, a business would try to hide from outsiders that it was not meeting costs. And in the hothouse atmosphere generated by the pretence of living in the business world it actually requires an effort of will to remind oneself that Consultancy Services Branch is a unit of public administration. Many of the parties from whom we are keeping information are also units of public administration.

(iii) The third matter from the August 28 minutes which I wanted minuted was the query I had raised in the meeting over the propriety of the branch's taking on a commission which we were offered by a particular unit of public administration. My query had followed the announcement by another consultant (i.e., officer) that this job was in prospect; but my query had been elided from the record. At the meeting, her announcement and the revenue it promised were greeted with enthusiasm unalloyed with doubt. Aside from mine. My doubt had motivated my query, and the query was unpopular, acting as a drag on the consensus satisfaction. Regardless, it happened at the meeting and should have been recorded. It elision reflected not a purposeful suppression of a contrary view, but a sincere non-attention to something that finds no place in the prevailing *Weltanschauung*, falls outside the groupthink. Therefore my insistence on its readmission to the warp and woof of our ongoing collegial governance of the branch (i.e., getting it into the record) created discomfort as a consequence of my colleagues' perception of themselves as doing nothing wrong[53]. All teams tend to develop unexamined, and usually unexaminable, shared ideological assumptions of which they are mostly unaware and which collectivise and compel their assent to things they might, as separate individuals, repudiate. The problem is not that our groupthink is more intense than most, but that it tends to elevate a consensus intrinsically pernicious, as well as being unsuited to proper public service. The motto that any income is good income (or, the customer is always right) has been contradicted only once in my experience of the Branch's meetings, by an officer who announced he had rejected a commission because it was not right to accept it.

[Aside from things I can personally attest to, my co-workers have reported (though not publicly) similar moral-free eagerness

---

[53] For this reason it would not be strange if my colleagues were to see my persistent querying as gratuitous hindrance.

on the part of the unit to accept paid jobs without examining the rightfulness of our involvement.]

(iv) At a meeting of the senior members (AO6, PO4, AO8) of Consultancy Services Branch's HRM team on August 1st this year there was discussion of the imminent departure of three AO6-level staff from the team. These were merely the latest in a long line of staff losses. The inevitable effect of our increasingly denuded state upon our capacity to meet our obligations to our clients was discussed. One of the AO6s proposed that the only sensible course was to admit the truth to our client departments: we did not have enough staff to meet their needs at the moment. The manager clearly rejected this proposal and articulated a different form of response to the clients, one which made no such admissions. Such obfuscation can only have been motivated, in my view, by the commercial imperative. That is, because admission of incapacity would lead to loss of face and shrivelling of the incoming work, both death to the consultancy's hopes, it was to be abstained from.

The following reflection is not an academic pastime, describing a particular ideology for sport or intellectual pleasure. It is presented to help make sense of the acts perpetrated by normally ethical public servants when recruited into the ideological community of commercialisation.

Just as no one involved in those transactions intends to encourage ignorance, no one who played a role in these four that I have offered from my own experience consciously chose to degrade their own or their subordinates' integrity. Regardless, it was nevertheless degraded. Thus here, where we are examining how we de-cultivate integrity, we need to try to understand the psychological mechanics of what's happening and how otherwise decent public servants, people of good will, can behave in these ways and continue to see themselves as acting in good faith. To understand it, I believe, one needs to think about the idea of ideological community.

Ideological group cohesion (i.e., community) arises in part at least as a result of the fear of being "outside". It serves our interests to stay within the safety of our clan. Then practices grow up and

Michael O'Neill

become entrenched, because they serve that interest. This happens instinctively. Then the practices are codified and enshrined as ideology. Next the ideology itself begins to generate fresh acts, and new recruits whose entire mindset is co-terminous with the ideology that spawned them. That is, the new recruits and their acts begin to fall into line with the ideology. The previous ethics of the agents of those acts, the moral precepts they were committed to before the new fashion assumed dominance, become irrelevant. What has now started to form is an ideological community, and within it its agents begin comprehensively and exclusively to act in ways the ideology makes OK. One can be born into such a community or one can adopt it as a result of finding it attractive or one can be told to join it. Who pays the piper calls the tune.

A good example of the intellectual technology which is spawned by the commercialisation ideology this submission is concerned with is the wide use of the tag "commercial-in-confidence", a device enthusiastically adopted in Consultancy Services discussions. Interactions among commercialised entities default to concealment, as anti-collusion legislation attests. Concealment is, by definition, antithetical to the public service values of transparency and openness. But commercial-in-confidence is a first resort and one unashamedly adopted among us now without any thought given to the way it detours around our ethical obligation to transparency. Commercial-in-confidence is equal to saying, Yes we are required to be transparent, but in this case (or that case, or whichever case we choose) we will not be transparent because it may damage our commercial chances.

### Issue 3
Diminution of intra-public service goodwill (social capital)

One consequence of Consultancy Services' adoption of the commercialised modality is a readiness to engage in self-promotion. This is a practice utterly endemic to the commercial world and, since the commercial world osmotically dictates the cultural atmosphere that contains us all, the way the sea contains fish, we are all always at risk of being contaminated by that practice. This means, I believe, that when the officers of Consultancy Services pick up the implicit instruction to adopt the practice of self-promotion officially the predisposition already present meshes easily with it. As a consequence, engaging in frank self-promotion does not even appear to embarrass us now. (Once boasters were reviled by conventional morality. No more.)

A difficulty arises, however, with the people in the departments who form the audience for this self-promotion. While we are proof against it, it does embarrass them. If they are among those whose actual experience as clients of ours has soured their view of our skills and capability (and these are legion), it embarrasses severely. And irritates. We put ourselves intentionally in the same category as toothpaste hucksters who ambush them on their lounge chairs every night with slick, 30-second TV ads. We invite our target punters to revile us for presuming to treat them like fools.

Even if it weren't true that many of our targets are aware of how far short of our claimed expertise we fall, our self-promotion would still be counter-productive. Our targets expect to be bombarded day in day out by self-congratulatory, over-hyped and deceitful messages from promoters trying to sell them soap, sausage and ski trips, but they resent it when it comes from public service units whose claims, which they know to be exaggerated, are presented with a straight face and the expectation of being taken at face value. The parties on both sides of these promotional transactions know that demur (or laughing out loud), though demanded by rationality, is prohibited in such situations because no one could bear the loss of face. But whatever face might be saved by the dependable devotion to decorum which we can count on in all parties, what is not saved is social capital[54].

---

[54] Below, where I elaborate upon Issue of Concern 4(ii), in the final paragraphs of the section on condonement of growback, I offer information indicating in

It is my view, what leads to this tension in the way units of public administration regard each other, a layered state where formal exchanges belie what lies below, is the direct result of adopting practices which take as their model behaviours *de rigueur* in the commercialised ethos[55].

Conversations about the quality of SSPs occur throughout the service. One person reports that his/her agency is the client of an SSP whose capability to manage the background, low level logistics that underpin the client's recruitment process is inept enough to have resulted in legal suits by disadvantaged job applicants against the client agency costing thousands of dollars and souring the atmosphere. But the SSP's capability had ineluctably eroded under the pressure of staff departures and consequent low morale. The higher the proportion of new staff, the worse the service provided. The worse the service provided, the greater the exasperation of the client agency personnel. The greater the client's exasperation, the lower the morale in its SSP. The lower the SSP's morale, the more its staff want to defect.

**Issue 4**
Practical difficulties arising out of Queensland's SSP model

(i) An under-utilised consultant cohort on life support: how it turns productivity into busywork

Although client departments are theoretically meant to buy their higher level HR services from their SSPs, it is a common complaint in the internal councils of Consultancy Services that

---

what bad odour Consultancy Services' ability is held. That information, while illustrative of certain matters in relation to growback, is relevant here as well, since it is equally illustrative of the parlous effect upon social capital among the state's public servants which the actions of Consultancy Services have contributed to.

[55] This same enthrallment to commercial ideals can also produce *inaction*, where the motivator is not image creation, as above, but image management.

"they" (the officers within an agency displaying unwillingness to send work to the SSP) don't want to "send the work here" because they will then have nothing to do and no way to justify their own existence. Now, in spite of the fact that the views held by "they" are quite opposite, they are equally sincerely held. It is not possible to avoid concluding from such lower echelon squabbles that Departments and Agencies are paying, and have been paying, lip service, while keeping going the arrangements they know bring home the bacon. That is, they have "grown back", or never pruned in the first place.

The effect upon consultancy services units within SSPs of the client departments' refusal to use them while countenancing growback at home is that those consultancy services units are withering on the vine. Because they are powerless to demand the work and at the same time required to show some reason for their continued existence, and because they are ideologically captured by the commercialised self-concept, these units of public administration, believe they must find income or go out of business. This is an actual fear expressed in exactly those terms during a discussion within CorporateLink, and, I expect, one not unknown in other SSPs. It is a fear real enough to cause these consultancy services units to pour a great deal of energy into trying to find a way to be profitable. And, because of the excesses and, ironically, the success, of the rhetoric that attended their birth, becoming profitable soon becomes their only objective. They become ends in themselves. That way only madness lies.

For the best such a public servant-staffed consultancy unit could hope for would be to become an independent profit centre that brought in not only enough money to pay for itself but also so much more revenue on top that the dollars would compensate the government for the embarrassment of the unit's existence and the hostility it would create in the constituency. There it would be in competition in the consultancy industry with slick private sector firms. And not even likely to win. Private sector consultancy firms are unconstrained by *Public Sector Ethics Act*-inspired Codes of Conduct, are staffed by people cultivated in the ruth-free private sector, and are unhindered by sheet-anchors like myself to whom the ethos of the private sector is not something to aspire to.

The reality, then, in fee-for-service outfits is that a significant number of public servants who would still be earning their keep had they been allowed to remain in their Departments doing exactly the same kind of higher level HR work they are ostensibly situated in an SSP to do, are instead devoting their energies to profitless (I use the word advisedly) busywork and endeavours bent on bolstering the charade of commercialisation. One of those endeavours is the seemingly endless pursuit of a perfect system of measuring our consultants' "earnings". An unconscionable proportion of our human resources, i.e., of our work time and energy, goes into meetings, planning and experimentation concerning such arcana as hurdle rates, revenue streams, billing styles, accounting systems and charging protocols; and getting right the important ratio of billable hours to non-billable hours, or, in other words, getting the balance perfect between time allocated to administration and supervisory duty and other "down" time and time that can bought by our clients and thus turned into "money" for the improvement of our "bottom line". Furthermore, this is a ratio that must be perfected differentially, i.e., for each level in the hierarchy. Such complex calibration, though diverting, is not easy. The ratio has to be determined, then revisited regularly and determined all over again.

(ii) Condonement of agencies' misrepresentation of the purposes of recruitment (growback)

This issue arises from the behaviour of those agencies, who meet their post-July 2003 (i.e., the SSP start date) needs for higher level HR services by redeveloping their own internal expertise. In short, by "growing back".

Originally this activity was camouflaged by devising creative ways to rename functions so that they wouldn't need to be relinquished to the SSP or re-categorising existing functions as strategic in order to keep them; but increasingly those pretences are being dropped and open recruitment of HR Officers whose work mirrors the work of officers in the SSP occurs. A cluster agency whom Consultancy Services offers Workplace Health & Safety services to appears to stop requiring our service. The Consultancy Services officer who liaises with this client reports this at a meeting in the unit. Someone asks, "Who's doing their workplace health and safety?" The answer is an unremarkable, "They've done growback."

This new recruitment is not a difficulty for the departments doing the growing back. They would appear to have decided that the prohibition, to which they have given formal consent only, simply must be flouted for the good governance of their organisations. It is a practical difficulty, however, for the body which oversights the SSP initiative, probably the Shared Service Agency at this time, since the alternative to condonement of this departmental disobedience is to confront the matter and risk exposing to public view the frank assessments which departments make no secret of in corridor talk but are more diplomatic about in formal settings. Thus a client department of CorporateLink advertises for a half dozen HR operatives to do higher-level HR tasks which CorporateLink was created to do and meets with tactful non-interference.

It is not put.

The conviction motivating the influential persons in the withholding client agency above would be hard to dislodge. It is clear to all that the particular CorporateLink unit concerned haemorrhages staff constantly, many finding a berth among the very client agencies whom last week they were supposed to be servicing. That staff movement phenomenon, when seen from the losing side, is vilified as "poaching" of our staff, the word used in Consultancy Services' inner councils. The trace of indignation in that expression is a leftover from before the speakers moved into the brave new commercialised world. In this world such poaching is par for the course and, like all else here, devoid of moral tone. Viewed from the side of the staff members trying to get out, this jumping ship is merely a career survival necessity. Job applications are escape pods. I am almost the only staff member in my group who has not been applying for jobs elsewhere. All of the haemorrhaged, of course, had done so.

(iii) Consequences of an organisational self-concept removed from reality

Consultancy Services Branch, encouraged by the official rhetoric to see itself as a player in the consultancy industry, sells or tries to sell higher level HR and other services not only to Departments and Agencies in its cluster, but also to other Departments and, increasingly, organisations not state public service entities. This conception of itself as a commercial agent who relates to other parties via a cash nexus has led to internal debate about the practice of "selling" services among internal elements of CorporateLink itself, establishing that same fee-for-service nexus between subparts of the Branch itself.

The nonsensical nature of such internal charging has flickered across the consciousness of at least one CorporateLink person, whose discussion paper for senior management canvassing internal charging, warned that transactions between our own subparts might mistakenly be thought to be trade in real dollars, but nevertheless accepted the validity of our cash nexus with outside agencies, the dollars we exchange with whom are implied to be real. The unenthusiastic reception this paper got might indicate some have seen the unwisdom of carrying the commercial self-concept that far. Perhaps it is seen as safe to eschew this insanity within our four walls where such a lapse won't be seen and won't attract the charge of treachery; but I believe there is little hope that CorporateLink will see that it is itself engaging at a sector level in the same charade, and, as a result eschew commercialisation. The turnaround will not come from within. The nil response to my December email, I think, confirms this.

However, it would, I think, be reasonable for the SDPC to take that flicker of insight and magnify it to the scale of the public service as a whole and place it before the state government. It may be, of course, that it makes sense for the Crown to charge the Crown for services to itself in situations that lend themselves by virtue of some peculiarity to that prima facie nonsense, but it is hard to see ours as one of those situations.

The fee-for-service modality which CorporateLink at least, if not all of the other SSPs, subsequently embraced as its praxis[56] needs to be looked at. I attach an account (Attachment 2) of a process within Consultancy Services which illustrates the consequences of imagining our continued existence depends upon the image we create in some fantasised "marketplace".

Fee-for-service, however, is itself mere symptom. Our captivity is more profound. Investigative journalist Brian Toohey once complained that Tony Fitzgerald, in his Commission of Inquiry into Possible Illegal Activities and Associated Police Misconduct, upon which Fitzgerald reported in 1989, didn't deliver enough scalps. It's probably true. Fitzgerald delivered us a blueprint instead. He was interested in a remedy beyond the next day's headlines. As a result, much that grew out of his work represented institutional structures intended to prevent the

---

[56] Fee-for-service is a practice increasingly associated with SSP operation in Queensland. Its insidious effects upon public service integrity are canvassed in Issue 2. Those effects are perhaps more likely to spread for the following reason. The fee-for-service operating style is a jealous God. Like Capital itself, from which it springs, fee-for-service cannot tolerate the co-existence of other modalities in the "marketplace". It must dominate and convert all, and for the same reason as its progenitor. Pockets of genuine industry and humaneness in which individuals merely want to work will always spontaneously re-appear and will tend to expose fee-for-service's inanity and threaten it. Thus some of an SSP's staff may desire not to operate on a fee-for-service basis, but before long the SSP will be brought to heel. Otherwise it may become obvious that better work can be done at lesser cost when there is no cash nexus, but a mere agreement between client and SSP to do the work and get better at it and more familiar with the client's nature over time, just as used to happen when staff within the client agency did the work.

growback of corruption by altering the conditions that nurtured it and providing different formative influences to redirect the practice of citizenship in Queensland towards integrity and away from the corrosive phenomenon of loyalty: the CJC, EARC and ultimately codified exhortation like the *Public Sector Ethics Act 1994* and explicit encouragement and support in the form of the *Whistleblower Protection Act 1994* for those who would individually extend the range of Fitzgerald's work.

The Act, Queensland Transport attests, calls for "public sector management to be ethical, professional and accountable". Not just managers, but management. The abstract noun is significant. For while integrity is not hard to understand, Fitzgerald's societal or macro-level vision and pedagogy were a big ask. We can't sustain them most of the time, and less so the further into the past his work retreats. We find it easier looking at individual perpetrators and instances. Big pictures require too much mental and moral effort, creating exhaustion commensurate with our anti-intellectualism. We keep our eyes down, steadfastly averting them from the behaviour of our collective whole. We do not protest or call in the Integrity Commissioner when entire segments of the public service suddenly take a right turn from the ethical path and explicitly, proudly adopt the livery of that very ethos of which "those greedy coppers" with the famous taste for sweet little fish were merely symptoms. We don't see it when the very System itself is captured, bushwhacked and brainwashed by the fad of the times. Greed is good, profit is its priest, the marketplace its church and we merely serve. Our catechism is re-writ. What once were vices are now just ways of doing business. We ape the minutiae of the ways of the Captains of Industry and hope some of their "success" rubs off on us. Fitzgerald's hard won principles end up as pieties in a parallel world, the one we used to live in.

For what Fitzgerald couldn't predict – it was more than ten years away – was the coming of Shared Service Provision to the sector. When that adventure first loomed the folklore began to grow around it, proclaiming that the inhabitants of the sector, long contemned in the popular imagination (that bond slave of the bond slave of Capital, the Media) for their presumed second-rate "public service mentality", would move boldly and at one stroke on to the very catwalk of business style, dressed in bottom lines, draped in business development, comely with competition, *décolletage* with contracts and commerce. The shared service provider push was a progressive force lifting us higher, making us better. Soon we'd be business class. (We were already calling our agencies businesses.) Our efficiency and productivity would rocket upwards under the famously energising influence of that way of life. We would be the poor cousin working in Capital's home as a domestic keeping her house running no more. We'd be participants in the larger world of the private sector. We'd have a *part*[57].

A clear indication of the hazard of self-concept removed from reality and a captivity so profound as to be almost invisible is to be observed in the connection our SSP has with a particular for-profit organisation which runs workshops purporting to be professionally oriented. Our CEO has received their award, or so it appears from International Quality & Productivity Centre's (IQPC) brochure advertising their October 2006 three-day conference titled Shared Services For Government 2006. That brochure encourages organisations to become sponsors of IQPC's money-making activities and tells these prospects that becoming a sponsor will give them direct "access to your target market", will enhance "your company or brand position", will increase "your competitive selling advantage" and achieve for them a "high profile association with a key industry event". We are publicly, and I presume proudly, thoroughly integrated into this commercial venture. Price of attendance: $5149.60. There doesn't appear to be any going back. Our lot is cast in with them. Keeping a decent

---

[57] This passage from an unpublished work of fiction dealing with the modern public service expresses the attitude being defined here: "Enron? What's that? Pretty soon, Man, we be toolin' down the freeway in the Merc. We be behind the wheel, Man; and sittin' right beside us, Capital, and she got her hand in our *crotch*. We be players, man, playing a part in the private sector. *Private* parts, Man! This sexy or what?" (By permission of the author.)

separation between state and market no longer appears on our radar except as something we should zap like an enemy sub. We're bought. This philosophical sell out is not merely of interest to dilettante ethicists. It has practical consequences.

Dr Phelps, past AMA President, now does television commercials for a health product. Her public defence of medicos going into this level of marketing blithely undermines the ethical obligation upon the medical profession to refrain from exploiting, even unconsciously, the unequal power and influence ratio between doctor and the patient for whom the product may or may not be prescribed[58].

Whether spruiking from the footpath with straw boater and loud hailer or perched on the podium with three-piece suit and PowerPoint, a huckster's aim is profit and his ethics equally at risk. Perhaps more risk surrounds the latter, for the pronouncements from the podium penetrate the listener's scepticism more surely and their having been bought and paid for is harder to spot. Our endorsement of IQPC, be it ever so discreet, joins us up with this world nevertheless.

(iv) The inbuilt obstacle for SSPs offering consultancy to Departments

The location and nature of the field of operation in which higher level HR services to a Department or Agency are delivered are organisationally intimate. That is, the work is done deep in the bowels of the client organisation and requires that detail of the client's inner workings become known to the SSP consultant. It follows that much background or environmental information is learned and local practice observed by the agent delivering the service, regardless of where that agent hails from. Add to that that the bad news about any less than optimal management behaviour or organisational dysfunction which such work reveals ought to be available to the Department or Agency concerned, and available in

---

[58] *The Australian*, 22 September 2006.

ways that cannot be glossed over or shelved unresolved. Departments and Agencies serious about maintaining a watch on organisational health and the eradication of bad management practices that periodically develop within them have long understood that such diagnostic intelligence has to be assiduously pursued and responded to. There is enough corporate memory, experience and awareness of these traditions in most agencies to know that the best functionaries to discover such information and feed it back up the line on a progressive basis are its own officers, whose tenured security, coupled with commitment to the organisation they have a long-term psychological contract of employment with, embolden them to tell it the way it is[59].

Corporate memory, experience and awareness are some of the reasons many agencies were reluctant to give over tactical (as the jargon of the time had it) HR and other organisational functions to their new SSPs – some were not merely reluctant but recalcitrant enough to refuse – and many of those who did comply began immediately to countenance grow-back, as discussed above in 4(ii).

(v) Myths and Reality concerning accountability and efficiency

The lodestar of accountability is used to justify commercialisation generally, and the fee-for-service modality in particular. The argument is that there has to be a translation of all our effort and actions into cash equivalence so that we, as recipients of services and as taxpayers footing the bill, can use the same methods to assure ourselves we are not being dudded as obtain in the commercial world. That is, if the service is not up to

---

[59] This is true in spite of the startling spectacle from time to time produced by gun outside consultant reviewers who find the results of chronic neglect when called in after the utter collapse of an organisation. Their work is cut out for them precisely *by* an organisation's avoidance of progressive diagnosis and treatment.

the mark, take your purchasing dollar elsewhere; or see what a service costs in the free enterprise world and assume it costs the same in the public service world. If it costs more, we are "entitled" to conclude it is being inefficiently done. Aside from the fantasy of the private enterprise world's real nature that this is built upon, it ignores the fact that accountability and efficiency are not in the exclusive possession of that world. Public servants of integrity have understood and practised accountability and measured efficiency for decades before this alien mode enthralled the minds of those recently advising governments. Integrity is the *sine qua non* of our endeavour, and accountability its guarantee. Without integrity, no amount of modish fee-for-service practice will produce genuine accountability. If the government's real spur to action is the conviction that the public service needs reform, then that should be addressed head on, without recourse to the stalking horse of commercialisation. The Commonwealth public service adopted that honest approach to streamlining itself in the 1980s, with the support of the unions, and succeeded without abandoning what makes civil service unique. False beliefs about where accountability is to be found make public servants aspire, as I put it in my December 2005 plea to management, to "behave like the free-wheeling private sector, exercising ruthless choice and rejecting those whose capacities we, in our pursuit of excellence, judge second rate". The unglamorous reality, however, is more like what happens in CorporateLink when it takes delivery of an unserviceable product. For example, CorporateLink pays (one assumes, at any rate) for an attendance recording system for staff called Alloc8. Alloc8 does not allow staff to truthfully represent their hours of work in certain situations. This shortcoming has been canvassed in official fora, including some I have attended. There are important reasons to do with workplace health and safety and maintaining the legal right to workers compensation in the event of accident occurring during unrecorded working time which make this deficient software unacceptable. We continue to use Alloc8.

In December I also attempted to throw a spotlight on to the increasingly common commercial style determining SSP activities. Unconvinced readers of the present submission might be sceptical enough, as I put it then, to "pooh-hooh the idea that such a widely accepted practice could ever be seen in a different light" from that which it presently is seen in, and to go on to say, "everyone is doing it, what can go wrong?" One who sets out to rebut those readers' defence of the status quo might supply a substantive answer to the question and point to the various inquiries that have illustrated that something indeed can go wrong and will need to be inquired into, no matter how widespread the abuse is. That eventuality will be (and has been already for some) an experience of public service accountability from the sharp end.

Yet we defend deception and lies, which we do not see as deception and lies, by resort to the rubric of "commercial-in-confidence", modelling ourselves on the profit-driven. We are encouraged in that action by those in influential positions who "scientifically" promote the fee-for-service modality as the style for the new public service and, if they do see the potentially corrupting effect of it, justify it as merely a method of securing accountability; and without accountability, they argue, how will our customers know they are getting value for money? That we are referring here not to "customers" but to fellow public servants or citizens of the state seems now a truth too far buried below an overburden of free market conditioning to even register.

A more useful tack to take for one attempting to disabuse public servants of these beliefs might be to look at failure of the public service community to critique in genuine and ruthless way the "business case" that was put forward for changing the way the public service supplies itself with corporate services. That case was received so confidently, despite its assumption that public servants could without detriment to precious things switch to an alien way of operating, that one must ask[60] how it could have gained credence and adherents in the first place.

_____

Writing in the *Harvard Business Review*, Dan Lovallo and Daniel Kahneman, a business scholar and a psychologist, examined the phenomenon of monumental scale organisational and business failures, citing three examples from across the developed world with a combined price tag of cost overruns and share market losses of scores of billions of dollars and decades of completion timeframe blow-out.[61] Lovallo and Kahneman reject the conventional wisdom explanations of such debacles in favour of seeing them as the result of flawed decision-making based on "delusional optimism". They draw attention to some disturbing facts: Most large capital investment projects come in late and over budget, never living up to expectations. More than 70% of new manufacturing plants in North America...close within their first decade of operation." The vast majority of efforts to enter new markets "end up being abandoned within a few years." (p. 58) The authors identify the culprits as cognitive and social phenomena that magnify what they call "people's native optimism". The third of these culprits they call Organisational Pressure, an intra-organisational political behaviour that seeks to "emphasise the positive and downplay the negative":

Organisations also actively discourage pessimism, which is often interpreted as disloyalty. The bearers of bad news tend to become pariahs, shunned and ignored by other employees. When pessimistic options are suppressed, while optimistic ones are rewarded, an organisation's ability to think critically is undermined.   The optimistic biases of individual employees become mutually reinforcing, and unrealistic views of the future are validated by the group. (p. 60)

The same insight is expressed by Michael Leunig in an article[62] subtitled "The time has come to be honest with ourselves

---

[61] Delusions of Success: How Optimism Undermines Executives' Decisions, *Harvard Business Review*, July 2003. Their three main examples included a combined project mounted by the national governments of four European countries, with an original proposed budget of $20 billion.

[62] Lest we forget, A2 supplement, *The Age*, Saturday, October 14, 2006, p.16.

and stop pretending we live in nicey-nicey, happy-clappy land." Leunig refers to Norman Dixon's *On the Psychology of Military Incompetence*, from which we learn that one of the principal factors in military disasters is "the inability of commanders to heed bad news or inconvenient intelligence reports; preferring to lie to themselves, their troops and their nation and to rely on triumphal thinking."

We also were offered an "inconvenient intelligence report". Everyone, nearly, agreed quietly to ignore its essence, dismissing it as something we could learn from merely[63]. Otherwise, from within the ranks of the cheering spectators the nakedness that the promenading emperor's arse displayed utterly escaped notice because of our eagerness to be like the private sector.

## The Elephant

My experience over the last three years and five months, that is, since CorporateLink began, has been curious. The sense that something is wrong and only I can see it obtrudes itself upon consciousness first as mere discomfort, then as a self-denigrating conclusion that one's discomfort is invalid because one's ideas are mistaken and so on through a series of manifestations until, all others explanations having been eliminated by their obvious inadequacy, one has to face the fact that there is an elephant in the room, between us and the picture window, blocking the view.

---

[63] In late 2004 a Performance Audit by the New South Wales Auditor-General exposed the actual savings for the first real year of that state's shared services exercise, the earlier predictions of whose success were a vital influence upon Queensland's adoption of the idea, as a mere $13.6m, or 5% of the projected accumulated savings by 2006 of $297m, and at the same time revealed the implementation cost to be $79.4m. Queensland's response was to issue an analysis of the NSW audit and to show how we were avoiding that state's errors of implementation. By then we were near a year and half into implementation, and no one suggested stopping. Not in public anyway. Saving, after all, is self-evidently important, face especially.

Everyone is calmly going about their business, commenting on the lovely prospect without as though the elephant were invisible. The elephant at last is not invisible. If only its handler were here to coax it away. But alas, he is not, and nobody here speaks elephant.

**Attachment 1** (to Nobody Here Speaks Elephant)

**To:**      "name suppressed @ Corporatelink" <name suppressed@corporatelink.qld.gov.au>
**cc:**      name suppressed <name suppressed@corporatelink.qld.gov.au>
**From:**   Michael P O'Neill/cp1/qdot/au
**Date:**   19/12/2005 02:55:10 PM

Subject:   tender

Dear D......

Thanks for the voicemails Friday and today asking me to help write [The Department]'s tender response. Your request brings a serious problem which we are all facing into sharp focus for me, and I will try here to make a start on explaining it, not only to you but to myself as well. I will cc this reply to S....... and B....... because the whole issue is very important to us all, it seems to me.

I think that a worrying trend developing in the public service is illustrated by [The Department]'s tender process, and particularly by their neglecting to proactively ensure we were at least welcome tenderers.

When the government chose two and half years ago to implement shared service provision in the public service clustered agencies were intended to accept the services being provided back to them. Alleged economies of scale, believable perhaps in relation to some unsophisticated HR functions, made sense on that basis. Then some clustered agencies arrogated the right to NOT take services from their ssps. These agencies put, and are putting, the work out to tender. (I, at least, haven't heard of any policy reverse by government that justifies this.) The result is that the public sector is being turned into a buyers' market in which an agency can shop around for private consultancies to do their work for them, in the process nurturing and husbanding the expertise of private sector consultants with taxpayers' money, while simultaneously facilitating the deterioration of the same kind of expertise in the public service and allowing it to atrophy. Unfortunately, however, the lure of being seen to behave like the free-wheeling private sector, exercising ruthless choice and rejecting those whose capacities we, in our pursuit of excellence, judge second rate, is seductive.

As far as I can see, this all runs counter to the public statement of Premier Beattie about reversing the trend towards outsourcing public service work to consultants and dumbing down the public sector. As well, I suspect it has policy implications for this and successive governments, which, to my knowledge, are not being discussed frankly with government, or sanctioned by government. The responsibility to alert government to debilitating trends which our vantage point in operational work makes us intimate with is not central agencies' exclusively.

Departments are flouting the principles espoused by the Premier, in my view, and this creates a Toni Hoffman situation for us. I think we are in danger if we simply collude, or, worse, participate enthusiastically in the delusion, all the while telling ourselves we will somehow "go out of business" - a concept that makes sense in private enterprise only - if we don't get in step. The danger is that we will be seen in retrospect to have been complicit when a Geoff Davies-type inquiry occurs. One might pooh-hooh the idea that such a widely accepted practice could ever be seen in a different light than that which it presently is seen in. One might say, everyone is doing it, what can go wrong? Drs Buckland, Scott and Keating and Mr Nuttall and Ms Edmond and Mr Leck certainly thought that way. But if the emperor is naked, it will out.

The apparent impropriety of action such as [The Department]'s in seeking tenders for HR services rather than accepting that CorporateLink has the commission ought not, in my view, to be tolerated and humoured.

For my part, I used to be in the advertising and marketing industry in the private sector, where my job was to engage in bullshit. I gave it away as an immoral occupation and began to practice the vocation of public service. Touting for business, with the smudging of the truth it entails, and the implicit acceptance that such practices in the public service are ethical, is, I'm afraid, beyond my moral boundary. I conscientiously object and may not do it.

In fact, it's my opinion that none of us should. We should rather challenge and confront it formally, as an agency. The word on the street is that departments served by other SSPs wish we were their partner because CorporateLink is seen as the leading SSP. Whatever virtues brought us that reputation, I think it can't hurt to add more integrity and courage.

Regards

Michael O'Neill

**Attachment 2** (to Nobody Here Speaks Elephant)
How Did We Fall For SSPs?

The Queensland Public Service had suffered from being, as Professor Peter Coaldrake observed, "professionally unattended" for a very long time when, seventeen years ago, Tony Fitzgerald first alarmed the people of Queensland with his revelations of a public service with degraded ethics. The high profile police corruption he examined was merely its most prominent feature. The condition of the service has been, more or less well, addressed by a series of persons and programs of recovery since.

However, it has proven resistant to treatment. The professional inattention Coaldrake identified had left deep damage and many elements of the service remained withered and in need of succour.  Its incapacity, for initiative and responsiveness, especially, has continued to hamstring governments which during the nineties and in the new century have desired to respond to the society they governed, but found themselves shackled to a public service with traditions which fitted an earlier era.  That era was a time when authoritarian regimes of thought and loyalty-based forms of interaction were predominant, and informed the service's real nature, albeit lightly overlaid with an upbeat, modern palaver, a coloration it took on perforce in the immediate aftermath of Fitzgerald.  The direct link, for example, between loyalty the seeming virtue and its potential for engendering corruption was still, despite the object lessons sent to jail, not understood – except by the cynical and disaffected, and by those ambitious enough to exploit it for their own ends.

Aside from tearing its hair out, government needed to act.

Independently of that problem, someone has the useful, if overdue, idea that economies of scale lie waiting to be realised by combining some fundamental services, like payroll, which agencies each are currently having done separately.

Now someone else conflates the proposed solution to the duplication of services problem with an idea for solving the responsiveness problem, but the hybrid solution is based on an inadequate understanding of human complexity and organisational behaviour, and an unfortunately accurate idea of how biddable people can be made even in the absence of genuinely logical argument.  A one-size-fits-all solution is proposed: "Your public service is not responsive enough.  The workforce in the private sector is very responsive.  In the private sector things happen because money changes hands.  Let's do it in the public service.  It will have the same effect here.  Let's set up bodies which can charge the agencies money and which depend on getting that money to stay afloat.  That'll make everyone edgy and sharp.  Take this SSPill and wash it down with fee-for-service water and you'll be right."  Government, desperate, buys it.

Michael O'Neill

Unfortunately for the people of Queensland, including its public servants, an inadequate understanding of motivation is just that. Public servants, too, know something of human complexity, their own and that of the citizenry they serve. They know something of motivation, too. Their work throws them hard up against the way human complexity impedes and interferes with the task of motivating people to cooperate with and not obstruct the implementation of legislation, a process which it is the *raison d'être* of public servants to facilitate.

Were their first-hand understanding of these things to be elucidated and validated, there is no reason to suspect that Queensland's public servants would need gulling with a commercialisation sales pitch to generate dedication. That is, there is no reason to assume that they won't respond to a straightforward reform agenda as well as, or better than, they respond to one organised by the gung-ho whose motto is, if it moves make money out of it. The deep irony in our situation, of course, is that this "money" is as phoney as the sales pitch whose central tenet it is.

But all of this is hard to follow and takes time and, even worse, faith; and then you have to mix in the right amounts of each.

So what'll it be? Real McCoy?

Nah, I'm in a hurry, Mate. Just gimme the snake oil.

What, straight?

For Pete's sake! All right, drop of Clayton's. Can you break a fifty?

Aah, Mate! You won't get much change out of that.

# TOOLKIT ITEM 5
## Using the Machine's Own Rhetoric against It

ORGANISATIONS issue policies and statements of vision filled with motherhood and spin. Education Departments proclaim child protection policies which purport to preserve kids from abuse, but are repeatedly shown to do no such thing. What employee-cum-abuser desists when he suddenly remembers there's a policy statement against what he's doing? He doesn't need a policy statement to know what he is doing is wrong. The policy is in place to protect the organisation, not the child.

Such policies, and they're issued on a wide range of subjects, proudly and publicly adopt postures which functionaries of the organisation routinely violate in camera. When they do, it's a useful tactic quite often to turn, on behalf of the victim, the organisation's rhetoric back upon itself.

This principle underlay my response to a situation of oppression my clients and I faced and enabled me, on their behalf, to tactically stymie my organisation's attempt to gain access to my confidential records of the issues clients sought my help with. In this case it was the policy governing the operation of the Employee Assistance Program.

The lead up to the crisis situation involved, like the Friday Afternoon Email adventure, a fairly routine email. Not one I sent, but one I received from the Freedom of Information officer asking me to release my case files on counselling interactions with a certain group of staff to him for scrutiny. Legal and Legislative wanted all my files which related in any way to a particular staff member who knew I had seen these clients and wanted to know what they had said about him. For the FOI officer this was an unexceptional request and consistent with the legislation. For me it was a violation of the confidentiality provision written into the EAP policy, which had been adopted by the Department years earlier.

My refusal to release my files was instinctive and immediate. Only later did I realise that it brought about a stand-off between the official EAP policy and the absolute obligation upon

Departments to comply with the law, which, after all, is what they exist to implement. When the cloud of emotion inside me cleared I saw what I needed to do next. It began to fit together as though it was planned strategy. If it was planned, the planning happened in a split second with no conscious input from me.

What was the strategy? I shall let someone else answer.

At about the time this was happening I was asked by a Social Work academic to be one of 30 practitioners contributing ethical dilemmas they faced in their workplaces to her thesis research [64]. I became case three. This is how she described the strategy:

In the third case, [he][65] mounted a highly strategic course of action when faced with the threat of release of confidential counselling files. His strategy focused on forcing an open confrontation with the department designed to trigger disciplinary action against him for refusing to release the files. In describing this strategy, he said:

> *My intention was to force the department to announce publicly that they were disciplining me for refusing to break faith with their own policy...[B]y bringing down upon my head the discipline which I would immediately appeal I would move the theatre of operations into the wider world.*

Another part to this strategy was his prediction, stated clearly to higher authorities, that he could foresee legal action being taken by his clients against the department if they became aware that their files had been released.

The stand-off was eventually resolved in favour of upholding the confidentiality provisions of the EAP policy. My files were

---

[64] McAuliffe, Donna, Beyond the hypothetical: practitioner experiences of ethical dilemmas in front-line social work, Ph. D. thesis, University of Queensland, 2000

[65] The thesis used pseudonyms.

exempted from scrutiny by order of the Director-General. (The FOI applicant could have appealed this decision to the Information Commissioner, who was independent of the Department. As luck would have it, he didn't.) But don't relax. For although this story suggests the great, heaving bulk of the status quo is somnolent and vulnerable to guerrilla initiative, its retainers never rest. You will not get to use twice any scrap of policy that you turn back upon the organisation in the cause of justice. The immediate sequel to the success story I have just told you is an education on this point; this is how it fell out:

An official rewrite of the EAP policy to obviate future opportunities for ambush found itself on the agenda quicker than a stock market correction. Because when someone wins, someone else loses; and, our species being what it is, when two parts of an organisation contend, both having right on their side, the losing side can feel sharply the need to have the last word.

Now, the particular bit of its own rhetoric I had used against the Department was, providentially, of my own design. For employee assistance was new to the Department when it appointed me, but not new to me. So, I drafted the new EAP policy myself, informed by wound-licking reflection upon past struggles, slipping in the fateful confidentiality provision. I was taking advantage of the penchant of organisations for motherhood statements, which they generally don't expect to later bite them.

But, as we've seen, bite them it did, and the hides of the defeated officers of Legal and Legislative bore the evidentiary tooth marks. These officers, however, were minions of The Law, and between their own teeth sucked upon a more august teat than I, Themis to my Dike. They proposed a *grand*motherhood amendment to the policy, which re-ordered the mammarian hierarchy. Confidentiality was OK as long as it didn't conflict with The Law. This found favour higher up - how could it not - and the loophole closed.

C'est la vie.

# TOOL KIT ITEM 6
## You get fired enough, you get to like it

A CONSEQUENCE of my expulsion from the service is that my interest in all this tactical and strategic information becomes increasingly academic. I miss the whiff of grapeshot, of course, and the scent of singed $500 suits, but not having to don the greasy overalls every day has cut the urgency to confront ugly, unethical action.

If you're still in the thick of it, however, and were attracted by the word subversive in the title, I put this *Manual for Square Pegs* together to round up some stuff I'd learned from conflict between my idea of what was a good thing and the organisation's.

Sometimes as a social worker you can begin to doubt your grasp of reality. That's a useful corrective at times. However, when those doubts arise as seemingly the only explanation for your inability to make your organisation (as embodied in your boss) see sense over a matter of ethical choice, there can be something more going on. It may well be that you have come up against the mismatch between your social work ethics and the ethics of your employer. We often delay admitting to ourselves that things have come to such a pass, for mostly the two sets of ethics rub along OK and a certain complacency grows up which we don't want to disturb. Admitting that conflict exists, on the other hand, arouses emotions we'd rather not feel. Nevertheless, it happens. It's handy then to have a manual for threading your way through it. Better still to have one beforehand. So I have put a very simple one together here by trawling over the bouts I have had with the dragon[66] in my work. A poor thing, but mine own.

---

[66] I have been told that I default to the negative. What my advisors mean is that I automatically think the worst in every situation and of other people; that I have, to use a cliché, a jaundiced eye. Maybe they're right. For example, here I have characterised those in my organisation of opposing views as the dragon.

At a few really important points I'll be setting homework. There'll be a test.

### Step One, drink milk

I remember being advised in my youth (when I could still do such things and not pay for it) before getting on the piss to drink milk, to "put a lining on your stomach". Allegedly one could handle more grog that way. Well, the equivalent advice when you're lining up to take on the particular kind of dragon we're on about here is: keep the faith.

I don't mean that as mindless instruction to be positive. What I'm suggesting is that you revisit a magical fact. For you may have forgotten how uplifting it was when you first recognised, at some moment in your training, the miracle of social work's existence and its toleration by society, of which it is oftener than not the great accuser. There is a loveliness about the continued presence of this fruitful tension for which not just we social workers but everyone ought to give thanks. It is as if Society magnificently tolerates within itself a sharp critic, and, as it were, licenses social work to give it curry at will. In a metaphorical sense, we're authorised to control one of the main spigots for the milk of human kindness and identify and shame those who might block its flow.

This, however, though true, is a deeply buried truth. Up on the surface everyday society, in the person of its power-wielders, takes a short term-approach of hostility to to the critique by social work. The same underground/above ground ratio obtains on a micro level within each organisation we work in. Even those organisations which only exist to provide social workers to the citizenry, hospital social work departments, the welfare end of agencies like Centrelink, etc., are not immune from the strong

---

You will find that throughout this paper, demonised opponents, larger than life. I decided to leave it that way. Here at least it serves a purpose. It makes my catechising and your grasp of what I am saying easier. Just remember to make allowances for it. In real life, your opponents will look more like ordinary people.

tendency to become hostile to the values of social work and captive to the conventional values of organisations. CEO-ism, the inclination to automatically defend the organisation against criticism, especially *valid* criticism, and spin one's way out of any tight spot that threatens the "good repute" of the organisation, is now endemic and on the rise.

It can, nevertheless, be quite reinforcing of one's flagging will to fight on in the face of bureaucratic stonewalling to simply remember that this lovely truth, this gift of human transcendence over ego, is there below.

My own practice is in employee assistance. I offer an internal staff counselling program, i.e., an EAP, in a large government department. Because my clients are employed by the same organisation which employs me and most of what they bring to me are problems with their employer, some ethical dilemmas are sharper focussed here than in other fields of practice. That's not because of the tension between my roles as Staff Counsellor and co-worker to these clients. That is relatively easy to manage. The tension which spawns the truly riveting ethical dilemmas is the one that exists between my role as Staff Counsellor and my (necessary and proper) subordination to my employer's authority, since my approach to practice demands I join in a particular way with my clients. Now, while this makes those dilemmas easy to see and articulate, I don't think it makes them essentially different from the dilemmas social workers employed in any organisation face. What makes it fruitful for our educational purpose right here, though, is it also makes that underlying miracle I mentioned before easier to see. An internal EAP depends upon that same miracle of human insight into, and discipline of, self on the part of an organisation's decision-makers, on the delicate umpiring of internecine forces. Decision-makers in organisations that tolerate an EAP have to have magnanimity – a gift that comes from God knows where – which outweighs their immediate ego needs; or, to define it more realistically and identify the self-interest at work, when such senior managers are discomfited by the gadfly's bite *and have learned that ego supplies delayed are non-perishable,* they can acquire a reputation for generosity of spirit which is money in the bank as far as their career is concerned.

### Step Two, prepare for battle

Girded with milk and faith, then, let's look at some detail. We'll start with a little sympathy for the devil and look at some of the forces at work in your enemy (it'll be good for your soul).

### Rubric 1: Who pays the piper?

Next time you are standing dumbstruck at the intransigent position your organisation's Top Brass is taking in opposition to an action or decision you see as self-evidently ethical, think about this.

Top Brass live under a ceiling which is also a floor, a floor upon which walk their political masters. Their political masters do not appreciate learning about bad stuff happening in their departments first from the newspapers. They expect the departmental Top Brass on the floor below them, their downstairs tenants, to forewarn them, like rent in kind. Those tenants need, therefore, either to know the bad stuff that's coming, or to prevent it ever happening. If what you want to do is ethical, but controversial, then it's better it never happen.

Let me be a little plainer about this. The values (from which flow their ethical postures) of very senior people in the organisations which employ most of us – i.e., government departments of one kind or another – are much influenced by their proximity to the political heat from the Ministers or other elected (and thus voter-focussed) shot callers who inhabit the floor above. This often results in their need to silence those below who may want to raise for debate or action the plight of those whose condition of life it has been, and is, the responsibility of the political masters to do something about. Very senior people in your organisation are thus caught between competing obligations to facilitate the discharge of *your* social work duty to the organisation's clients, on the one hand, and to protect their political masters on the other. This latter obligation derives from a pact between the politicals and Top Brass which is, except in the Humphrey Applebys, unconscious, certainly unmentioned at least. The pact between Top Brass and you is minor by comparison. Under our system of government this all may be unavoidable.

Of course, I am talking here about our *de facto* system of government, not the Westminster form we espouse. Ideally, Top Brass give frank and fearless advice to politicians, regardless of how unpalatable it is, and rely on the safety provided by tenure to be bold in, for example, upholding your right as a social worker to implement your ethics. Senior public servants now, however, reverse the traditional direction of flow and *take* their cue from politicians. That means seeing an upbeat picture of the world at all times[67], making sure downbeat stuff doesn't happen, and reflecting that picture back upstairs to the politicians (like two kids each with a torch and mirror).

In any case, it is sometimes fun (while you're licking your wounds) to watch the virtuoso sophistical footwork of senior Fred Astaires top hat and caning between their governors' demands stage right and face preservation in front of little Tommy Aquinas, who's naively expecting to be supported in some ethically OK endeavour, stage left.

Laughing out loud at such times, though, can be dangerous.

---

[67] Dr John Scott, not long since removed as Deputy Director-General of the Queensland Health Department, testified on 13 September 2005 before the inquiry conducted by Commissioner Geoff Davies, QC, into malpractice at Bundaberg Hospital and related matters in the Department of Health. Dr Scott said, "I was probably more of an activist for the Government and the minister than perhaps I should have been." He recalled issues that needed addressing, but weren't because they were "not attractive politically". Dr Scott said, "It was and is the case that more money is required to produce an optimal service." His clear implication was that asking for that money was precluded by the absence of the necessary prior recognition of the parlous state of the health services, a recognition that was, by unspoken agreement, off the agenda.

<u>Rubric 2</u>: Hubris and human frailty

There will be times when you know what you're about to do or already have done with or for a client is going to get you in Dutch with the organisation, but you are surprised to see that your boss is OK with it.

But let me tell you a cautionary tale of hubris and a time when I experienced a similar pleasant surprise. My immediate boss, let me call him Hans, and I conversed about a potentially controversial action I had taken and he raised no objection. I couldn't really read how he felt about my action, but had assumed the best (odd for me). What I was unaware of when conversing with Hans on Monday afternoon was that Siobhan, who was Hans's immediate boss, had been away for a few days. She would return the next day. Having no knowledge yet that I had taken it, Siobhan obviously had formed no view of my action. Once she reappeared and acquainted herself with the controversy, however, she adopted an attitude (disapproving) and it sucked his into its slipstream at once.

What this rubric is trying to focus your mind on is not so much the possible presence in the chain of command above you of wishy-washies, but one of the multiplicity of ways the ethical competition presents itself in practice. The hold the organisation's ethics has on the individuals who represent it on the field of battle can fluctuate with the brown-nosing needs of the person you're dealing with. Understanding that can relieve the sense of the surreal such conflicts can engender (and making tactical use of that knowledge might even undo the effects of hubris).

Rubric 3: Worthy of your mettle: Attempts to minimise the validity of your ethics

You will meet opponents worthy of your mettle. I did. It went like this:

I had decided it would be useful to my colleagues in the small network of officers (a hundred souls) within the organisation who had responsibility for the industrial welfare of the rest of the staff to do a spot of education. This group included people doing a wide selection of functions like industrial relations, workplace health and safety, and grievance resolution. One Friday I categorised all the types of difficulties my work had shown me had plagued the lives of our four thousand fellow workers that week, and circulated it amongst the small network. My intention was unremarkable, merely to deepen empathy for our common clientele. (I didn't set homework.)

It was naïve. I offended a basic, but of course unespoused, value of the organisation: Avoidance of unpleasantness at almost any price. My Director took immediate remedial action and published an upbeat counter message to the network. In it she adopted, for didactic purposes, the role of seeker after knowledge and (addressing me by name in a missive formally addressed to the whole network) said, 'Michael, I was trying to work out what was your purpose – a "wave" for assistance perhaps?' She went on, in seeker after knowledge mode, to reject that interpretation and plump for a more sinister, but the purpose had been achieved. My action had been reduced to a symptom of my own fatigue. It was a neat thrust.

Rubric 4: Worthy of your mettle: Attempts to redefine your role to exclude whatever it is you're trying to do

The great advantage your betters have is that they define your role. They don't, if they're subtle, simply issue a new Position Description or Statement of Duties (you could contest that in the appropriate tribunal), but float almost in passing their own idea of what you are employed to do and couch it in such superficially reasonable language the re-write is achieved without ever declaring itself.

In Siobhan's counter message, as a preamble to something else she was going to argue, she alluded to the characteristics of my role in a way that implied there was consensus about them. It was an apprehension of the role which perfectly suited her coming argument.

> ... In your role, Michael, you can contribute to the success of shaping positive environments by encouraging and acknowledging the good news that people are generating, and not sending out a message that ... we are experiencing some unusually large barrage of misery targeted at the people of [the Department]...

This Dale Carnegie redefinition by stealth of my duties suited her argument against my making (relatively) public the shit that was regularly going down for Department staff. And its upbeat tone implied such a rosy prognosis    for the overall industrial and morale climate for the wider staff group and fitted so perfectly the received temper of the times that one felt a churl to gainsay it.

Definitely worthy. But don't despair. She went on to add,

> I am not advocating a denial of the bad things – I am talking about inspiring people, creating energy to copy some of the good things happening, so that we can achieve together, and use some of that energy to help those having a rough time.

A paragraph of gratuitous overkill, yes, but have another look at the disclaimer in the first line. The bald denial of what she is at this very moment doing, that is, her denial of her denial, is the tip. She knows at some deep level what is obvious to anyone not defending an investment.

Your homework: Perceive those inward conflicts[68] and, as in Rubric 2, make tactical use of them.[69]

Rubric 5: You are not emotionally invulnerable

Well, I wasn't anyway. I will just confess to this, and leave it at that. There isn't much to say about it. All I want to do is not hide the dreadful way struggles like these can get you down. I felt overwhelmed by this cloud of arrows, as if the victim of some modern Boadicea's ranks of archers who had loosed a thousand feathered bolts at once, obscuring the sky above me, the shafts sliding this way and that, but all homing on my heart. At the same time I wanted to blunt and break the point of each in turn before their sheer numbers did for me. But want as I might, I did nothing. A paralysis, which I told myself was detachment, overtook me.

Rubric 6: Think hard about the consequences of actions, yours AND theirs

Occasionally you will find that your opponents will camouflage even from themselves the real cost of their obduracy. And since they are always, by definition, more powerful in the organisation than you, this cost is not going to be counted and the quality of organisational life will be diminished.

In the situation I described above where the Director sought to negate my "depressing and negative" publication of facts about the vicissitudes of life for departmental staff, it was not my allegedly debilitating effect upon the life of the organisation which was her target, but the liberty of the HR network to engage with

---

[68] We must be grateful for the unconsciousness in some of our opponents that results in their leaving these revealing little tags on show for us to read. And we must also be grateful for our training, which teaches us to be alert for external signals to the internal world.

[69] This denial of one's own denial is not confined to the bad guys. At Rubric 12, below, I return this and to denial as a human failing in general.

difficult professional matters such as the purposeful nourishment of empathy that was actually in the cross-hairs. On the face it, counterproductive. One might, rather, have expected engagement in such an endeavour to attract approval from her. And, I am sure that, if it were put to her in theoretical terms, it would gain approval. That liberty to grow professionally, then, died from friendly fire; but it still died.

Your homework: Work out what is really in their cross-hairs. It may just make a difference, if you can articulate it. (I don't mean just in the test.)

Rubric 7: Work out the real values that govern life in the organisation

You can waste a lot of energy on outrage simply because you have never sat down with a sceptical eye and measured the distance between the organisation's espoused values and its values in practice. (A few run-ins with the organisation usually are enough to force you to do this exercise.)

There are two steps. Number one is the more fundamental. There's a falsehood – a fiction that is a convenience of discourse, really – which personifies organisations, treats of them as if they were human individuals. We'll go along with it for clarity's sake in what follows, but (and here please let me nag you for a minute, Catechumen) you have to remind yourself, and remind yourself again, that for all that its boosters (for their own ends) like to portray an organisation as if it could think and feel, it can't. When, for example a university's publications declare that "the University of Hicksville welcomes foreign students", in other words boasts a value it wants you to believe it lives by, that claim, ubiquitous as such claims now are, is bullshit. (I'll tell you what it really means in step two.) Some one person employed by the university may welcome a foreign student, maybe even two will, but the whole entity does not because it cannot. So, begin by recognising that talk of an organisation (e.g., The University) acting is camouflage for the fact that individuals within it act. This sounds obvious, but we do tend to forget it, to our consternation.

Now here's the second step. Even when an organisation (always through the agency of some individual) behaves decently, the desire to exploit that virtuousness springs up at once like a weed,[70] (again, in the heart of an individual – but this time some *other* individual – within the organisation who has an eye to the main chance) and the decent act will be promoted, with more or less sham humility, as indicative of the organisation's culture. The aim behind this other individual's action (i.e., the boasting) is at bottom self-promotion, and once we see that we are getting closer to the actual values that dictate the organisation's behaviour and notice we are quite a distance from the warm welcome bullshit. If we forensically pursue it, we will see that first vaunted value transmogrify into something more like, "the University of Hicksville welcomes foreign students' fees" (and perhaps "will cut a deal by cutting a few corners on the way to your degree").

This is all part of a bigger problem and not one unrelated to ethical contests. Laura Penny has declared that the world is drowning in bullshit[71]. She draws attention to our obfuscation

---

[70] I have enshrined my despair, irrational I know, over this inevitability in a rave too big for a footnote here. It appears in a text box in the "Statement: We Don't Like Talking about That" section of *Darkness and Denial.*

[71] In her book, *Your Call Is Important to Us: The Truth About Bullshit,* (Crown, 2005) she writes: "Your call is important to us" has been chosen from a very deep reservoir of bullshit phrases for the title of this book... Like most bullshit, the more times you hear it, the bullshittier it gets. This is why bullshit is best served quickly, with many visuals, in mass quantities, with no questions from the floor. Penny was interviewed on ABC Radio National, Wednesday, 31 August 2005, and 2 September 2005 about her book (Crown, 2005). On 2 September interviewer Steve Austin editorialised: Laura Penny says phoniness "not only alienates us from each other but degrades public discourse, breeds apathy, and makes us just plain stupid". She says the sheer volume of commercial communication and the technological advances that spread it has

compulsion, our devotion to pretty falsehoods, which degrades the public discourse that should conjoin us all, on almost every topic it touches. The senior managers who will be opposing your ethical endeavours when ethical conflict occurs are not, in their role implementation, immune from the corrupting effect of all this bullshit upon our understanding of what's proper and acceptable. Neither are we. These reflections are salutary. Step careful.

Your homework: Remind yourself that if individuals find it hard to hold themselves to a standard and know what their in-practice values really are, organisations find it even harder. Which is really to say that persons upon whom an organisation devolves power, those whom Hamlet set forever in aspic, puffed up insolent and clothed with a little brief authority, and whom Ricky Gervais embodied *par excellence*, find it harder. For they conflate or confuse their own agency with the activity required of them by the organisation. This inhibits tremendously that concurrent monitoring of oneself for falseness and hypocrisy which is one of the marks of the human. The nose for bullshit, your own included, is rendered inoperative by ego inflation.

And read Laura Penny.

Rubric 8: Think about going public

Going public can be scary. Fear of being done for bringing the organisation into disrepute is a powerful dissuader and bosses rely on it. But don't succumb to quietism straightaway. Organisations resort or threaten to resort to this silencer on the assumption that their case will be proven against someone whose actions have the indirect consequence of adverse publicity (as opposed to someone

---

(sic) led to an explosion in bullshit. "Advertising and PR make one thing and one thing only, and that is shit up. Making shit up is not to be confused with outright lying, although lying is sometimes involved. Making shit up is more like painting the lawn green when the Queen comes to town. The grass may be green to start with, but it ain't that green," she argues.

Michael O'Neill

who explicitly blows the whistle, in relation to whom the *Whistleblowers Protection Act 1994* now gives them reluctant pause) merely by showing that adverse publicity has occurred. What is rarely given the chance to see daylight is the counter argument that it is not the action of the staff member that brought the organisation into disrepute but the pre-existing negligence that produced the circumstances which justify the disrepute.

(Homework: Think as well about the various ways in which one can go public, and the different meanings public can have.)

Rubric 9: Watch your flank

Beware the organisation's attempt to solve the problem of your conscience by making apparently unrelated, innocent-sounding but uncannily convenient and "timely" restructures of the organisation, or some small part of the organisation. Which just happens to contain you.

When things with me and my Director had deteriorated irretrievably she placed before her own boss a plan to "restructure" the EAP. The key proposal in it was to subordinate my role (internal provision of counselling to the staff of the Department) to the external EAP provider whom I had used as a back-up. I had contracted with this firm some years back to step in when there were too many clients seeking help and as my locum when I was on leave. My Director declared that this restructured EAP would eliminate the need for my clients to log their requests for my help by leaving a message on my answering machine. This alleged inconvenience for my 10 clients had never been the subject of comment before, but now acquired such importance that a comprehensive organisational restructure was imperative to remove it. The external firm had a receptionist who actually spoke into the phone. It would be much more personal, nicer. We simply teach Departmental staff a new number to call when they need help, and Voila! Bob's your uncle. A footnote in the plan was that, henceforth I would be professionally and clinically supervised by the head of that firm. Firms on a yearly contract to an organisation

254

generally do not give the organisation much trouble of a philosophical kind.

If you suspect that a proposed restructure which involves your position is an outflanking move of this kind, monitor your feelings after they tell you about it. If you get a feeling consistent with overhearing someone relaying your co-ordinates, duck. And weave. And organise, as Joe Hill posthumously advised his mourners.

As a senior management control tactic, restructure has acquired some notoriety. For example, the following quotation, found on tea room bulletin boards, which is often attributed to Petronius Arbiter, master of elegance at the court of the Roman Emperor Nero, is not in fact to be found in the surviving text of his *Satyricon* so may well be of modern provenance. Certainly, it speaks to many of us who have felt utterly demoralised by bureaucratic doggedness in the pursuit of restructure and "improvement":

> We trained hard, but it seemed that every time we were beginning to form up into teams, we would be reorganised. I was to learn later in life that we tend to meet any new situation by reorganising; and a wonderful method it can be for creating the illusion of progress while producing confusion, inefficiency and demoralisation.

It can also be a wonderful method for disappearing some ethical irritant. If it is an invention of the modern mind, the desire to found it in the distant past suggests that the human characteristic it defines is intuitively seen as deeply entrenched in human behaviour.

Your homework: Have a closer look at the noticeboard in the tea room.

<u>Rubric 10</u>: Moral authority

Keep moral authority in mind. It is, after all, what these contests are about in the end. In disputes like these, when your oppressors are ostensibly defending what they fondly desire to see as a competing, superior *and official* set of values, remember that valid moral authority is not exercised with blunt instruments (public floggings, open reprimand) in one hand and words, weasel or not, in the other. It is not bundled with the administrative authority one acquires when appointed to a management position. Moral authority is voluntarily bestowed upon one, and only when undeniable virtue, wisdom, courage and compassion attract it. This is so for Presidents, Popes, Prime Ministers ... and senior managers. To behave as if one has it by right or *by appointment* is simply to misread the world and the way allegiance and professional integrity function and interact.

Moral authority is where it is. It may be with you.

Your homework: Expect some senior management people to assume its mantle anyway, whether the colour suits them or not.

Rubric 11: The problem of loyalty

Until one is forced to think about it, the idea that loyalty is a problem rather than a virtue comes as a surprise. It is, however, actually one of sources of the adamantine opposition displayed by senior managers to an action you may wish to take on ethical grounds.

This is the paradox we have to grasp to begin with: Loyalty looms large and problematic in organisational life, especially where sycophancy is king, since for senior managers to not shield those to whom they "owe" loyalty (i.e., *very* senior managers, CEOs and politicals) from bad news about the organisation is, if they are where the buck stops, to endanger them, and thus to be *dis*loyal. When so expressed it is a conundrum redolent of Shakespeare's comedic maestros, but it is not funny.

To unravel, I will begin by asking you to listen to John Kleinig, Professor in the Department of Law, Police Science, and Criminal

Justice Administration at John Jay College of Criminal Justice. When Kleinig visited Brisbane and gave this address on 20 April 1994 he was editor of the journal, *Criminal Justice Ethics.* In an address he gave to an audience which included Queensland public servants he elaborated on the idea of dissenting from a prevailing view within one's organisation, which he termed loyal opposition:

> Those in power, whether elected or appointed, and who, for personal reasons, cannot cope with criticism, or have something to hide, or feel insecure, or may even have an absolutist understanding of loyalty, will have little interest in fostering a notion of loyal opposition. In some circles, a loyal opposition has been all but extinguished, as those in power have gathered around them a coterie of yes-men and women.

> Yet I want to suggest that it is absolutely crucial to the good name of loyalty, and, for that matter, acceptable whistleblowing, that loyal service allow for appropriate, vigorous, and conscientious criticism. Only a loyalty that allows for – and indeed encourages – some form of critical appraisal will be responsive to the complaint often made that loyalty involves the sacrifice of one's autonomy, and constitutes a form of slave mentality. Only a loyalty that allows for critical appraisal will serve the interests of the organisation or institution or system that requires it.

Another way to come at this is to recognise that loyalty is a tribal virtue, and in that sphere a proper one. In a society that has, by contrast, avowed allegiance instead to the rule of law and subscribes to the belief that all are equal before it, it is finished. This logic is unassailable. Those declaring it, however, are not.

In Queensland we had a course of steroid injections to help us acclimatise to the moral present and shed the tribal past as the daily revelations twenty years ago from the long-running Fitzgerald inquiry exposed the consequences when integrity plays second fiddle to loyalty. But the dose needs to be repeated regularly, and I'm afraid we are late for our appointment.

This tension between loyalty and integrity is a growing pain for the human species. But for those top hat and cane men we met earlier, it's also a show that must not go on.

Rubric 12: Understand denial

In much of what we've looked at here it's implicit that denial is playing a big role in the opposition you will be facing. There have even been a few mentions of it in passing (and you may find yourself doing a bit of it, too.) So, it deserves its own dedicated rubric.

Playwright and iconoclast Arthur Miller, towards the end of a long life of suffering condemnation for his clear view of things, wrote usefully about the endemic denial in his fellow citizens which he constantly disturbed in his autobiography *Timebends A Life*. There he reflects upon on his post-war tour of Europe. On page 523 he speculates about how the farmers and villagers of an area "still famous for its anti- Semitism" must nevertheless have learned not to look up as "trucks packed with people whined up [the] road" to Mauthausen concentration camp, near Hitler's birthplace.

For another score and more pages he riffles through historical and cultural examples of denial ranging through history and across the globe, coming to rest for our edification upon a little classic from his own experience. He looks at the conviction and ultimate acquittal of a suspect named Reilly, accused of slaying his mother, and the revelation that prosecutors simply denied the existence of evidence which would have exploded their obsession with Reilly's "guilt" and their convictions about his motivation, which they had explained as oedipal rage. It was a case Miller had been personally involved with.

On page 556 he writes,

> The Oedipus complex may or may not operate universally, but the sheer animal reflex of bureaucracy in stonewalling against embarrassing truths surely does, and no less so [here in America]

than in Russia or China or anywhere else ... because man is what man is, *nature's denial machine.* (my emphasis)

Like Miller, I am convinced that denial is our default mode. It is an inbuilt incline in us (more like a cliff face, perhaps) precipitating us into episodes of denial so easily that it fairly clamours to us to both resist *and* understand it. Denial is so close to our normal condition, one baulks at calling it pathological. The usual theological sidestep around this hesitation, conceptualising us as Original Sinners, is tempting. It seems there must be a conscious effort made not to manifest the illness, and striving engaged in to become a graduate of some unnamed rehabilitation program. We all know people who have flunked that program. Our newspapers provide us plenty of examples of people coming unstuck as the endgame to denial, and indignant amusement at seeing denial writ so large and public and safely located in others is comforting respite.

However, it is also defensive. The non-graduating group from that rehab program is rather large. We may be in it. So, if we are to penetrate the mystery of denial, we will have to go beyond the disbelief, rage and weary despair these revelations generate in us and see our very selves as part of the problem and admit that denial is more than merely ghost in us. That is, we have to go further than the conventional there-but-for-the-grace-of-God admission of a tendency and acknowledge that we ourselves, at moments where telling the whole truth would 13 result in embarrassment, try to put the best possible face on things, if not actually lie or deny reality, while scrabbling around for a rationalisation.

So our cycle of rage, resignation, insight and *mea culpa*, might bring us to these three huge questions:

> 1. When a challenging truth is put to us before it has become so publicly known that it can no longer be hidden, i.e., while it is still known only by those whose silence (we think) can be coerced or cajoled, what fosters in us this readiness to deny?

259

2. For those truths we ourselves first see and should utter, what stills our tongues? Is it the fear our ribbon to Power's maypole might be cut? Is it Power's pure aphrodisiac subversion of our self-respect? Or is it Power's plain, old-fashioned threat, which we suss and succumb to in an unnoticed instant, thereby sparing Power the embarrassment of those locutions which would unface us both and which it would rather employ only when the chips are down? ("If any of you mention this [report, submission, statistic] outside this room, you may be in breach of your obligations under the Code of Conduct to not bring the Department into disrepute. OK?")

3. If we perceive who or what has offended the Gods and, like blind Teiresias, are asked to speak the unvarnished truth, may we be forgiven for taking refuge with him, in fearful silence, and crying out, "Alas, alas, what misery to be wise/ When wisdom profits nothing!"; forgiven, that is, for our despairing avoidance of those dimly perceived and terrifying insights about ourselves that, like death, have undone so many?

Tradition tells us St Peter, when the cock's crow ended his long three dog night of declarations of denial, was dismayed to see he'd lived out a humiliating proof of his master's predictive insight. That agonised awareness of being subverted by one's own cowardice may be step one towards renewal, but is utterly aversive. None choose to experience it. So when we have fallen prey to our own denial, we all, I think, work hard and darkly to avoid knowing it. For we know that should we ourselves or anyone else, naïve, confront us with our sin, we will be thrown into crisis. Which means we must *deny our denial*.

And thus cement it in place.

Few, of course, engage in the self-renewal I allude to, choosing not to resolve the crisis that is composed of knowing-but-refusing-to-see the truth; and crisis shunned long enough can end with one flying to one's fate like Oedipus. Therefore, best avoid the crisis altogether. Call in an air strike: attack is the best defence, and easy to do, if all this is set inside an organisation and the naïf urging the truth upon us is subordinate to us. Dead messenger, dead easy.

Your homework: Stay alert.

Rubric 13: Who's calling the shots?

"The dilemma for organisations is an insider who pricks their consciences and bites the hand that feeds him/her was observed by Elizabeth Hutchison in 1989. Writing about an organisational setting in which social workers, by attempting to fulfil their professional ethic, stir conflict with people implementing other functions, she said:

The social work profession has difficulty coming to terms with the reality that society employs social workers as agents of social stability and seldom as agents of social change. The profession should struggle, honestly, with the nature of its societal mandate"[72]

Clearly, it is not just the social worker, counsellor or other worker attempting to ameliorate social relations who must struggle honestly. Conflicts like the ones which blow up around us are inevitable in our line of work. Some human beings are not interested in social change, if it disturbs their comfortable grip on reality. They also, sometimes, believe in their way of doing things, and with equal passion.

That's why many counsellors working in my game within organisations would subscribe to this rule of thumb: if you are not getting into serious strife with someone senior in the organisation at least once a year, you're not doing the job. Let me use here the

---

[72] Elizabeth D. Hutchison 1989 "Use of authority in direct social work practice with mandated clients", *Social Service Review*, vol. 61, no. 4, pp. 581-598

experience of a fellow EAP counsellor, rather than my own, to illustrate that the struggle can take forms other than mine took. This colleague faced a struggle to hold fast to his professional duty, as he saw it, to be free to advocate for his clients in the face of a boss whose worldview was offended by this idea.

He presented his circumstances to his employer this way:

> The problem for the Department is that while it may, from an administrative perspective, legally delineate my "duties" as a Counsellor, it may not, from the broader societal perspective, delineate with any authority (other than that of a corporate or societal citizen offering an opinion) the content of the sociological status, Counsellor. It is simply not the Department's, or even the government's, prerogative. Rather, it is the helping professions which, in the aggregate and/or by individual profession, assign meaning to and define the status, Counsellor. In turn, every Counsellor, via the strictures and ethics of her or his individual discipline or profession – in my case Social Work – maintains allegiance to a set of ideas and actions thus constellated that delineate what's included and what's not included in the practice of counselling. The professional and social legitimacy or otherwise of advocacy's place in that constellation is decided thus, not by administrative fiat.[73]

For him, advocacy and its legitimate role in his work were the particular sticking point. For me it was the permission to tell my colleagues the truth about what *our* clients were really facing in

---

[73] A reinforcement of this perspective on settling the relationship between managerial and professional authority and on what can be included in it and how, is to be found in a legal judgement by Wilcox, J, in which are set out some of the pertinent arguments. See in particular, paragraph 36 of Geoffrey Preston v. L. Carmody, J. Cauchi and J. McAuliffe and Chief Executive Officer of the Family Court of Australia.

their working day. For you it will be something different. But for all of us the essential tension is the same.

<u>Rubric 14</u>: Work out who your opponent is

When I was a student we were encouraged to read a text by an English social work academic and practitioner whose name I wish I could remember, but whose luminous (though now controversial) pronouncement, "private practice in social work is a contradiction in terms", I have never forgotten.

His words, along with a library of others (including some equally luminous pronunciamentos from Tom Aquinas, whose uncompetitive dancing we had to watch earlier) came marching to my aid a couple of years ago when the state government decided to trial the idea of shared service provision for the corporate services needs of the public service. Roles such as mine were identified for centralisation in the new shared service provision (SSP) agencies; and, as an unkind fate would have it, those SSP agencies fell victim to a piece of snake oil known as the fee-for-service modality. We public servants in this new body were asked to adopt a commercialised approach to our delivery of services to other public servants. This was meant to make us more efficient. Me it just made sick. For ideological reasons. I resisted passively for a long time until I was served a show cause why I shouldn't be disciplined for refusing an instruction (to keep a special time-capture record used to "charge" other departments whose staff I counselled). I fought all the way to a Fair Treatment Appeal, the public service equivalent of the High Court, and lost. My line was, commercialising our activity breeds contempt for any criterion other than profit and inevitably leads to unethical behaviour by public servants sworn to a higher code.

I was at first puzzled (as well as suitably outraged) by officialdom's blank look when the fundamental question of whether my argument was correct or not came up. (I had, of course, provided recent examples of corruption of public servants' behaviour that the fee-for-service modality had already achieved.)

At last, however, it came to me that we, the public service corporately, were following in the train of a government enchanted by the odour of Capital. It was simply not possible for officialdom to countenance the idea that a method of organising social endeavour, indeed whole societies, namely Market Forces, which had captured the government's philosophical apparatus, and apparatchiks, could be dissented from.

And it is not only our modern worldview, the market system (which Heilbroner[74] identifies as the third of only three ways humankind has ever tried of organising for social survival – he calls it the "astonishing game") which hypnotises us once we become government officials. That same susceptibility to the onset of moral impenetrability existed long before coming of the worldview Adam Smith described. Listen to these thoughts from Chinese history of the late sixth century A.D.

At this time the people abandoned their family homesteads to assemble within the fortifications of walled towns. There was nothing to provide for themselves. Although what was in the granaries and storehouses was still very plentiful, the minor officials all feared the regulations and none dared to assume the responsibility of distribution of provisions for public relief. As a result there was increased distress. At first everyone peeled the bark off trees in order to eat it. Gradually they went so far as to eat the leaves. When bark and trees were all exhausted they then boiled earth. Some pounded straw to powder and ate it. After this men then ate each other.[75]

(One is reminded of Arthur Miller's inclusion of China in his assertion above about the universality of bureaucratic stonewalling.)

---

[74] *The worldly philosophers: the lives, times, and ideas of the great economic thinkers*, Heilbroner, Robert L, Fourth Edition, Simon and Schuster, 1972, pp. 17 and 18.

[75] From the *Sui-Shu* (official dynastic history of Sui, written under Tang supervision,) quoted in *The Rough Guide History of China*, Wintle, Justin, 2002, Rough Guides Ltd., London, ISBN 1-85828-7-642, page 141.

Your homework: Look behind the person who seems to be the one stopping you. There may be an army there you haven't noticed and they may be impenetrable zombies.

<u>Rubric 15</u>: The bowels of Christ

The bouncy tone of my catechism so far may have given the impression I believe that there is always a clear choice a social worker can make about which side to be on in these contretemps. To be honest, that is my view – almost. However, history, and the twentieth century in particular, I will have to admit, have produced a number of men whose names have by now probably become household names in Hell. With sobriquets like, "_____, the Butcher of This Place" or "_____, the Scourge of Somewhere Else", they got to that eminence by being absolutely sure they were right. I don't want to bunk with these guys for eternity, so it's time I let someone from a little earlier put this plea to me: "I beseech you, in the bowels of Christ, think it possible you may be mistaken." I may. Thus, I confess there are some situations I have encountered which defy easy choice. It *is* possible for those opposing social work's ethical demands in certain situations to be at least sincere, and maybe sometimes even right to resist us.

I was once ordered to give up my case-files on a small number of clients who had been victimised by a particular manager. The organisation, to its credit, had sacked him after a thorough investigation. He had then applied under Freedom of Information legislation for much material he intended to use in a bid to have his sacking overturned in the industrial court. This man had a reputation, well-earned, as a taker of unofficial reprisal against subordinates who crossed him. If my case-notes fell into his hands, he would, I feared, identify and do ill by those clients. I was not prepared to surrender them to the departmental Officer whose obligation it was to collect them from me.

The dilemma consisted in this. That officer was discharging a duty under the law, a law of which I, of course, in a general sense much approve. This, then, was a contest with right on both sides.

I tracked a path through this minefield, one way or another, and it was eventually resolved by the CEO of my organisation in favour of preserving my case-files from exposure; but that path led through lowering clouds of doubt and fogs of moral imprecision. One of the dicta I held to my heart to comfort me on the journey was Dylan's agonised line, "to live outside the law, you must be honest". At the time, my chosen clinical supervisor was Peter North. I had chosen Peter, so by definition, I respected his judgement. But even between us there was disagreement and one tactical bridge I crossed which was a bridge too far for him.

Judgement about the ethical status of my actions I will have to abandon to ... who knows whom. Final arbiters are hard to agree upon.

Rubric 16: The big picture

Ethics, while it may seem to some of us passionately straightforward, is, like everything else, a product of the ruling culture, if not exactly the ruling class, of the day. We had better give it some thought so we can situate ourselves in a context historically and philosophically. It may just help us not to think we have to die in a ditch over some ethical position we hold to.

Marx made us understand that a society's cultural superstructure is determined in the interests of its ruling elite – in our case Capital's minions – and even its most basic features (education objectives, healthcare delivery, ownership of exploitable resources) is arranged ultimately to suit them. This means, I believe, via a long chain of dialectic I won't bore you with, we each have to construct a commitment to an ethical framework of our own. Notwithstanding the sterling and protracted efforts of the AASW, (neither) the ethical framework of the generic human activity called social work, nor that of any individual social worker, is definitively described. Nor can it be. This may sound heretical at first, but in the final analysis, when the crunch comes for each one of us, we will either have to align ourselves with the AASW's (or some other group's) or rely upon our instinctive own, none of them perfectly suited to all situations. The latter choice, relying on one's own, is, in my view, preferable; but doing it without ever having become comfortable with one's ethical self – however one does that – is no mean feat.

After coming all this way with me, you may be expecting a parthian precept like the ones I've essayed above. I have to disappoint you. In the territory this rubric assays, we are all as alone as we are in birth and death.

(No homework.)

Last things

Reading all this may depress you. But, mate, don't quit the field. Even though it may be your doom to be shot, metaphorically, as Messenger and be (not metaphorically) reviled as a naysayer and nark by those your ethics make uncomfortable, and your life for a while become as ugly as, to borrow an unloved expression from across the water, all get out, don't. If we get out, they win. That is, when social workers withdraw, anti-social workers (who are in senior management positions quite often) have their backward-looking way and we're all the lesser for it.

# TOOLKIT ITEM 7
## Tools de Chardin

I MENTIONED in *Michael, we really have to talk...* Teilhard de Chardin's observation that evolution has reached a point where we are offered a part. In his view, our conscious and willed involvement in deciding the future is required. Well, if so, who's requiring? Teilhard's answer and mine would differ. There is a mind at work, or there is not. Whatever the truth of that, you can respond to evolution's alleged invitation, if you choose to. From my viewpoint, social workers especially have already chosen.

I have argued that for a species defined by socialness, we have not yet skilled up much. Our progress toward productive cooperation is slow. We do war reasonably well, and one or two other endeavours, but our grasp of pure sociality, organised human life, seems at best patchy. Paul Gibney once observed that if you set up the head offices of three organisations, the army, the church and a legal brothel, side by side in three different buildings and set them going, when you came back twenty years later you wouldn't be able to tell them apart. Organisation succumbs so regularly that standing commissions of inquiry into police and other corruption proliferate embarrassingly. Brilliant moral initiatives come into the world. To persist they must be organised, minimally or not. They then lose the point.

In this setting, it's widely, if not quite universally, acknowledged that social work has a mandate. Miraculous. It's not a mitred mandate and wears no shiny badge; it's of the intellect. The omega of all the training, regardless of academic coloration, is seeing where the dysfunction of the world is and not turning away. The work is done one cup of coffee at a time on the pre-dawn streets or deep and quiet in the heart of the beast. It is all subversive.

The living weight of this falls on me and on each and every one of social work's cohort. Off-loaded, it cannot live. Expressing it in the world requires many tools. They all look different and there's one you cannot see. It's courage. Choosing it and using it is a skill like any other. You can call it a virtue, if you prefer, a virtue one decides to own, and every such decision nails it to your mast afresh. Know the terrain, of course. Then stand.